D0459305

International Business-
Government Communications

International Business-Government Communications

U.S. Structures, Actors, and Issues

Jack N. Behrman
University of North Carolina

J.J. Boddewyn
Baruch College
City University of New York

Ashok Kapoor
New York University

Lexington Books
D.C. Heath and Company
Lexington, Massachusetts
Toronto   London

HD69
I7B416

Library of Congress Cataloging in Publication Data

Behrman, Jack N.
  International business-government communications.

  Includes bibliographical references and index.
  1. Corporations, American. 2. International business enterprises.
3. United States—Foreign relations administration. I. Boddewyn, Jean J.
II. Kapoor, Ashok, 1940-   III. Title.
HD69.17B416   382.1   74-28974
ISBN 0-669-98046-3

Copyright © 1975 by D.C. Heath and Company.

All rights reserved. No part of this publication may be reproduced or
transmitted in any form or by any means, electronic or mechanical,
including photocopy, recording, or any information storage or retrieval
system, without permission in writing from the publisher.

Published simultaneously in Canada.

Printed in the United States of America.

International Standard Book Number: 0-669-98046-3

Library of Congress Catalog Card Number: 74-28974

Contents

Preface

The Department of State has been questioning for several years the role that the multinational enterprise and other emerging forms of international business would and should play in the formation of foreign policies of the United States. It has proven quite difficult to come to grips with the policy implications of a structure of business that cannot be segmented according to functions, but cannot be treated as an aggregated whole either. A variety of functional activities—exports, imports, taxation, pricing, competition patterns, investment, disinvestment, technology transfers and licensing, etc.—are conducted by the same company but are under the surveillance of quite different agencies of the U.S. government. There is greater coordination of these activities within the international companies than there is within the U.S. governmental agencies concerned with them.

Further, U.S. policy tends to be formed on an overall basis rather than on a disaggregation of dissimilar types of activities—that is, policy distinctions are not made among extraction, manufacturing, and services nor within these sectors according to the impacts of specific operations abroad. It is difficult to formulate appropriate policies unless the diverse effects of business operations are taken into account.

For this reason, the Bureau of Intelligence and Research asked for a study of the ways U.S. businesses abroad interact with U.S. embassies and with host governments thereby potentially impinging on the formation of U.S. foreign policy. It has not been possible to cover all types of activities, so it was agreed that we should concentrate on the largest segment—manufacturing. We recognize that the conclusions drawn will not necessarily apply to other sectors or to all countries.

To obtain our information base, we traveled to some twenty-five countries—from Algeria to Zambia and within Latin America, Europe, Africa, the Mid-East, South Asia, and the Far East. We interviewed general managers of companies and banks, consultants, Washington representatives of companies, embassy officials, host government officials, and officials in the U.S. Departments of State and Commerce, amassing some fifteen hundred pages of interview notes plus other materials. In addition, we interviewed officials of the parent companies, of which more than thirty cooperated with the study and some half-dozen provided extensive introductions to their general managers around the world. We chose these few so as to make certain that we had a fairly clear picture of their worldwide network of activities and information flow on external affairs, rather than trying to piece together bits and snatches from a larger number of companies. Adding this more intensive picture to the extensive interviews of a larger variety of companies, we felt certain that we acquired a fairly accurate picture of what is going on in government-business relations.

In addition, we undertook several case studies of the negotiation process in which U.S. embassy officials were involved, reading the State Department cables over a period of years related to each case; in this we had the invaluable help of Mrs. Williams in State's document service. The results of this process were not always satisfactory, because the cable record is spotty. The published record could be supplemented adequately only in three of the five cases we examined. The published materials were researched and drafted by Anita Benvignati, but the inability to make a thorough study led to a decision not to publish these studies in this book.

The time constraint of completion of the project within fifteen months meant that we each had to draw extensively on our own prior activities in the area in order to shorten the research time. J.J. Boddewyn had five years of experience in business concerned with market research, systems analysis, and industrial management. During the past ten years he has been teaching in the areas of European business systems, comparative management and marketing, and international business-government relations. As part of his research in the past five years, he has interviewed over three hundred corporate executives, government officials, and intermediaries in Western Europe. His writings have related to foreign government policies toward U.S. international companies, international business-government relations, and external affairs of U.S. companies around the world. Ashok Kapoor has taught for nearly ten years in the areas of international marketing and business-government relations and has lectured around the world and before officials of the AID. In connection with his research, he has interviewed over eight hundred individuals in Western Europe, South Asia, the Far East, and the U.S. His research includes books on international business negotiations, international mixed ventures, the negotiation era and the multinational enterprise, plus ongoing studies of international business-government relations. Jack Behrman conducted early studies on foreign licensing and direct investment during the late 1950s; in connection with these and later studies on the multinational enterprise he has interviewed over one thousand officials of companies, governments, and various law and consulting firms concerning international operations and public policies concerning foreign business.

These interests and experiences dovetailed so that Boddewyn undertook responsibility for Part I, Kapoor for Part II, and Behrman for Part III. Although these were the primary responsibilities of each, we hammered out in joint sessions not only the research design but also the choice of interview results used in the study and our conclusions.

The study would obviously not have been possible without the wholehearted cooperation of officials of many international companies in the U.S. and abroad, that of embassy officials, and many officials of host governments. We agreed not to identify them or cite any company or officials unless from already published statements. They will remain unlisted, therefore, but our debt to each is great.

We profited also from the continuing interest and criticism of an advisory group from agencies of the U.S. government as we proceeded with the research design and progressive drafts.

Finally, our thanks go to Mrs. Betsy Pierce and Ms. Faith O'Neal, who typed several drafts of the manuscript. Needless to say, any remaining faults are the responsibility of the authors.

Jack N. Behrman

Acknowledgment

This study is one of a number done by academic and other research institutions for the Department of State as part of the Department's external research program. These studies are designed to supplement the Department's own in-house research capabilities and provide independent, expert views to policy officers and analysts on key questions with important policy implications.

This study was proposed by the Office of Economic Research and Analysis in the Bureau of Intelligence and Research (INR) and developed in discussions with officers in several Department bureaus. It was monitored by Warren H. Reynolds, Senior Program Officer in the Bureau of Intelligence and Research, with the assistance of an interagency working group, which provided thoughtful critiques of several drafts. However, the views and conclusions contained in this study are those of the authors, and should not be interpreted as representing the official opinion or policy of the Department of State.

1 Introduction and Conclusions

U.S. international companies are affected by governmental policies at home and abroad, and are often the target of special policies because of their being foreign or transnational in perspective. The overall policy of reception (the "climate for investment") and the specific policies concerning entry, expansion, operations, and exit produce the setting for communication between governments and the international companies (ICs).[a]

More important, there is an increasing need for governments and companies to communicate on problems of international business. Governments are tightening controls, and are asking for more and more information. And national governmental agencies are not the only ones doing so; various provincial governments are adopting policies on inward direct investment, and the United Nations has examined the need for controls over multinational enterprises. It would seem that better policies can only be formed out of an adequate dialogue among the actors on the issues.

The Issues

It is frequently said by both home and host governments that ICs are little concerned about the goals of the countries where they operate, and that they generate unique conflicts of national vs. corporate interests and loyalties. These conflicts are made more complex by the fact that many governments are *both* home and host governments; that is, the United States has long been a strong exporter of direct investment capital but is increasingly an importer, while Japan has been an importer but is increasingly an exporter also. The same duality is arising in countries such as India, Canada, Brazil, and Mexico; and it has long been the case for Europe. It is not yet clear whether this duality will create new and greater tensions, increase understanding of the "other fellow's" viewpoint, or create a kind of policy schizophrenia within governments. The likelihood is for greater tension until conflicts can be resolved, however. The existence of these conflicts also means that there are opportunities to build new relationships

---

[a]The abbreviation ICs, used throughout, refers only to U.S. companies operating abroad. It should be stressed, however, that the spread of ICs based in other countries is likely to alter the dialogue in both substance, intensity, and structure. The existence of ICs from several foreign countries in a host country is likely to reduce concern over foreign government interferences and increase attention to *company* operations. Any move to joint ventures will accelerate this shift.

1

among governments and between them and the ICs. The relationships will differ according to the sectors of activity—extraction, manufacturing, commerce, finance, and services. This study focuses primarily on manufacturing companies.

Interdependence

The relations between ICs and governments at home and abroad represent a mixture of conflict *and* cooperation, as well as of risks *and* opportunities; and these mixtures affect the policy-formation process. On the one hand, home and host governments have varying expectations about ICs ranging from controlling and using them internally and externally (the extreme nationalist and imperialist views); falling more or less under their control (a variant of the technostructural and imperialist doctrines); and loosening control over them (the limited supranationalist view). On the other hand, many international companies want to be accepted as legitimate economic actors within each nation and in the international economic sphere; but others either do not seem to care about their contributions to host economies and societies or are barely aware of the fact that conflicting positions exist; and still others have opposed any systematic program for developing information on the economic, social, political, or cultural effects of their operations.

Legitimacy

Companies want and need to have their power legitimized by government and other relevant groups and individuals (e.g., public opinion, industrial elites, or the intelligentsia) because the possession of legitimacy facilitates access to policy makers, increases influence over policy making, and reduces criticism, thereby maximizing the use of other company resources. Legitimacy comes either from established rights or from acceptability by the company; and it may be accorded to the roles played by the company, to their occupants, or to their decisions—the strongest position resulting when legitimacy is accorded on more than one basis.

In obtaining legitimacy, international companies encounter special problems because there are no international rights and supranational organizations under which they can claim to exercise their powers. Instead, the rights of the parent company and of its subsidiaries stem from national laws. Incorporation in any one country, of course, grants some measure of legitimacy to a firm, but few host governments see themselves as giving the parent company the power that it does in fact exercise in the host country. (At the same time, the U.S. government does not wish to relinquish any power it has over IC operations overseas through the parent company.) Consequently, the acquisition of legitimacy by international companies rests largely on the acceptability of their actions in the eyes of the host and home governments and of other beneficiaries of their activities.

Such acquistion is particularly difficult by the classical (or colonial) type of IC and the more recent multinational-enterprise type. The colonial type originally gets its legitimacy from its home government, since it serves mainly the home country; but this source is now almost extinct, following the independence of colonies. The subsidiaries of an IC that are operated separately and largely as "national" companies are more likely to be seen as operating in the national interest, and in favor of national sovereignty and identity; and legitimacy is easier to obtain in this event. The multinational enterprise, on the other hand, is usually seen as having too many nation-servants and not enough nation-masters as it pursues its "least-cost"-oriented operations from country to country. Conversely, because it cannot serve the interests of *all* of its host nations at the same time, the multinational enterprise sees itself as having too much interference from each government.

Besides, whatever legitimacy is acquired in one country generally cannot be extended abroad. A good example of this situation is provided by those American subsidiaries which are incorporated in any one of the member states of the European Community and thus benefit in principle from the "freedom of establishment" guaranteed by the Treaty of Rome. Yet countries such as France and the United Kingdom have discriminated against such U.S. subsidiaries when they launch an investment into these countries *from* other EEC states because they do not consider them as truly Belgian, for example, on account of the American-based control exercised over them.

Mutual Adjustment

Moreover, any acceptance is not stable, because national and company objectives and personnel change and because the relative bargaining power of the parties changes over time. In general, the new foreign investor has greater leverage at the outset, if he is wanted by the host country. Later on, he is much more likely to be taken for granted, unless he threatens to move or is increasing his contributions to the host country.

Because of these shifts, ICs must continuously redetermine the proper scope and manner of their relations with governments at home and abroad in order to adapt to or to influence the processes of policy formation and implementation. Not all companies perform this function equally well; and among those that do, most are only recently giving it a high standing within the corporate hierarchy, as analyzed in Part I. Part II addresses the issues and actors in the dialogues between business and governments; and Part III assesses the criteria of successful government-business relations and some alternative approaches open to the U.S. government for their improvement.

Given the widespread knowledge of the expanding interfaces between business and government around the world, the primary hypothesis from which the study started was that the ICs and the international economy were developing in ways that required close and continuing business-government dialogues on problems and solutions. This dialogue should be based on the exchange of information on policies and practices, for it has become clear that the market is no longer the sole or even primary source of information on which business policies are based.

Study Focus

A complete study of impacts on policy formation would have required an examination of the relationships of all U.S. business to the Congress, and of headquarters companies to various departments in the Executive Branch, including the White House; but some exclusions were necessary. The empirical base, therefore, was narrowed to primarily manufacturing companies through some banks, and petroleum companies were interviewed. Within the interviews it was not possible to examine the impact of personalities on the communication process; this is left to later research.

The focus of the study, therefore, is on the patterns of communications among foreign governments, ICs in manufacturing, and the U.S. government, and the means of their improvement. Examination of the three actors is carried throughout the book, even though each part focuses primarily on the relationships of one with the other two. The recommendations for reorientation of the State Department are limited to its direct relationships with ICs—not to its general responsibilities in the political or economic realms, but these will, of course, be affected by any shift in priorities. An assessment of the fit of these various responsibilities would require a thorough examination of the mission of the Department and the means of accomplishing it.

Our investigation demonstrates that relationships of ICs with governments of advanced countries differ strikingly from those with governments of less-developed countries (LDCs). Dialogues with governments of advanced countries occur principally at the stage of entry, under a screening process or approval mechanism, and in a general climate of receptivity. Succeeding dialogues relate to specific problems that may arise in operation but do not require any more frequent communication than local enterprises, since the foreign enterprises are largely absorbed into the local private sector.

Contrarily, the IC going into a developing country has a set of negotiations for entry that begins frequently within a relatively hostile setting despite a desire to have the investment. Most government officials are often suspicious of the IC's motives and distrustful of its executives, as well as uncertain of their own ability to match the negotiating skills and information base of the IC executives.

On his part, the American manager is less capable in the LDC setting. Although he may give the impression of confidence and strength, his unfamiliarity with the situation, the mores and customs of the host country, and alternative approaches to negotiation itself make him also an ineffectual negotiator.

Besides, in LDCs, the political, psychological, ideological, and personality aspects of negotiation are more important than in dealing with advanced countries. As a consequence, U.S. embassies are likely to become more involved in the relationship, even though their officials in LDCs are less likely to understand business mores than those assigned to posts in advanced countries, simply because of the relative insignificance of U.S. business activities in the LDCs.

Consequently, the American manager is more attuned to the relationship that is likely to develop in advanced countries than in LDCs, and U.S. Embassy staff are likely to be more capable of playing their role in advanced countries, even though the greater necessity and pressure for close governmental relations on the part of both are in the LDCs. The capabilities and interests of the parties do not mesh; the result is an ad hoc treatment of the problems of business in developing countries, at a time when the base should be built for the longer-run role of the private sector within the existing and emerging framework of ideologies.

There are at least five policy orientations that might be used in this situation, each leading to a quite different pattern of relationships: (1) use of host-government edicts under which unilateral regulations are issued, without dialogue with ICs or the U.S. Embassy; (2) ad hoc negotiation resulting in special deals that cannot be used as a precedent for any subsequent contractual arrangement; (3) contractual or concessional arrangements made under established guidelines so that useful information can be obtained for future negotiations; (4) adaptation of the dialogues on a continuing basis so as to develop a set of guidelines and understandings of the role of the private sector and the foreign investor within it; and (5) extension of this last approach to a wider, regional or international scope employing international controls to the ICs. All but (5) involve bilateral or trilateral adaptations between the host government, the ICs, and the U.S. Embassy.

None of the three participants, however, are really prepared to handle the problems by any one of the available approaches. Instead, each begins with inadequate information about the activities and objectives of the other. Each lacks professionals with adequate preparation in the area of his responsibility and training in negotiation. Each lacks clear guidelines from superiors as to the limits within which he can negotiate or the objectives to be sought, which also take into full account the motives and limitations of the others. And few have adequate organizational structures to channel, assess, disseminate, and utilize the necessary information. Even though the IC is relatively more advanced and better structured than governments, it also needs improvement if it is to take an initiative.

From the standpoint of the United States, this state of affairs is understandable in the light of the chasm that has existed between government and business, each tending to stand apart or remaining suspicious of the other. Business has historically considered that government exists to serve the desires of business; while government has, since the 1930s at least, considered that business would not act in the interest of the country. It is difficult for U.S. international companies to form a close relationship abroad with either the host government or U.S. Embassy with this background of attitudes—particularly since embassy structures have not given a high priority to business problems abroad.

Many of the LDCs are simply too young to have formed their own structures for handling business, either at home or from abroad; and in many, attitudes have been negative toward the private sector in general, reducing their interest in cooperative dialogues. The advanced countries have tended to rely on the local business organizations and their normal business-government patterns to handle communication with the foreign investors. This procedure is becoming inadequate to meet problems that arise from the mere fact of "foreignness," and further adaptations probably have to be made.

The lesson from this analysis is that all parties will either have to give a higher priority to reordering and restructuring the relationship of business to government, or they will have to acquire the ability to withstand increasing tensions arising from mere muddling through with good intentions but little modifications of attitudes or procedures. A third alternative, of course, is not to do either, but to generate strictly ad hoc reactions and solutions that tend to disrupt if not destroy the existing system and the capabilities of the ICs along with it.

An accommodation is much more likely with the advanced countries than with LDCs, simply because the former tend to accept the phenomenon of ICs more readily. Besides, the nature of the dialogues is more specific and related to such problems as acquisition (vs. new establishment), 100 percent ownership (vs. joint ventures), sourcing, intracompany pricing, antitrust, exports, and employment policies. These governments tend to recognize the legitimacy of ICs also because they have their own nationally based ICs operating abroad, which they seek to promote and protect. This proliferation of mutual direct investment among the advanced countries will tend to shift the dialogue to that of mutual accommodation of problems within a larger setting of acceptability and legitimacy. This scenario is not likely in the LDCs, however.

This study takes the first alternative as the most useful one to pursue—that of reorienting and restructuring the relationships between government and business. But it focuses essentially on the changes that will need to be made by U.S. international companies and the U.S. government—namely the State Department and its embassies abroad. It was not feasible to examine foreign countries to determine the gaps and inadequacies in their own structures and orientations, although some evidence was gathered during the process of interviews and is drawn on for illustrative purposes throughout the volume.

Company Structures and Processes

Part I addresses the IC's approach to governmental relations (GR), showing that the GR function is a developing part of company policies, that there is increasing sophistication being applied by management to governmental dialogues, that there is considerable diversity of approaches and organizational structures for handling GR, that the personnel involved range widely in responsibilities and preparation (with some evidence of improvement in quality as the status of the GR function is raised in the company), that there is substantial geographic decentralization of responsibilities with little coordination at the top, and that intelligence gathering and circulating is a major problem. Companies are not yet certain what information they need, how to obtain it, how to interpret it, how to circulate it through the company layers involved, how to reintegrate the variety of assessments made by these layers, and how to use the results in negotiations.

If the approach to be adopted is that of reorienting company policy toward closer dialogues with governments, the *first* policy implication of the results of this study is that the GR function must be raised to a higher priority within the headquarters company, with the chairman or chief executive officer taking direct responsibility; but this requires a basic change in attitudes. The *second* policy implication is that the consequence of this higher priority will be a reorganization of the company grid to better disseminate, interpret, and use the information flows.

IC Attitudes

The changes in attitudes within the company toward GR should be achieved by top-level emphasis on the importance of closer dialogues with governments. Top-level commitment will then percolate throughout the organization both by example and by the explicit or implicit use of sanctions when actions are taken in ignorance of governmental views.

Changes are also needed within business and industrial associations, whose awareness and abilities in the matter of business-government dialogues vary significantly from country to country and sector to sector. The influence of key companies and "industrial statesmen" is crucial on account of their prestige and financial clout in the process of educating other international companies, and "least-common-denominator" positions of the membership would be avoided in favor of more forthcoming postures. In turn, these shifts would be reflected in new attitudes toward governments, through direct contacts by company executives and through collective action, but also through the encouragement of international conferences where governments discuss among themselves, with the assistance of international company representatives, the shape of the emerging international economic order and its consequences for triangular communications in international investment matters.

In this process, the quality of the men (line executives, staff, intermediaries) involved remains crucial. Americans abroad have had to learn on the job about the importance of this function and about its techniques, for lack of proper sensitization and experience at home. This situation, fortunately, is slowly improving as more U.S. managers and technicians have lived overseas, have acquired experience in dialogues with governments, and are being better selected and trained in the light of these new job requirements.

IC Structure and Skills

To improve the GR structure of companies and skills of IC officials, changes are required within companies and among them.

Within companies, a number of alternative arrangements for conducting GR exist in terms of the respective roles of line and staff, the centralization or decentralization of government activities, and their integration with other functions. Clearly, such structures and skills need to be scrutinized in terms of effectiveness. In particular, the establishment of goals and their achievement has to be linked to appropriate recruitment, training (both of the classroom and experiential varieties), motivation (including promotion), and reporting schemes. Besides, crucial decisions have to be made regarding the nationality, status, and geographic location of those executives and staff that interact with governments.

Collectively, international companies face choices regarding the proper locus, format, and focus of collective action. They must decide in terms of: (1) business-wide (e.g., the Chamber of Commerce of the United States) vs. industry-based (e.g., among chemical firms) efforts; (2) a multipronged and special-purpose approach (e.g., focusing on the Hartke-Burke bill) vs. a more unified and broader one—a dilemma reflected in the present proliferation of U.S. groups with different or overlapping objectives, geographic coverages, and memberships; (3) special associations for foreign subsidiaries abroad vs. fitting into domestic ones; and/or (4) grouping of only U.S. international companies vs. representing all international investors, irrespective of ownership or control of nationality.

The underdevelopment of the GR function is matched by frequent underdevelopment of intelligence networks within international companies. This condition results from the complexity of gathering information about the nonmarket environments of many countries, the significant "distances" among the various levels of international companies, and the lack of proper attitudes and skills among IC executives. More effective intelligence gathering is not easily achieved, and few international companies can boast of having progressed very far in obtaining and using intelligence at the planning, executing, and reviewing stages. This situation, however, is matched by that found in governmental departments vis-à-vis international companies, and it helps explain why international business-government dialogues are still at an infant stage.

U.S. Government

The U.S. government could stimulate these policy changes on the part of ICs by insisting that the companies tool up for better communication. This can be achieved both at home and abroad through official pronouncements, government-sponsored conferences, and U.S. embassy activities, and also through contacts with individual international companies. Such awareness, as with ICs, must start at the top levels. This was done in one case in the early 1960s when an assistant secretary of commerce and the Alliance for Progress coordinator encouraged several business associations dealing with Latin American issues to combine into a single group (presently the Council of the Americas), so as to facilitate and make more effective the dialogue on the role of private investment in Latin American integration and development. There was a felt need on the part of the government for a better dialogue, and the companies involved responded.

This could be done not only among associations but also within the ICs themselves, lowering the level of continuing dialogue but raising the responsibility to top levels so that there is full coordination across the company. Recent initiatives in the formation of a U.S.-Latin American Commission on Technology provide a new opportunity of close government-business dialogue at several levels. None of the parties involved is ready, however, and much planning and structuring will be needed.

Presently it appears that the role of the embassies with U.S. business abroad is better carried out than communications between business and the State Department within the United States. The distribution of information by U.S. embassies in the field for the local affiliates of U.S. firms is superior to that between the headquarters company and the State Department—superior not in the sense of accuracy, for State relies on the embassies, but in the sense of volume and relevance to specific problems. Embassy officials are closer to the problems and have some knowledge of the company needs at the local level, and can transmit information face to face that they might be unwilling to put into reports back to the State Department—or might simply lack time to do, given all their other reporting requirements. They can also transmit information to the local American Chamber of Commerce (AmCham), which they might not care to transmit in official and public reports.

Consequently, in the matter of intelligence, the U.S. government can reshape the diffusion of the valuable information it collects through its embassies, its Washington staffs, and the various studies it commissions. In particular, it can channel more of it within the countries where it is hardly available to foreign subsidiaries. Greater diffusion of its information through American Chambers of Commerce abroad provides a real opportunity in this respect.

In view of the importance of intermediaries in government relations, the U.S. government can also encourage and even assist their growth and improvement—

for example, by negotiating with foreign governments for the establishment of U.S. law offices overseas; by encouraging and supporting the development of more American Chambers of Commerce abroad (if this is shown to be an appropriate way of dealing with a particular foreign government); and by encouraging companies seeking U.S. government assistance in foreign investment (e.g., in the context of OPIC) to analyze the changing contributions of their investment over time and the likely reactions abroad. This would help develop a better government-business understanding.

Host Governments

The host governments can also accelerate the reorientation of company structures and priorities. They can insist on one of several channels of dialogues or patterns of relationships to induce IC responses. At present, few governments have taken the time to think through the desired relationships or the implications of any one approach for their own governmental structures used in handling business problems. Rather, one finds quite different structures among even the advanced countries with undeveloped structures in those LDCs where the private sector itself is preadolescent. In some countries, such as Brazil, governmentally directed business associations have been formed to be the channels of dialogues, and the foreign sector is more or less effectively included within it—or, in the case of Mexico, has found a niche completely outside the local associations.

The alternatives open to host governments in structuring the business-government dialogue cover a wide range. At one end the foreign investor is indistinguishable from local companies, while at the other end, they are set apart:

1. Insistence on foreign-owned affiliates becoming fully participating members of local associations so that the only dialogue with ICs is as part of the total private sector or relevant segments;

2. Insistence on association through local organizations, save for treatment of special (single) company problems that may arise;

3. Insistence on association with local groups, save for treatment of special problems having to do with generalized problems of all foreign-owned companies;

4. Separation of specific industrial sectors from local associations, when that sector is predominantly or wholly controlled by foreign interests—e.g., extraction;

5. Development of a "foreign-community" association encompassing all foreign-based ICs;

6. Development of foreign-country-oriented associations, such as the American Chambers of Commerce (AmCham's) abroad, including both local companies and foreign-owned affiliates, so that local interests can also be represented in foreign investment problems;

7. Creation of solely foreign-country-oriented associations, with each country having its own business association—e.g., Japan Chamber, German Chamber, French Chamber, etc.—each separate from the others and from the local community.

There are advantages and disadvantages to each of these approaches, and none is likely to be followed consistently throughout all governmental dialogues with ICs. On the contrary, negotiations about specific company problems or contracts will, obviously, be taken outside of any association structure. But at times, even macro problems can be settled by company-government negotiation (such as tax liability, interest rates, price levels, wages, and employment conditions). The approach taken will depend on national customs and mores and on the personalities involved within both the ICs and the host governments.

Government-Business Dialogues

Part II concludes that there is a wide gap between the perception by company executives and government officials of business-government relationships, and the reality of each party's views and interests. Further, there is a lack of focus within the host-government organizations responsible for business relations, an inadequate assessment of the costs and benefits of alternative IC relationships, an absence of criteria for effective communications (rather an ad hoc approach under which "appropriate" relationships are tailored for each case), a lack of trained personnel to deal with foreign businesses, an absence of trade-offs among policies of the U.S. government in support of business abroad, and a lack of a clear statement of expectations from the embassies on the part of business, the State Department, or the host countries. Besides, the three parties have quite different exposures and interests in closer government-business relations, facing potential loss, benefits, or null effects in quite different combinations in any given situation. This alters their bargaining positions, their effectiveness, and their interest in structuring closer communications.

The complex relationships among the three parties can be summarized under five broad categories: *information, attitudes, skills, structures,* and *initiative.*

Information

Information is a source of power and influence. The credibility, timeliness, accuracy, and relevance of the information possessed are some of the determinants of the extent of influence exercised.

The IC, U.S. government, and the host governments have developed a greater awareness of the closeness of their relationships. This recognition has created a need for more information and more effective transfer of information from one party to another. The LDCs are made suspicious by the fact that the IC and the

U.S. government have access to information that they do not possess, and therefore they feel at a disadvantage in dealing with the other two. In addition, LDCs feel that the U.S. government and the IC exchange information between themselves, excluding the developing countries. Charges of intellectual colonialism exist because the developed countries often have more information on a developing country than the country itself. Moreover, as the host government gains in experience in international business and economic transactions it develops a greater awareness of the role of information in dealing with foreign entities, both public and private.

The central policy implication that applies to all three parties is that the development of an effective dialogue will be strongly dependent upon and conditioned by the extent to which there is a sharing of relevant information among them on areas of mutual interest concerning policies and operations of the IC and governments. In fact, greater equality of access to information is likely to result in reducing the charges of collusion and collaboration between the U.S. government and the IC, which in turn will permit the host countries to see the U.S. government as an independent entity whose interests and objectives are not necessarily the same as those of the I.C.

The need for greater and more specific information is an important policy implication for the U.S. government itself, in order for it to understand better the nature of the IC and to influence it more effectively through formal and informal means. However, specification of the information needed must be in relation to the existing (or future) policy of the U.S. government toward the IC, as discussed in Part III.

The host government is also faced with a similar policy implication. In order to exercise greater and more effective influence over the IC, the host government will need to specify what type of information it seeks, from where it is to be secured, and why it seeks a particular type of information. The last question poses a basic policy question for the host government, namely, determining what role it assigns to foreign enterprise in the country's development efforts. Of course, seeking information about ICs will also have a bearing on the internal policies, personalities, and politics of the host country, because the information gathered from various sources might well prove that the interpretations and accusations by local interests of the IC and U.S. government are not correct. Therefore, information gathered by the host government for the sake of greater and it is to be hoped more effective influence on the IC is likely to create some realignment in the internal power structures as well as the policies of the host country.

The IC is faced with several policy implications regarding the role of information in the influence process. Increasingly, governments are beginning to gain greater (if not always more accurate) information on the ICs through international organizations such as the United Nations, and through sharing of experiences between countries. Publications of the U.S. government and congressional hearings are additional sources of information on ICs.

The fundamental policy implication for the IC is that it could exercise some influence over governments by *offering* information as against being forced by governments to provide information. However, the type of information furnished cannot be determined solely by the IC ("This is what we think you are entitled to"), but through dialogue with governments in determining what information is useful.

Of course, this approach to the exercise of influence requires significant revision of the traditional orientation of the IC about what is confidential information for purposes of competition or what is the appropriate scope of demands of a government in terms of seeking information from a company. The act of taking the initiative to provide information, therefore, reflects an important change of attitude on the part of the IC in the influence process; namely, the IC indicates that it is responsive to the needs of the host society *as interpreted by the government.* But governments themselves need to be more explicit about their policies, as well as candid about why they need the information.

Attitudes

The U.S. government, host government, and IC have different outlooks and expectations regarding the relative role, value, and priority of IC activities. There is an attitudinal gap between the U.S. government and the IC and an attitudinal chasm between the IC and many host governments, especially in the developing countries. The outlook of each group toward the others is determined by a range of social, cultural, political, and economic characteristics extending over long periods of time, since each party is a product of its particular environment. Yet, in the context of their emerging relationships, they have to interact and understand each other to a far greater degree than at present if progress in communication is to be made in the pursuit of objectives.

A fundamental characteristic of existing attitudes for all three groups is that, having come into being over a long period of time, they are not likely to change overnight. All parties to the influence process must recognize the need for adopting a long-term perspective to effectuate changes in attitudes. Conflict arises from the fact that the present and growing interrelationship between ICs and governments demands new attitudes *now*, while the attitudes are just beginning to change.

A more effective dialogue will require a change in attitude toward ICs on the part of the U.S. government and vice versa. However, changing attitudes will require strong leadership and support from the most senior levels of the U.S. government and from ICs, acknowledging the presence and the growing importance of closer interrelationship between the two. Besides, the development and implementation of specific programs to promote greater understanding between the U.S. government and the IC will contribute over time to a gradual reorientation of attitudes.

The host government is faced with a major policy implication because its belief of collusion between the U.S. government and the IC strongly affects its approach to dealing with the IC. But, if the perception is largely incorrect, the host government will be wasting some of its negotiation strength in dealing with the IC. What would be the approach of the host government toward the IC if its perception of collusion was to be proven incorrect? What would be the effect on internal political power relationships if the host government significantly discounted the charge of U.S.-IC collusion? Obviously, the dialogue between the IC and the host government would take place with much less of a diplomatic overtone and more along the lines of dialogues with local business or all other foreign investors. Consequently, strong leadership by senior officials of the host government will be required to review and reassess such existing attitudes toward the IC and the U.S. government.

The key policy implication for IC management is that it must develop a view that does not regard governments to be ineffective meddlers, seeking only to impede the IC's efforts to tackle problems of economic growth. In addition, the IC must recognize that considerations of sovereignty will transcend economic considerations; and that in relations with governments, the IC invariably will be seen as the junior partner. The IC will also need to assess its economic contributions to a country with reference to how each assists key decision makers in the host country to protect and promote their notion of the national interest, sovereignty, and identity.

Skills

Nationalism remains the critical dimension in relations between the IC and the host government and between governments over international investment. The emphasis on sovereignty has made most of the LDC governments highly sensitive to possible encroachments by the IC or the U.S. government. In addition, often because of its own tradition, the host government believes that the IC's economic interests are closely related to the U.S. government's politico-economic interests, and vice versa. Since many host governments view desirable IC activities in purely economic terms rather than in terms of *political* economy, the skills required by officials of the IC, U.S. government, and host governments include more than mere political or managerial talents.

Three general types of skills can be identified: economic/technical, political/ diplomatic, and human/personal. Interactions between the IC, U.S. government, and the host governments calls for different combinations of these skills according to the situation. The IC typically possesses relatively more of the economic/technical talents than the other two types, but the U.S. government's role and the host government's use of bilateral bargains to control the IC will demand greater economic/technical skills. On the other hand, the IC will need to gain greater political/diplomacy and human/personal skills in order to represent its interests effectively.

Efforts on the part of each to acquire a better *combination* of skills would reflect a basic change in attitudes and objectives, but it will probably have to wait for a recognition of a fundamental shift in the roles of each toward the others.

Structures

The existing structures in governments and ICs are inadequate, as is shown in Part I, but neither uses what it has very effectively in the interaction/influence process. Both gaps are likely to increase the pressure for new structures. The key policy implication for the governments and ICs is that they should review and reassess their existing structures from the standpoint of their effectiveness for particular purposes.

More effective structures for both ICs and governments will likely require greater centralization and coordination of information-gathering and dialogue-building. Some degree of realignment of relationships—parent-affiliate within ICs, and among ministries of government—will have to occur; and senior officials of each will have to set policies and determine the extent of delegation of communication and negotiation responsibilities to the field.

Especially in the developing countries, the internal political implications of realignment of relationships and responsibilities will be greater than in advanced countries. This situation means that even stronger and more decisive leadership will be required—a need made more acute by present attitudes and the lack of effective structures for dialogue even between the host government and locally owned companies.

The ICs face the difficult problem of potentially influencing several governments around the world at the same time, in different policy directions. A policy has to be developed, enunciated, and implemented over time with the active support of officials at several levels of corporate management. To do so, again, requires a recognition that governments are perhaps the most important single unit in determining the continued success of a foreign affiliate, and that governmental interest is not focused solely on economic impacts but also on political, social, and cultural effects—all of which the IC must be able and willing to discuss openly.

Initiative

Compared to the U.S. government and host governments, the IC has been by far the most active party in taking the intiative in dialogues, save when statutes require the government to take it. In the future, any effort to reduce foreign government intervention through the IC, or achieve harmonized treatment of investors will require governments (host or home) to take the initiative in dialogues with each other. Also, the need to specify the type of information sought from the IC will require a governmental initiative. To take such an initiative implies that the U.S. government and others know what they want from the ICs—something they do not at the present. Thus, they may be pushed by the U.N. or the companies themselves.

These policy positions should reflect considered views as to the desired mutuality of interests between the U.S. government and American ICs, and whether the U.S. government wishes to take initiatives apart from those of the ICs. Unless it does, the host government will believe that any U.S. government-IC initiative is one more evidence of the collusion that it has always thought to exist, creating additional difficulties for U.S. government-host government relations.

If the host government seeks to take the initiative, it will need to address first the question of what role it wishes to assign to the IC, and what methods it wishes to use (and in what combinations) in attempting to influence the IC. Once these are decided, the mere taking of an initiative will increase the need to change its existing attitudes, skills, and structures for communication.

The IC must recognize that, by and large, governments are unlikely to take any initiative in changes of policies or relationships that might be viewed as more desirable to the IC. Especially in developing countries, host governments are likely to take initiatives that will demand changes in IC practices and policies. By taking the initiative, the IC might be able to exercise some influence over the host government in the extent, nature, and pace of change sought. To be successful, this initiative must include adequate consideration of the needs and preferences of the sovereign states that make the ultimate determination of the desirability of the continued presence of the IC.

U.S. Government Policies

Part III focuses on the changes needed within the U.S. government in order to create a continuing and closer dialogue with ICs, both at home and abroad. Based on the findings of the prior chapters, Chapter 7 assesses the alternatives open to the State Department both in policies toward foreign investment and in reorienting its organizational structure in Washington and in the embassies. If the Department wishes to establish closer relations with business, it must first change its attitude toward business motives, and reflect that shift in departmental activities. On its part, business needs to do a better job in explaining its objectives fully and carefully. Unfortunately, business continues to assert that profit is its *single* objective when, in fact, profit is interrelated with the pursuit of a variety of business, personal, and societal objectives, and is a means rather than an end in itself.

With a more forthcoming attitude toward both business and other governmental agencies concerned with international economic and business problems, the Department could probably regain authority over international economic policy—centered in the White House's special adviser under the Nixon Administration—and pass this authority through to ambassadors and the regional bureaus in State. Only through a reorganization of responsibilities and reordering of priorities within the regional bureaus will any significant change occur within the State Department itself. The specific proposals made in this study are supported by the investigations of the Inspector General of the State Department and the White House's Office of Management and Budget.

This restructuring and reorientation of State Department priorities and activities would be more readily undertaken if there were a recognition that a dialogue between any two of the parties would be likely to involve the third, either directly or indirectly. For example, even in a bilateral negotiation between an IC and a host government, an embassy might consider that the company position is: (1) dangerous to the company itself, and should warn the firm; (2) harmful to the interests of the United States, and the firm should be counseled as to that interest; (3) harmful to other companies, whose long-run interests must be taken into account; or (4) harmful to the host government, and would thereby injure long-run relations of all parties. When embassies have seen these situations emerging, they have adopted quite different postures, from embassy to embassy—some not intervening and others intervening quite strongly, sometimes without the knowledge or support of the State Department.

The emergence of discriminatory policies toward international business (following the likely rejection of the U.S. criterion of "multilateral, non-discriminatory trade and payments") will increase substantially the occasions for interference by governments and the necessity for ad hoc dialogues. Negotiation will also continue, of course, but would be altered in substance by any adoption of new international rules.

In this situation, embassies will want some guidelines as to when to act, when not to, and how to do so effectively. Embassies could appropriately decide *not* to intervene:

1. When no significant interest of the U.S. government, third country, or company is involved;

2. When the market mechanism is deemed to produce an acceptable resolution of a problem, under the rules laid down by the host government;

3. When the host government's interest is perceived to be considerably greater than that of the U.S. government;

4. When interference would prejudice more important relations of the U.S. government with the host government;

5. When U.S. government interference would set a bad precedent for relations with third countries;

6. When the company requested nonintervention on the grounds that U.S. government interference would not be in its interest, and the U.S. government does not have an independent interest of its own;

7. When the U.S. government sees the situation as irreversible, i.e., it got in too late or the local forces are simply too strong;

8. When the embassy sees the situation is too murky and ill-defined for it to develop a defensible position; and/or

9. When the possibility of publicity is so great as to prove harmful to U.S. interests in the country.

In any of these situations, the embassy might still determine that it was necessary to make a *record* of protest, even if it could not alter behavior of the host government.

Conversely, the embassy could decide to enter the dialogue on the side of the host government or try to dissuade the IC from pursuit of the problem if: (1) the embassy considered the company in error; (2) the company's position was sound but its pursuit would damage significant U.S. interests; or (3) the company problem was deemed to be insignificant and not worth the time it would require.

Recognizing the lack of a single criterion and the myriad structures and interests, it is not possible to provide a "model" set of government relations for business, nor of business-relations approaches for either the U.S. government or the host governments. But recognition of complexity does not remove the necessity to achieve a more productive relationship in pursuit of mutual goals. This recognition of diffuse communication channels and of the need for organizational efforts toward an effective dialogue should go a long way to defusing the criticism that ICs and the U.S. government are so close as to form an imperialistic conspiracy against the host country.

If it can be accepted that the present dialogue and channels are inadequate to support continuing communication among the three parties, and that closer relationships are desirable to meet the emerging problems of development and the creation of a new international economic order, then each party will feel more confident that it can participate in that restructuring without fear of losing its fair share of the benefits of industrial advance over the world.

Presently, none of the parties seems able to take such an initiative, since ICs are oriented toward the past world order, although they themselves are changing it; while governments are mostly unhinged from the past rules but have not conceptualized a new set that might be acceptable. Consequently, the dialogues among the parties are either related to quite specific (ad hoc) problems or tend to flounder.

Any one party has the opportunity to take the initiative; but if the ICs do not, they will likely find a more hostile setting than would be the case if they were more forthcoming. This hostility is fed by the fact that, in the absence of agreed-upon rules, it often pays one player to be overly aggressive. If host countries adopt a policy that is seen as too aggressive, or merely creates an unacceptable level of uncertainty as seen by the ICs, the latter are likely to retract and to seek a more secure mooring in their home countries and more hospitable host nations. There is, therefore, a limit to what an aggressive posture on the part of any party can achieve. To reduce this reaction on the part of LDCs especially, the ICs will need to demonstrate openly and continuously that *all* players are obtaining equitable benefits from IC activities. In final sum, improved dialogue appears imperative, and international companies will do well to initiate it—on or within the rules laid down by governments—or at least to welcome it.

Part I
Company Actors, Structures, and Processes

2

The International Government-Relations Function

International companies have not yet given the government-relations (GR) function a high priority among management's responsibilities. Among the few that have, there are quite varied methods of handling the function; and no generalized pattern of behavior or performance can be discerned in this area, although some common elements are visible.[1]

Government Relations

Government relations are fundamentally concerned with changing public policy (or preventing changes in it) and/or with gaining favorable (or avoiding unfavorable) treatment under existing policy—with cases of influencing policy at the application state being by far the most frequent.

Yet the government-relations function fits into the broader "external affairs" of the firm, relating it to its entire *nonmarket environment* of "noncommercial publics." (Other names are also used: public relations, public and government relations, public affairs, corporate affairs, etc. "External affairs" is itself inadequate to the extent that it seems to leave out the *internal* public constituted by an organization's personnel.) This group includes not only (1) government, in its multiple roles of legitimizer, regulator, and promoter, but also (2) the trade-union movement, as a countervailing power group in society (witness the AFL-CIO support of the Hartke-Burke bill); (3) the rest of a firm's industry, as well as business in general in their collective roles of pressure group and regulator (when permitted to do so, as in more "corporatist" countries); (4) the intellectual, moral, and scientific communities as legitimizers and/or critics; and (5) public opinion at large—including actual and potential employees, stockholders, suppliers, creditors, and neighbors who must be convinced to offer and maintain their services and other forms of support to the company. Success in all of these areas bears heavily on the acceptability of the company's actions—i.e., its legitimacy—as seen by consumers, workers, managers, stockholders, the local community, and the government. At the least, the opposition of such groups must be minimized or negated but obtaining their support—moral, regulatory, financial, and other—is even more important.

Key Factors

Market Orientation[2]

One type of international company is essentially geared to the production and marketing needs of home country and parent company, as in the older *classical* or *colonial* type of investment linked with obtaining foreign raw materials and/or developing privileged outlets. Such a firm not only has to cope nowadays with new nations whose policy-making capability may be underdeveloped, but also has to face anticolonial reactions, atavistic attachment to natural resources, conflicts among developed and underdeveloped countries about international terms of trade, and various preferences for noncapitalistic forms of production.

These problems are sometimes mitigated by long and deep links and familiarity with the host country and elites on the part of the IC, which facilitate intervention in policy formation. However, there is often a tendency on the part of the parent company to act like an absentee landlord who does not care about local needs and aspirations; and such a posture does not make for good government relations.

The home government (the United States) is usually quite anxious to assist such investment, because of a critical need for imports of raw materials and for exports, but current international relations with raw-material exporting countries are such that relatively little protection can be provided by the U.S. government.

The *international holding company* (IHC) produces and markets its output in a set of countries pretty much cut off from each other. There is thus strong "local" orientation and autonomy, which are often reinforced by the employment of nationals as chief executives and cadres, and by joint ventures with local firms. Such ICs interact mostly with host governments in the context of protectionism and the realization of industrialization plans; and they are usually welcome when they contribute to their achievement. IHCs typically leave much autonomy to their foreign affiliates in dealing with local governments, and there is relatively little centralization in the system—a fact that militates against strong outcries over foreign-dominated decisions by the international company. However, domination of a key sector by foreign-owned companies still feeds the nationalistic qualms noted earlier.

For its part, the U.S. government is interested in IHCs to the extent that they support national-development schemes that contribute to the stability of LDCs, and that they help expand U.S. exports.

The *multinational enterprise* has a worldwide market orientation and operates in as many national markets as governments will permit to be served by local production plus imports. In addition, the foreign subsidiaries are locked together in a pattern of international logistics, financing, staffing, and research, which requires substantial centralized decision making. Its purpose is to seek least-cost and optimum-profit operations, which means that this type of IC is frequently able and willing to shift production sites, product lines, technology, or trade patterns, when it pays to do so.

This type of orientation makes for special conflicts with host national interest, sovereignty, and identity, because the multinational enterprise is frequently seen as elusive, foreign oriented (meaning bound to U.S. goals by U.S.

regulations), and "supranational" in the sense that it transcends and therefore downgrades or threatens all national sovereignties, even that of the United States. Their intervention in policy formation is thus often viewed rather warily by governments, who suspect that the commitment of the subsidiaries is wholly to the parent company, and that such an IC cannot possibly satisfy the goals of all the governments involved.

Type of Industry

Extraction is the prime example of an industry that prompts many governmental measures because of the strong nationalistic, mercantilistic, and peasant emotions associated with natural resources. In addition, a polluting industry is suspect nowadays; and there are strong prejudices everywhere against marketing operations.

Conversely, some industries and firms are very much desired because they can assist governments in achieving such goals as growth (if they add a lot of value), full employment (if they are labor-intensive), balance of payments (if they are export-oriented), and technological development and prestige (if they use sophisticated techniques).

Patterns of Ownership, Control,
and Association

The multinational enterprise prefers 100 percent ownership, despite the problems it creates; while joint ventures (whether of the majority, fifty-fifty, or minority variety) and management contracts are associated more with the IHC type, thereby mitigating some of these problems through the intercession of local partners. Mixed ventures with state enterprises, and many other forms of association (e.g., coproduction, compensation, complementation, and consortium agreements) are also likely to promote closer government relations.

The U.S. government has taken no position on ownership by American parent companies—except to take no position—despite the fact that majority ownership tends to give it more influence over U.S.-controlled subsidiaries through the U.S. parent company.

Other Factors

Size is often relevant, because larger firms—on either an absolute or a relative basis—have more resources, more exposure, and more communication with governments; and big firms are expected to have information, views, and influence not available to others. The overall size of the U.S. presence in a particular country is also relevant here because, past a certain threshold, it becomes more visible and is perceived as threatening various local interests.

Crises tend to generate new policies about foreign investment or more intensive application of existing ones—for example, some particularly criticized takeovers, layoffs, and pull-outs create demands for new regulations; and the energy crisis as well as the concerted action of OPEC countries have prompted a reconsideration of the role of international oil companies in petroleum supply. Conversely, competition among host countries ameliorates policies toward foreign investors in order to induce new investment.

Targets

Levels

National governments are the main targets of U.S. international companies because sovereign power over foreign investment still resides there; even though this power is often curbed by international treaties or by federal structures; and some new nations have relatively weak central governments. However, lower-level governmental units are also significant targets because, in a number of countries, they have the power of incorporation, and are important policy makers and implementers as well as influencers, since there are frequently pulls toward greater subnational autonomy—as in Italy and Belgium—as a reflection of increasing demand for more participation and democracy. Yet, even in the decentralized governments of Canada, West Germany, and Switzerland, the federal level retains significant and sometimes major regulatory power vis-à-vis inward investors—if only through exchange controls.

Supranational bodies require attention on account of their existent, incipient, or potential regulatory and/or persuasive powers—e.g., the European Communities (EEC), the Andean Pact Group, the General Agreement on Tariffs and Trade (GATT), the Organization for Economic Cooperation and Development (OECD), the World Health Organization (WHO), the Food and Agricultural Organization of the United Nations (FAO), the International Labor Organization (ILO), the World Bank (IBRD), and the United Nations itself (including its various regional branches such as the Economic Commission for Europe).

Typically, such bodies cannot directly regulate international corporations. The EEC is an exception as far as certain matters are concerned, but most work through the relevant national governments. Still, their studies, resolutions, assistance, and directives are frequently relevant, as they create the climate and provide specific data for national policies; but bodies such as the United Nations are increasingly assisting host governments in dealing with international firms. For example, the United Nations set up early in 1973 a study by a Group of

Eminent Persons to analyze the effects of multinational corporations on economic development and international relations—an outcome of the 1972 UNCTAD Conference in Chile—and significant analyses and recommendations were issued in 1973 and 1974. Besides, many developing countries turn to the United Nations for general and specific assistance in formulating technical codes for industries and other areas of activities influencing private enterprise, both domestic and foreign. They are now to be coached on how to negotiate with foreign firms.

The complexity of government relations is increased by the fact that what takes place in one international body or in one nation-state is frequently affected by what is happening elsewhere. Since governments often join, imitate, and counter each other, an international company can optimize its influence only by coordinating and integrating its policy-formation activities. For example, influencing the European Communities' authorities requires approaching the EEC commissioners (and their staff) who propose regulations, *and* the national governments whose permanent representatives to the Commission examine these proposals, and whose ministers sit on the Council of Ministers and make final decisions. Consequently, in order to enhance their influence, IC subsidiaries in EEC countries must adopt similar stances in order to come up with compatible information and requests; and they must seek the support of European companies, leading to the formation of a more-or-less official advisory group.

Government Policies, Structures,
and Processes

Governments have a variety of policies, structures, and processes which complicate the government relations. In the first place, few countries (e.g., Mexico, Argentina, Malaysia) or groups of countries (such as the Andean group) have a law or code that embodies all or even most of the goals and instruments of a policy toward foreign investors. Instead, most nations (particularly the developed ones, including the United States) have a variety of more or less coherent laws and regulations bearing on such inward investment. Numerous bilateral agreements (such as the Treaty of Friendship, Establishment, and Navigation between the United States and Belgium) as well as a few supranational treaties and conventions (such as the Treaty of Rome establishing the European Economic Community, and the OECD Code of Liberalization of Capital Movements) restrict governments in these matters—at least de jure.

Second, the actual application of such codes, laws, regulations, and treaties typically differs from their formal contents. For one thing, many of these documents are only enabling acts that state broad objectives but leave it to various governmental units to issue implementing decrees and directives. Besides, the guidelines and application criteria are often vague as a reflection of the complexity of the subject matter, the anticipated fluctuations of the environment, and the preference of officials and bureaucrats for discretionary powers in performing their function.

Third, government policies toward foreign investors are typically riddled with conflicting objectives and multiple criteria of effectiveness that reflect the varying interests of the different parts of a government—one ministry being interested in the jobs created by foreign firms, for example, while another opposes such jobs on account of their impact on the industrial structure of the country.[3] Reconciling such conflicting goals is very difficult, and leads to delays if not indefinite postponements in obtaining the necessary permissions to invest. In addition, priorities change, and affect the ranking and reconciliation of such objectives.

Fourth, there is usually a variety of ministries and bureaus to contact in order to obtain information, permits, and incentives, although a particular department (typically, the ministry of finance or of industry) may well be the leader or coordinator of the various units, with large investments being handled at the highest level of government (e.g., the president's office or the council of ministers). Governments differ too in the policy role assigned to the bureaucracy, and in the role permitted local industry in the process of making and implementing policies toward foreign investors.

Fifth, governments exhibit differing scopes of interest over the content and life of a foreign investment. Some regulate only part of the investor's decision (e.g., where he will locate, or whether he can acquire a local firm), while others are more comprehensive in their reach. They also differ in terms of whether they have an overseas bureau to attract foreign investors, a "welcome-wagon" to assist them in getting started in the host country, and a "follow-up" service to monitor the execution of the investor's commitments and his continuing contribution to the achievement of public policies.

Sixth, it is well to observe that it is practically impossible to appeal administrative decisions about foreign investments for lack of effective judiciary or settlement systems at the national and international levels. Of course, some companies are more effective than others in avoiding or resolving unfavorable outcomes; and the U.S. government is sometimes able and willing to intervene on the basis of bilateral and supranational treaties, and of the various instruments it can use to influence foreign governments (e.g., the Hickenlooper amendment).

Organizing for Government Relations

Line and Staff

Even when there is a staff, a good part of government relations is handled by line people at the very top. The fundamental reason for this situation is that the acquisition of legitimacy and community support (typically bestowed by government, public opinion, and other legitimizing elites) attaches to the man at the very top who represents the corporation in this search. Normally, this role is the responsibility of the board of directors, and many U.S. subsidiaries abroad use the local board for this purpose, particularly when local nationals must be members (as in Sweden, Mexico, and Indonesia).

A more operational reason GR cannot be delegated downward is that, as one executive put it: "Only real power can face power in important negotiations and deliberations with government and other groups." Staffs and lower-level managers can obviously prepare the ground and carry out routine or less crucial transactions; but only the man or men who know and represent the total firm and control its resources can speak with full authority when important matters are at stake.

This requirement is reinforced by the fact that in many countries, there is a long tradition of centralized authority whereby companies speak only through their top executives (for example, within trade associations and with government officials). Having a lesser executive represent the company in major external contacts is actually interpreted as a slur on the other party, and is not conducive to open and productive deliberations. Protocol thus also brings about top-management involvement in relations with government and other key groups.

However, interacting with government officials and bureaucrats is not limited to the chief executive, who typically interacts with the highest levels, while middle managers and functional specialists (e.g., the personnel manager and the treasurer) deal with their technical correspondents in government.

Despite the fact that GR responsibility rests at the top, few companies (not even the largest) have incorporated this task in the job description of the general manager abroad. This omission is little short of amazing in view of the fact that the managers in LDCs spend between 30 and 60 percent of their time in government relations. To pick the right man for this task is quite different from selecting a mere "plant manager," but many U.S. firms are still accustomed to staying away from government at home.

Thinkers, Go-betweens, and Doers

When needs and resources warrant it, there is frequently some GR or EA staff to provide expert advice, although it will not necessarily exist at all geographic levels (local, national, regional, and world) nor on a full-time basis. Nationals are normally found here, although Americans and other Anglo-Saxons are still used in public relations on account of greater U.S. expertise in this area. Three types of skills and functions are evident in these staffs, although they overlap to some extent and are sometimes combined on account of small size.

1. Some staffers are mainly *intelligence gatherers*, skilled at obtaining,

interpreting, and reporting information about political, legislative, and regulatory developments. Some information is of such a highly technical nature (e.g., food regulation, antitrust, etc.) that skilled technicians must be employed; while generalists with liberal-arts backgrounds are used to handle broad environmental data. On the other hand, when the intelligence is of a more confidential or strategic nature, people with high official and personal contacts have to be used.

2. *Door openers* are people with connections based on family ties, social position, education, and/or previous employment (e.g., a general, a political figure, an aristocrat, or a former high-level bureaucrat). Most foreign societies are elitist in nature and readily allow for the use of connections of this sort, so that some members of the organization are recruited precisely because they possess such a marketable asset besides being, it is hoped, qualified to serve in some other capacity—on the board of directors of the subsidiary, in the general manager's office, or as head of a department.

3. The *doers* group is made up of implementers in government relations. While this is a function from which top management cannot divorce itself, a frequent problem is that the expatriate general manager's previous experience may have prepared him poorly for external relations—a difficulty often compounded by his lack of familiarity with the country's environment. In such a case, an associate "doer" (e.g., a personal assistant to the president) is imperative until the general manager is able to assume his proper role in this area, or to complement the latter.

Full-timers and Part-timers

Most ICs do not have full-time GR or EA staffs abroad, because their needs and resources do not justify them. Even large companies have moved slowly in creating full-fledged staffs, for lack of relevant models to copy and for fear of overdoing it. Besides, important policy developments may be few and far between, and can be followed without any elaborate intelligence or communication apparatus. Company attitudes are also important here. As one official commented in comparing his company to another which has given considerable attention to GR: "They are willing to get much closer to governments than we are."

Another element favoring a small staff or no special staff at all is that part of this function is carried out by other people or departments within the firm. Thus, some of the relations with government pass through the legal, financial, accounting, and marketing groups; production and engineering people get involved in trade-association committees dealing with such matters as industrial standards, and they handle part of the contacts with the scientific community; some of the relations with employers' associations and the labor movement are handled by the industrial-relations department—and so on. Clearly, this diffusion calls for coordination and common servicing, but not all external relations must pass through a single, specialized internal staff.

An additional shortcut consists of using the services of a "big sister" company. This approach is common in petrochemicals, where the petroleum company is considered to be the GR/EA expert for all affiliates of an IC in one country; or one subsidiary is designated as the "senior company" among all affiliates in a particular country (e.g., Bell Manufacturing Company for the other ITT firms in Belgium). A higher level within the IC (e.g., the European management headquarters) also acts as a substitute when a new subsidiary lacks the size, experience, or competence to handle some or all of its external affairs. Furthermore, a local partner can provide its EA expertise to the joint venture overseas.

The lack of a formal GR or EA staff in international companies, even large ones, is not necessarily a good yardstick of company effectiveness in this area, because information exchange, decisions, and implementation are achieved through frequent corresponding, telephoning, and visiting—especially when the organization contains people who have been assigned to a variety of foreign or international posts and who know each other well. Thus, many ICs have a European (or African) director, located in London, who travels a dozen times a year to the U.S. headquarters and to each affiliate in his region, and who is frequently visited by U.S. executives, in addition to a constant flow of letters, telephone calls, and telexes.

Insiders vs. Outsiders

What tasks can be performed inside the firm is also partly a function of the ready availability of external sources of information, assistance, and influence. Countries like the United Kingdom have an excellent politico-economic press, which simplifies the collection of data and interpretation of external developments. The spread of several worldwide intelligence services has also been useful in providing analyzed data. International law firms, banks, consultants, and engineering companies also guide prospective investors in their approaches to governments; and international public-relations services are becoming more readily available. Practically everywhere there are counselors of various backgrounds (including former prime ministers, generals, and members of parliament) with ability to advise, open doors, and intercede. Furthermore, briefing sessions by the U.S. ambassador and conferences organized by a trade association or the American Chamber of Commerce (AmCham) often provide ways of keeping up with significant developments in the nonmarket environment.

In Washington, a number of international consulting firms have been created to assist ICs in keeping track of U.S. legislative and regulatory developments and in monitoring foreign-government relations. They also engage in quasi-lobbying activities (e.g., in preparing position papers for ICs or even in making direct representations as bona-fide interest groups)—as do major business and industrial associations such as the U.S. Chamber of Commerce, the National Association of Manufacturers, the Machinery and Allied Products Institute, and such specialist organizations as the International Economic Policy Association and the Emergency Committee on American Trade.

Personal vs. Impersonal Communications

Some targets, such as the broad "public opinion" or some segment thereof, are reached through mass communications, although the ultimate target of such exercises may well be some politician or bureaucrat who pays attention to these groups. However, more personal approaches are often indicated.

For one thing, most foreign countries are still traditional in orientation, and they prize personal relations over impersonal ones. This situation is magnified when the country is dominated by a small elite where the key decision-makers (public and private) know each other and frequently interact socially and otherwise. In addition, reliable sources of economic and political information (censuses, business periodicals and services, trade associations, etc.) are frequently lacking abroad. In such cases, good intelligence, real understanding, and effective communication depend on the mutual trust and respect that result only from personal relations between individuals in business, government, and other relevant societal units.

It is of course difficult for the itinerate expatriate manager to fit quickly and readily into elite groups. To develop good personal relations typically takes more time than is given him at any one post—a problem frequently magnified by local suspicion of the foreign firm. Such obstacles can be overcome only by long and active involvement in associations, consultative and planning bodies, and conferences where the elites interact, and by deliberate efforts at informal meetings with politicians, bureaucrats, members of the intelligentsia, local business executives, etc.

Unfortunately, many U.S. executives assigned overseas have not been conditioned through experience and training to conceive of the importance and mechanics of such personal involvement. Until their appointment abroad, they have usually devoted their energy to technical and internal-management matters in the parent company, while GR/EA activities have remained the province of experts and of top management. Consequently, it takes much time and a new orientation for general managers abroad to understand their new role of spokesman and negotiator. This learning process can be facilitated by the use of assistants, advisers, and intermediaries, although frequently it is not begun unless there are specific orders from headquarters or a strong tradition of government relations in the parent company.

Individual vs. Collective Action

In gathering intelligence as well as in approaching government and other relevant groups, ICs use a blend of individual and collective approaches.

The classic rationale for collective action is that of economy and synergy in informing, advising, representing, and otherwise assisting a collective of international companies. Besides, group action adds credibility to some relations with government because a single firm may find it harder to press for a given policy change if members of its industry do not share the same problems and views (e.g., fiscal regulations that discriminate against importers). On the other hand, collective action can be slow, cumbersome, costly, and at the level only of the lowest common denominator. Much time may be spent to discover only that there is no agreement within the group as to appropriate action.

ICs typically face a choice of collective groups, ranging from national industry associations (e.g., the Sindicatos in Brazil) to overall organizations such as the French Patronat and including special IC collectives such as the AmChams abroad and some ad hoc groups of multinational corporations of several nationalities (such as were created in West Germany to oppose certain proposed revisions of the German tax code, and in Venezuela to discuss the new petroleum law). The variety of groupings reflects such factors as the importance of international firms in a particular country, the existence of special problems, company leadership (as when one U.S. firm reinvigorated the Association of British Pharmaceutical Industries), the reaction of local industrialists (who generally want U.S. companies to play a role in local associations), and the attitude of host governments.

In fact, representation by a group of ICs has been rather gingerly used in dialogues with governments because it evokes an image of massive "American intervention." Moreover, the grouping of American or multinational companies exacerbates the fear that they may overlook the national interest and ignore local sensibilities. Furthermore, some companies as a matter of policy want to be separated from other U.S. firms in any discussion with governments, and prefer separate dialogue.

The stigma of special pleading can be somewhat reduced by the use of such outsiders as lawyers, bankers, public-relationists, and U.S. embassy personnel. Adverse reactions against "foreign interference" can be eliminated also through collective action in *local* associations and chambers of commerce. Membership in some of these associations is compulsory in such countries as Mexico, Brazil, France, and West Germany; but even domestic associations are now increasingly aware of the need for all private firms of whatever national origin to band together in order to defend the private enterprise system; and they are increasingly urged by their members to defend the principle of free movement of capital and other resources since more non-U.S. firms now invest abroad. These factors make them increasingly receptive to accepting and supporting U.S. subsidiaries, although the latter seldom occupy key executive positions in such associations. For that matter, U.S. subsidiaries are seldom represented in those formal advisory bodies that counsel governments on economic and social policy, although this lack is compensated for somewhat by more informal contacts with the authorities.

However, some U.S. firms abroad keep their distance from local groups for lack of understanding of their actual role and functioning; while some of these associations resent the challenge to their economic and social leadership represented by the ICs. Still, at times, such foreign leadership is irresistible as when U.S. automobile firms dominate that industry in a country, or as in the case of petroleum and pharmaceutical products in Sweden, which has few indigenous firms in these fields: such associations are obviously more congenial to international companies. Moreover, some domestic associations take on the nature of cartels, and U.S. companies (sometimes large in relation to local firms) are asked to take leadership roles, but U.S. antitrust laws are interpreted as prohibiting acceptance.

In the United States itself, the international committees of the National Association of Manufactures and of the Chamber of Commerce of the United States are active in GR/EA tasks, but there are also special-interest associations such as the National Foreign Trade Council and regionally oriented groups such as the Council of the Americas, the Japan-U.S. Trade Council, and the Asian Society. At a more global level, the International Chamber of Commerce and the Business and Industry Advisory Council (BIAC) to the OECD perform similar functions. On a still broader (politico-economic) level, IC officials meet together in groups such as the Conference Board, National Planning Association, and the Council on Foreign Relations.

Patterns of GR Coordination and Development

Overall Organization Structure

International companies are normally organized on one of three bases: functional (where the major divisions are production, marketing, finance, research, and development), geographic (country and/or region); and product. Most IC organizations are hybrid, and mix two or three of these; and they are frequently altered because of changing personnel or environments. Companies organized on either a functional or a product basis often have an "international division" that assists or coordinates overseas exports, investments, licenses, contracts, etc.

The *geographic* basis matches the nation-state structure and is better geared to follow up government policy, but it loses some efficiency when a variety of products makes it difficult to keep track of legislative and administrative changes in policy. The *product* basis avoids this problem of diffusion of attention to different lines, but it raises problems of coordinating the GR efforts of affiliates when there are several product divisions that operate in the same country or region. The *functional* basis of organization is best suited to single-product companies, and can be coupled easily with a regional staff concerned with national policies. *Conglomerate* firms face different problems of organization, because no single structure suits all its parts.

Because of the lack of a clear "fit," ICs frequently reorganize, but shifting from one organizational form to another can be troublesome. Reorganizing a geography-based IC to a product basis can jeopardize years of effort spent in building constructive relationships with key government executives and other influential elites—particularly in less-developed nations, where personal relations are quite important.

Conversely, a priority on the GR function can affect the choice of organizational structure because good external relations may preclude a more centralized pattern of decision making. For example, there is no ITT-France which directly controls the various French affiliates, because a major ITT affiliate produces telecommunications equipment sold mainly to the French government, which prefers to be seen buying from "French" firms. Such an obstacle does not exist in the case of other ITT subsidiaries, such as Sheraton, where the very fact of belonging to an international network is a positive marketing asset and presently is perceived as having little "nationalistic" significance.

Coordination

The use of line and staff, insiders and outsiders, full-timers and part-timers requires coordination so that the head and the parts can complement each other fruitfully and efficiently. This classical organizational problem is complicated by three major factors in the case of the GR/EA functions. First, these functions are "polycentric," in that they need to be closely tailored to the local environment, if only because the relevant targets are national by definition, even though some supranational and subnational units are becoming more important. Consequently, as in the case of industrial relations, foreign solutions are not exported easily.

The GR/EA tasks are complicated also by the fact that many headquarters companies are not experienced in this field. The parent company has less experience to contribute on GR/EA to its overseas affiliates than in marketing, production, finance, etc. In fact, affiliates have often achieved greater sophistication in GR/EA activities than the headquarters company because of the earlier need for such competence abroad, where there is a longer tradition of relations with government and other elites. In addition, the parent company finds it difficult to supervise the GR/EA activities of its foreign affiliates because of a lack of sufficient information and perspective to appraise what is going on abroad and what the appropriate response and performance should be.

The corporate headquarters assumes a triple role still underdeveloped in most international firms: coordinating and supervising the GR/EA activities of subsidiaries around the world; handling GR/EA in the United States, including the relaying of U.S. government regulations and policies to overseas subsidiaries; and planning, executing, and controlling its GR/EA objectives and operations directed to "world" targets, such as the United Nations Assembly and Secretariat, the International Chamber of Commerce, and the OECD.

Despite their far-flung operations, American ICs are still primarily oriented to the United States because U.S. operations are the main reference point for IC executives and the place where most of their stockholders reside. For example, one American IC that claims to be a "multinational enterprise" admitted that it was really only "mid-Western" if one looked at the composition of its board of directors and the orientation of its management. Even companies such as Exxon, organized on a worldwide basis, with regionally separate companies, are still considered as U.S. companies, and the subunit in control of U.S. operations (i.e., Exxon Co., U.S.A.) is not seen as *the* U.S. company. Thus, in the context of the energy crisis, the president of Exxon Corporation (the headquarters company) and not that of Exxon Co., U.S.A. was queried by U.S. government officials and others concerned.

One outcome of this situation has been the rather loose relationship between the U.S. parent company and its subsidiaries as far as government relations are concerned. Although some GR/EA centralization is afoot in a few ICs, the common pattern appears to be an advisory one, ("pure" staff function) rather than of "functional control" by the world level—that is, there is much more "showing" than "telling" (and still less "doing") vis-à-vis the regional and national subsidiaries.

Usually, the GR staff reports directly to the chief executive of the subsidiary rather than to the GR staff in the parent company or international division, so that foreign autonomy prevails. Consequently, GR staffs at the regional and world levels typically exercise influence over the foreign subsidiaries' GR/EA activities to the extent that they are asked by top management at headquarters to comment on budgetary requests and on activity reports. However, informal contacts (mail, telephone, and visits) and personnel rotations contribute to coordination, mutual trust, and understanding among the various geographical levels.

Three major stages of coordination are evident in organization structures for international government relations: "minimal" arrangements seem to characterize about two-thirds of U.S. international companies; another 30 percent are at an "intermediate" stage; while some 5 percent exhibit rather "advanced" capability in this area. These estimates are based on research by the authors, but the labels "minimal," "intermediate," and "advanced" should not be used to judge the adequacy of IC effort in this area, since obviously many internal and external factors move firms to do more or less, as well as better or worse, in relating to their nonmarket environment. There are some very effective (and some rather ineffective) large staffs and some highly productive one-man and part-time units.

Minimal Pattern

The great majority of American subsidiaries abroad deal with their GR/EA problems on an ad hoc and firefighting basis on account of: (1) their small size, which facilitates a low-profile approach; (2) the recent nature of their investment, which is conducive to a honeymoon period with host societies; (3) lack of parent-company experience, which does not alert or prepare them for a more sophisticated approach; and (4) a tradition of noninvolvement with the U.S. government, which is extended abroad.

Typically, there is no government-relations or external-affairs staff at the national and regional (e.g., European) levels—or even in the parent company—outside of some public-relations capability. Whatever needs to be done is handled by the general manager abroad, some appropriate subordinate (e.g., the firm's Corporate Counsel or the Financial Director), or someone with "good connections" on the board of directors or elsewhere (actually, part of the staff may have been hired precisely because of their outside connections). Banks, law and CPA firms, and regional development boards concerned with attracting foreign investors are also used as intermediaries with government. Some subsidiaries rely on a local partner or a "big sister" company to help then when necessary; and *in extremis*, officials of the U.S. embassy are drawn upon.

Intermediate Pattern

Growth, age, the activities of rivals, or crises (including shifts in government policy) usually force the subsidiary to come up with something more explicit and permanent. A transitional phase starts then, aiming at developing some more formal GR/EA capabilities on a regional or national basis.

Regional Coordination. Frequently, the regional (European, Asian, Latin American, or African) level is the first one to build up GR/EA competence abroad. This emphasis on the *regional* level is logical in that it represents a halfway house between the *world* level, which is too heterogeneous and complex and generally lacks the commensurate international expertise, and the *country* level, which usually does not warrant a full-time expert. It is also a good learning-and-teaching level, as it gives the international company an opportunity to gain some perspective about the nature and possibly the commonality of its GR/EA problems and to educate country subsidiaries about the importance of these tasks. The regional level is also able to demonstrate appropriate techniques, frequently on the basis of pooling experiences. When there is frequent rotation of country managers, the regional headquarters also provides some stability in external affairs.

The regional center is also important in balancing national claims within a region. The presence of several subsidiaries in a single region can create conflicts of national sovereignties, interests, and feelings when the IC has to choose among several neighboring countries as to where it will locate a new plant. This decision requires some multinational coordination and supranational representation.

Developing GR/EA capability in the regional headquarters is further justified by the growing importance of supranational bodies. Thus, the European regional headquarters is a natural vehicle for surveilling such institutions as the Common Market (EEC), OECD, FAO, WHO, and Economic Commission for Europe; and for keeping them informed of the IC's views and problems. Similarly, the Economic Commission for Asia and Far East, the Asian Development Bank, LAFTA, the Association of Southeast Asian Nations (ASEAN), and other such institutions require regional-level contacts. Most of the supranational institutions lack a sufficient research staff, yet are expected to take stands on measures that affect international trade and investment. A number of ICs have, therefore, concluded that such bodies should be offered assistance in designing and conducting studies and in formulating policies.

A related reason for regional coordination is that national governments increasingly keep track of what other governments are doing, now that they have access to greater information, have assumed more responsibilities, face a corresponding number of problems, and are continuously searching for new solutions to such issues as pollution, consumer protection, inflation, and ballooning costs of social-security systems, as well as entry, exit, and operating conditions for inward investors. Since many problems and solutions are thus no longer purely "national" but rapidly acquire a "multinational" dimension, the regional level is an appropriate one to keep track of country developments that have potential repercussions on neighboring nations.

U.S. citizens usually serve very adequately in a regional capacity because of the lingering prejudices and rivalries among nations in a single region, although in Europe a significant number of Britons serve as GR/EA officers in U.S. firms and appear well accepted; Australians, Dutchmen, and Britons are active in that function in Asia because of their greater knowledge of the region on account of former colonial experiences; and many Europeans (particularly Britons) perform this role in Africa for the same reason.

National Orientation. The national level may be underdeveloped at this intermediate stage, especially if the regional level substitutes for activities by the smaller subsidiaries. Even in this event, the country managers remain responsible for identifying GR and EA problems and developments, and for initiating the appropriate responses within the country.

This stage often involves some personnel specialization, such as a member of the board of directors, the company lawyer (or some other appropriate functional manager), or a personal assistant to the general manager, who devotes part of his time to external relations. Such people are typically local nationals who have (or are supposed to have) particularly good introductions to government and/or other relevant groups. At the plant level, the local manager deals mostly with "nuisances" (pollution, noise, traffic congestion, etc.), although he may loom much larger if he is the main employer or taxpayer in the community.

The problems they handle vary on account of their size, stage in company growth, type of industry, etc. But a key function at this level of development is following up on new regulations.

Advanced Pattern

Very few ICs have reached the stage where full GR/EA capability—both line and staff—exists at the world, regional, national, and local (community) levels, with these tasks integrated throughout the company and all levels sensitized to their importance. Some petroleum, computer, pharmaceutical, and telecommunication firms are quite close to having achieved such an advanced pattern, however. Companies in these sectors are closely tied to governments because the latter are major customers (telecommunications, pharmaceuticals, and computers), or regulators (pharmaceuticals), or owner and taxer (petroleum). Pharmaceuticals and food firms are faced with an additional level of control through international organizations (e.g., FAO, WHO, EEC). The chemical and automobile firms are following suit, because host governments are scrutinizing the centralized control of the parent company and the worldwide rationalization and integration of production—a process that always exacerbates problems with the authorities, unions, and local communities.

Given the divergence in sectors and varied approaches of top managers, it would be surprising if companies even at this level did not exhibit quite different techniques of GR/EA coordination around the world. Thus, Western Europe is typically better coordinated but much less is done in Latin America, Asia, and particularly Africa.

National Line Executives. Companies at the advanced stage have top line executives in affiliates spending anywhere from 10 to 70 percent of their time on four major GR/EA tasks:

1. *Identifying problems, discussing them with subordinates and assigning responsibility for them;*

2. *Gathering environmental information* through meetings with various elites

in government, business, labor, the press, academia, etc.—either singly or collectively in the context of trade associations, major conferences, and exclusive groups (e.g., AmChams, seminars sponsored by the American Management Association, by Business International, by the Council on Foreign Relations, by the Council of the Americas, by the National Industrial Conference Board, etc.);

3. *Obtaining general support for the firm's actions* (past, present, or contemplated) from decision makers (e.g., legislators, government officials, and bankers), opinion makers (e.g., the press, financial analysts, critics), and other relevant influencers such as stockholders, employees, suppliers, and neighbors. This is achieved through discussions (including press interviews), speeches, testimonies, and letters;

4. *Negotiating with external decision makers* when the man who symbolizes the entire local organization is considered to be the only valid spokesman.

Several managers can share these tasks, because there are usually two or three positions that are considered "top." Thus, in one major electronics firm, the chairman of the board of each national subsidiary serves essentially as an "industrial statesman" who cultivates the elites on account of his renown and connections, and thus prepare the way for the "politicians"—the general manager and other key-line executives—who carry out the negotiations. There is also usually a "chief of protocol" (it may be the director of government relations or external affairs or a special assistant) who prepares materials, provides introductions, and softens up the targets—but this is really a staff job.

Lower-level line executives are active in external affairs either singly when lesser matters and lower-level counterparts are involved; or in a supporting role during negotiations or in negotiating with higher governmental levels—after having been properly introduced by top management, who may well reappear when the negotiations are to be concluded, the documents signed, and the ribbon cut. The many details that must be followed through are handled at this level, while the senior levels limit themselves to broad policy matters.

National EA Staff. This staff assists the line executives in their gathering of information, in obtaining public support, and in negotiating; and it engages in various activities for which the line provides policy guidelines and the necessary budget.

Largely reflecting the relatively small size of the national subsidiaries of U.S. international companies, few companies have broken down their EA function into separate subunits such as government relations and public relations. Instead, an emphasis on one or more of these subfunctions is usually evident as a reflection of current environmental factors, company tradition and experience, and the background of the staff executives. Where GR is handled separately from other EA functions, it usually reports to higher line officers than, say, public relations. One U.S. oil company in Europe distinguishes between "public-administration relations" concerned with the day-to-day problems of obtaining licenses to import, authorizations to increase prices, favorable tax rulings, etc.; and "political relations" concerned with developing ties with key decision makers and with forecasting the evolution of parties, coalitions, personalities, the electorate, and government policies.

A full-fledged EA department usually includes personnel with such backgrounds as: (1) *researchers* who gather and interpret information, prepare speeches and reports, etc.; (2) *mass-communication specialists* who plan and execute PR campaigns, handle visits of the firm, speak to the press, and so on; (3) *program experts* in the charitable, artistic, conservation fields, etc.; and (4) *personal-relations* men in such areas as government, trade, and scientific relations. Its activities are almost entirely performed by nationals of the host countries with the assistance of the regional and world headquarters and their more multinational staffs. Yet one also finds a few Americans, Canadians, and Britons who handle them at the local levels on account of their expertise in some aspects of external affairs—but no citizens or neighboring countries are assigned to these tasks, because national antagonisms linger on in most regions. Such expatriates tend to specialize in mass communications and in coordinating the whole EA effort, rather than in personal relations, which are typically left to nationals.

Regional External Relations. At the advanced stage, the regional headquarters has a fully developed EA staff operating along the lines detailed above under the intermediate pattern. This staff is normally smaller than that found in the large national subsidiaries, because its role is more one of assisting, coordinating, prodding, developing, and educating national staffs than when the national subsidiaries are less equipped to handle their own external relations.

The regional EA director relays information about significant U.S. developments, such as the progress of protectionist bills and government policy toward East-West trade; and it often passes judgment on the relevance of American themes and materials for the region. However, some communications go directly from the parent company to the subsidiaries, because certain announcements must be released nearly simultaneously all over the globe in order to match the instantaneous travel of press news from country to country.

Where supranational problems are already apparent (e.g., in petroleum and food regulations), the regional EA level also interacts regularly with the appropriate international bodies, either alone or in conjunction with other firms. Some respondents commented that most supranational institutions are rather difficult to approach and influence because of the large variety of nationalities and interests they contain, and because business firms have been reluctant to act collectively. Besides, organizations such as the United Nations only hear governments but not private parties.

Since for most international organizations, the formal and real channels of communication and influence pass through the member governments, the greater part of the lobbying has to be done through the national bureaucrats, politicians, and trade-association officials that represent their country. (The U.S. Mission to the EEC is another channel of information, communication, and influence, regarding that supranational body.) This requires that the IC coordinate its stances and lobbying activities—either by having some sort of an "ambassador" to supranational institutions, and/or by holding regular regional meetings of national GR directors in order to agree upon what to tell the national delegates to such organizations. Again, the regional headquarters is the natural locus for such coordination.

The World Level. This is the least-developed part of international government relations—even at the advanced stage. For one thing, many American ICs are only beginning to face the new governmental challenges to their existence abroad and now at home. As mentioned before, within the United States many large American companies have only recently begun to develop their GR/EA function in the fact of the new (or newly discovered) problems associated with pollution, consumerism, youth, women, and other minorities. For example, in the 1960s, only about fifty companies had a permanent Washington representative; and the post of Washington representative for international affairs is a relatively new one in many firms. Furthermore, the existing GR/EA staffs of the parent company are typically busy with American problems—including antitrust actions. As one executive abroad put it about the parent company: "They have their grass-roots problems, and sometimes the grass grows pretty tall!"

In addition, GR experience developed in Latin America, Asia, or Africa is not particularly relevant to Western Europe or Japan and vice-versa. Finally, the men who, on account of their experience and disposition, are capable of handling GR/EA on a worldwide basis are very scarce. Hence, there is still relatively little which can be contributed by the U.S. parent company or the international division.

This situation, however, is changing as experience is obtained both at home and abroad, and as supranational institutions develop. The role of the world headquarters is growing because of instantaneous communications that require quick uniform responses in many overseas locations, because of the precedent-setting effects of the decisions of other governments, which demand coherent reactions, because of the apparent trend toward more centralization within international companies, and because more top executives in the parent company are now returnees from overseas assignments, where they learned the importance of external relations abroad. Consequently, the embryo of a worldwide GR/EA staff and global orientation on the part of the world line executives is gradually emerging and world headquarters of some American ICs are keeping track of the supranational agencies located in the United States—particularly the United Nations, the World Bank (IBRD) and its affiliates, the International Development Bank, and the International Monetary Fund.

Finally, the world level acts as a transmission belt between the U.S. government and foreign subsidiaries, since it has to "screen" decisions made abroad for their conformity with U.S. regulations (e.g., in antitrust and export-control matters).

Special Patterns

We saw earlier that the regional headquarters may serve as some sort of "uncle" for national subsidiaries that do not have an GR/EA staff, but one subsidiary may also help another in the same nation or region. Such a "big sister" arrangement usually reflects the fact that one company, on account of its age, size, product line, etc., has more experience that is relevant for younger, smaller, and/or related subsidiaries of the same parent.

The foremost example is that of the petroleum companies assisting their petrochemicals companies in a region and/or nation. Thus, in one of these firms, the chief executive of the petroleum company has prime responsibility for government and public relations for both the oil and the chemicals companies. At all levels in both companies, responsibility for external relations remains with the line people, who are assisted by the EA staffs at the world and regional levels. At the national level, only the petroleum company has an EA officer and staff, while a fairly highly placed line executive in the chemicals company is designated as the "contact man." The latter serves as relay between the oil and chemicals subsidiaries, but he often conducts some EA activities of his own.

In another variation used by very diversified firms and conglomerates, the key officers of the largest (or oldest) subsidiary have assumed responsibility for the external relations of the others. Typically, this subsidiary has more GR/EA experience; and its senior officer, who is almost always a national, carries a lot of prestige and has excellent connections with various elites in the country. This form is also used when for various reasons the subsidiaries cannot really be brought under a country umbrella—for example, when some of the subsidiaries must look very "national" because the government is a major customer (the ITT situation in France, for example), or because association with American ownership may otherwise harm the company's sales (e.g., in the field of traditional foods).

Another incipient pattern is that of the big petroleum companies in Europe that have apportioned government-relations responsibilities *among themselves* on a country basis, since one of them usually predominates in a particular nation on account of its nationality, size, or GR experience. Thus, Shell exercises a leadership role in The Netherlands as far as government relations of oil companies are concerned.

3

Intelligence Networks: The Collection, Evaluation, and Dissemination of Information

Effectiveness in influencing policy formation and implementation requires an intelligence network both within the company and through outside services and intermediaries (including U.S. embassies).

The Intelligence Function

A distinction can be made between information and intelligence to the extent that the former is more general in nature and even publicly available (e.g., about the investment climate in a particular country); while intelligence (including its interpretation) is more related to the specific needs of a company and less public, thereby requiring greater efforts as well as pronounced reliance on personal contacts. The problems connected with collecting, evaluating, disseminating, and using such information and intelligence are both general and special in nature.

For one thing, business executives tend to react to their environment as developments come to their attention, rather than to anticipate them through systematic forecasting; and they prefer personal sources of information based on networks of oral communication over impersonal ones (e.g., newspapers and magazines)—particularly at higher echelons.[1]

In addition, executives are unable or reluctant to acknowledge the relevance of strategic environmental information—especially when it comes from inside the company. This phenomenon seems to be related to a lack of confidence in their subordinates' ability to recognize or interpret the real significance of external developments; but it results in subordinates lacking proper feelings or instructions about what their superiors want in the way of information, in a "mountain of facts without meaning," and in discouragement about the pointlessness of intelligence work.

Higher levels often have privileged sources of information that they do not share, if only to test the quality of the information they receive from their subordinates. The latter are asked to transmit information that will be used to evaluate their performance; and they tend consequently to filter what they communicate upwards. Long lines of communication are also likely to increase distortion; while the status of the information-bearer bears heavily upon his credibility and influence.

While specialization is essential for the efficient command of knowledge, it is antithetical to the meaningful sharing of intelligence because it encourages rivalry and the concomitant withholding of information, and because specialists operate in different universes with their own frame of reference, which hampers the understanding of staff people by line people, of government-relations experts by others, of international-business operators by domestic ones, etc.

Environmental Intelligence

Generally speaking, it is easier to generate information about the internal operations of a firm than about its external environment (e.g., government), because the former are under the control of management and are more readily quantifiable, while the latter are not. Besides, scanning the nonmarket environment is still in its infancy because the appropriate models (e.g., what matters, why, and how), data, and techniques are largely lacking in this area.

While it is not too difficult to become aware of potential or emerging risks and opportunities in the nonmarket environment, it is much more arduous to figure out the likelihood, magnitude, and timing of such developments. This is a case where judgment about the "unfolding of the relevant environment" matters more than information; and formal forecasting systems, whether or not based on social and political indicators, have not replaced knowledgeable persons with a feel for the situation. Furthermore, whatever noneconomic environmental information is obtained is rarely embodied in corporate strategy—and there is relatively little strategic planning of the sort, even in large firms.[2]

International Intelligence

The variety of economic, political, social, and cultural systems around the world multiplies the amount of information to be collected and complicates its reporting to upper levels and other affiliates. Physical distance, time differences, and lack of good communication links (mail, telephone, telegraph, telex, etc.) further complicate the sharing of information and its use in decision making.

There is now a fairly sizeable literature on gauging political risks and opportunities abroad.[3] They vary from quick "go/no-go" analyses based on a single factor (e.g., the presence or absence of a "leftist" government), to more sophisticated weighting and probabilistic assessing of a large number of factors, and to the use of factor analysis of the correlations between social, economic, political, and cultural indicators and the experience (cash flows, sales, profits, assets) of the company in various milieus. All of these methods are still very imperfect because of the international company's limited experience in handling them and the complexity of relationships, which makes them less amenable to measurement and statistical manipulation than traditional economic and commercial factors.

Consequently, not too much in the way of foreign intelligence is adequately collected, interpreted, and communicated within international companies. For that matter, much company-generated and -circulated intelligence about broad political and economic developments is inferior to what can be read in the politico-economic press of the company or in major publications such as *The Economist, Business Week*, and *The New York Times*. This observation, however, is less applicable to very specific information—such as a bill to limit oil exports from Canada, which the Canadian subsidiary of a U.S. petroleum company can readily follow and report.

On the more personal level of contacting, interacting with, understanding, and influencing people in different environments, there are communication gaps stemming from differences in values, expectations, social mores, national loyalty, and interpersonal attitudes and relationships.[4] Particularly obvious are problems connected with: (1) varying amounts of sophistication among affiliates regarding environmental assessment and influence, which complicates the task of integrating intelligence work around the world; (2) differing cultural attitudes toward working with others (superiors, peers, and subordinates) and toward using staff people (e.g., to gather intelligence); (3) lack of familiarity with foreign languages; (4) the absence of good sources of information in many foreign countries; and (5) further complications arising from having to enlist the assistance of minority partners (private or public) when joint ventures are used.

Furthermore, perception is very important, because it is not so much "objective reality" but rather "perceived reality" that matters in decision making. Thus, what happens in a foreign country tends to be perceived more negatively than if it had taken place at home (e.g., political demonstrations), although things may not be what they seem—as when frequent changes of government are interpreted to mean "political instability" when it may merely be "more of the same" (e.g., in Italy or Brazil).

Another crucial fact is the selectivity—whether judicious or not—exercised by business executives when investigating foreign governments and investment opportunities. Not only do they fail to make a broad analysis of the latter, but a few factors tend to overwhelm the rest of their limited analysis. Thus, when executives believe that a foreign government is comparatively unstable (and most believe they know when a government is stable or not), they also tend to believe that it is corrupt and that investment opportunities in that country are risky and unprofitable—consequently, they are overlooked. And when they perceive a foreign government as anti-American, they also tend to think that it is obstructive and that it restricts investment opportunities—irrespective of what the actual government policies are.

Moreover, foreign nonmarket environmental data are often wished away or ignored, as evidenced by repeated pleas that host countries create a "favorable investment climate"—a plea that translates into "one in which environmental conditions are similar to those of the United States," so that foreign business decisions may be based on commercial data only.

Few IC subsidiaries have a full-fledged body of experts for collecting and interpreting environmental intelligence. Instead, they rely on the partial expertise of one or two people who have to combine various assignments requiring distinct skills rarely found in a single GR/EA staffer.

Such a difficulty is compounded by the poor sensitization of many U.S. top executives to the importance of government relations, if only because their background has typically been in marketing, finance, engineering, and production, which require different mental orientations and social skills (former legal counsels fare better in this respect). This group is learning fast on the job, and they carry their new awareness and ability to subsequent positions, although the frequent rotation of IC personnel does not allow them to use their learning for very long on the spot. Besides, it does not appear that the selection processes and training programs of international companies provide for much systematic learning about, and exposure to, government relations.

These various factors help explain: (1) why most ICs experience difficulties when it comes to obtaining, processing, transmitting, and using intelligence about the nonmarket environment of international business; and (2) why decentralization tends to prevail in these processes.

International Intelligence Sources

Affiliate Intelligence

Media. Outside of the United Kingdom and a few other developed countries, general-circulation media are usually limitedly interested in economic matters and their regulation. In addition, newspapers and magazines tend to be politically aligned, thereby distorting their choice and analysis of relevant topics. Fortunately, this situation is improving in many countries as the equivalents of *Fortune, Business Week, The Wall Street Journal*, and *Forbes* are becoming available—sometimes as joint ventures with U.S. publishers. Moreover, international services such as *Business International* (and its various regional publications) and *The Economist Intelligence Unit* and a number of national (e.g., the *Galling Report on Italy*) and international newsletters and reports (e.g., of large banks) have multiplied and increased their circulation. Such "international" media are also available to the parent company or world headquarters, which can thus follow up on many foreign developments and/or check on the intelligence provided by the affiliates.

These sources are quite important, because they are often the first ones to report major events in the political arena on account of their networks of contacts in government and industry; and they provide at least one interpretation of such developments.

Still, a major problem in using local media arises from the lack of knowledge of foreign languages on the part of expatriate managers, who must rely on their native subordinates or superiors to follow up on these media. Personal contacts provide a partial compensation, but even that source of information is often restricted to foreign nationals who speak English.

Business Associations. In every country surveyed, there are organizations grouping businessmen, executives, and professionals along general, sectoral, size (small vs. large), nationality (domestic vs. foreign), ownership (private vs. public), professional skills (e.g., public relationists), and other lines. Unfortunately, their relatively small size, fears of U.S. and local antitrust prosecution, insufficient knowledge of the local language, and the frequent rotation of executives—together with some clannishness on the part of business-association officers—result in many U.S. subsidiaries maintaining their distance from such groups, or not using them very much even if they belong. This is mainly true of expatriate executives, while native general managers, lower-level managers, and staffers use associations much more, thereby benefiting from their monitoring of legislative and regulatory developments and other services.

It was also mentioned that international business associations, such as the International Chamber of Commerce, are useful in keeping track of regulatory developments in a number of countries and in such supranational bodies as GATT, OECD, and the European Communities (where UNICE is the capstone organization for those industrial associations that deal with the EEC authorities).

American Chambers of Commerce. This type of private association, often labeled as the "collective voice" of American business abroad, groups the owners and/or managers of U.S. affiliates and enterprises overseas, together with native importers and exporters that trade with the United States and make up the bulk of their membership. AmCham directors and officers must usually be U.S. citizens, although the "nativization" of top personnel makes it increasingly difficult to satisfy this requirement. The score or so of official AmChams (which may have several branches in large countries) are affiliated with the Chamber of Commerce of the United States, which provides them with information and offers them political representation in the United States.

AmChams publish magazines containing articles about local economic, political, and sociocultural developments; they organize seminars, lunches, and briefing sessions for their members, nonmembers, and new U.S. investors; they have committees that prepare and circulate reports on various topics; and they even commission studies about U.S. investment in their country (e.g., in Spain and Austria). Such activities provide opportunities for American managers and technicians to learn about the foreign-investment climate (including government regulations) at home and abroad, and to exchange information among themselves in a more informal way.

AmChams follow regulatory developments in the U.S. and abroad. This knowledge is then analyzed in committee work, diffused through AmCham publications, and discussed at various general meetings. Although AmChams are generally underbudgeted and understaffed, they have benefited in recent years from the participation of international lawyers, consultants, and bankers (typically very active as officers and board members), who are excellent sources of information about regulatory and political developments.

There is usually a fairly close relationship with the American Embassy, which frequently has an economic/commercial officer serving as adviser to the AmCham. They exchange information, and the AmCham helps select invitees to briefing sessions by the ambassador. When treaties between the United States and foreign countries are being negotiated or revised (e.g., on establishment and double taxation), AmChams are typically consulted by the U.S. government; and they occasionally present their views to the U.S. Congress via the Chamber of Commerce of the United States.

There are now regional organizations of AmChams in Asia/Pacific, Western Europe, and Latin America, which are dedicated to coordinating their activities and to strengthening weak chapters. Thus, the Council of American Chambers of Commerce, Europe and Mediterranean, was created to observe and influence the European Communities regarding policies affecting U.S. investors in that region—for example, the possible exclusion of American subsidiaries from the "European Company" form of incorporation or from national subsidies and public purchases. (Normally, the EEC opposes such practices.)

American Embassies. U.S. embassies follow many economic and political developments abroad that are of considerable interest to U.S. international companies. They report some of them, as well as major U.S. events (e.g., new bills and legislation), to Americans overseas. However, the major reporting responsibilities of embassies is not to American companies abroad but to U.S. government departments in Washington, so their intelligence gathering has a different orientation than that of the ICs.

The embassies have an Economic Commercial Section staffed by economic officers largely coming from the State Department's Foreign Service and by commercial officers, frequently assigned from the Department of Commerce but also sometimes coming out of the Foreign Service. Responsibilities of these two types of officers (where there are sufficient numbers in a section to permit specialization) are divided between macroeconomic problems in the host country, economic relations between the U.S. and the host country, and the microeconomic issues affecting company activities.

In addition, intelligence desired by the ICs comes out of other sections of the embassies—Political, AID, Military, Agriculture, and Treasury—each of which has responsibilities determined by the U.S. department to which it reports. Information gathered by each of these is supposedly known also to the Economic Commercial Section, which can determine whether to pass it along for the use of

U.S. business. However, such pass-throughs do not always occur, even when information is relevant or important.

The types of information gathered by each section are dictated by the department in Washington, which seeks to serve its own programs with this intelligence system. Economic/commercial reporting has been determined by a program jointly developed by State and Commerce. It seeks to provide adequate information on economic events in the host country, its balance of payments problems, specific issues with the U.S. on trade, legal matters, finance, investment, etc. Emphasis in this program shifts according to the overall objectives of the U.S. government. For example, until the late 1960s, U.S. embassies were instructed largely to ignore American investors in *developed countries*, because the traditional orientation of the State and Commerce departments was to emphasize foreign *trade* rather than investment, since the latter was considered as a drain on the U.S. balance of payments. In fact, until around 1970, there were official instructions to U.S. embassies *not* to assist visiting Americans investigating investment opportunities abroad, but to refer them instead to the local foreign government, to American Chambers of Commerce abroad, and to other intermediaries such as lawyers and banks. A number of foreign service officers chose to ignore these directives, however.

The normal flow of the intelligence collected by U.S. embassies is back to Washington to the relevant "country desk" in the State and Commerce departments, rather than to the field where it is collected and written up. Some unclassified reports are directly available on the spot for those interested, although they seem to be sparsely used by American investors. Washington then decides about the diffusion of some of this information through government publications and field offices, and by making some of the files available to qualified publications and inquirers.

This system as well as the type of information collected reflects the export-trade orientation of the embassy network, which is still viewed as some sort of a scout investigating and reporting export opportunities to the firms back home, rather than geared toward providing field intelligence to U.S. subsidiaries in the country where both operate. Yet there is some increased distribution of embassy information through American Chambers of Commerce, on account of the frequently close links between embassies and AmChams.

Recently, and in repetition of orders issued periodically since the early 1960s, the State Department has instructed American ambassadors (assisted by their commercial and economic officers) to meet regularly with the managers of U.S. subsidiaries in order to discuss with them various developments at home and abroad. However, this instruction has not been implemented consistently from country to country and from ambassador to ambassador, if only because the quality and interests of American representatives vary a great deal.

Hence, the impression remains with many ICs in developed countries that U.S. embassies are not particularly inclined to assist them. This observation, however, applies much less to *developing countries*, where U.S. private investment has been seen as supporting economic development programs, and has itself been supported by investment guarantees from AID and OPIC. Besides, underdeveloped countries typically provide much less in the way of intelligence and influence services by government, banks, law firms, etc., so that U.S. embassies represent a greater source of help to U.S. investors in such nations.

Besides, in some countries there are now hundreds, if not thousands, of sizable U.S. subsidiaries which, unlike import-export houses, are often spread all over the country and are thus much harder to reach. Much of the information available to embassies is of a sensitive nature and cannot be communicated to U.S. subsidiaries otherwise than through personal communications with one or a very few IC executives. This requirement severely limits the number of people who can be appraised of embassy intelligence, although there is some multiplier effect to the extent that confidential information is repeated to other executives or picked up by AmChams or the specialized press (with or without attribution to the embassy).

Furthermore, there is the problem of the nationality of the affiliate's general manager, who increasingly is a local national: should a Frenchman or Indian be invited to briefing sessions by the U.S. ambassador? In some nations (e.g., Sweden), there is no alternative because there are very few American managers operating there. Besides, in European countries such as Belgium or the United Kingdom, there are relatively few fears that a professional manager who is a local national would act as a spy for his government and thereby possibly embarrass the ambassador. Such fears are greater, however, in underdeveloped countries, where there may be less professionalism as well as closer personal ties among the various economic and political elites (this is particularly true in the case of joint ventures with family firms). Last but not least, U.S. ambassadors are more at ease with U.S. citizens who speak their language and understand more readily the background of U.S. developments, decisions, and interpretations.

U.S. Missions. The U.S. government has various missions to supranational bodies, e.g., the U.S. Mission to the European Communities (in Brussels), to the Central American Common Market, to the OECD, to NATO, and to the United Nations (in New York and in Geneva). They are the arms of the State and other U.S. departments which make the policies and take all the important decisions in Washington. Consequently, an American subsidiary bothered by some EEC policy, actual or anticipated, may well prefer to inform its parent company in the United States, who then contacts Washington directly or via its congressmen or senators.

Still, there are also direct contacts between ICs and these missions. Thus, the U.S. Mission in Brussels gets inquiries about EEC policies and regulations as well as expressions of concern from U.S. firms; and it approaches the Common Market authorities in order to obtain their views and to lodge formal protests under orders from Washington. American subsidiaries in the EEC countries also influence this regional body via the member governments and via their membership in the industry associations, which are in turn related to industry advisory groups with more or less formal ties to the EEC Commission (e.g., UNICE). Similar routes are available to the OECD through the European Industry Committee and through the parent company's membership in BIAC; and to NATO through the NIAG.

Other Intermediaries. In countries where they are authorized to provide legal advice and other services, American *lawyers and law firms* are frequently used by U.S. international companies. Such firms usually employ foreign law graduates and lawyers or have them as associates, besides relying on the counsel and court-related work of indigenous law firms.

They provide good sources of information about U.S. regulations and policies, besides being very qualified to interpret similar foreign developments to U.S. affiliate and parent companies. In most countries, however, foreigners are not allowed to provide such legal-advisory services; and the IC must then turn to local law firms, which are typically less informed about U.S. laws and policies, although their capabilities are fast improving.

Some of these firms—mainly American-owned or -influenced—have developed their political intelligence and brokerage functions and thus constitute excellent if costly sources of information and intermediation that are most valuable when entry permits as well as other authorizations and subsidies are applied for, and when regulatory developments must be followed.

Banks are also important sources of foreign information—particularly regarding capital-investment and exchange controls and incentive programs of financial assistance. Frequent contacts with domestic (some of them state-owned) and international (mostly U.S.) banks allow the financial officer and, to a lesser extent, the chief executive of U.S. affiliates to tap these banks' knowledge of the current investment climate, government priorities, and pending regulations. Parent companies also avail themselves of such information.

Public-relations firms serve in a variety of capacities abroad, whether they are local firms or branches of U.S. companies. For large firms, PR companies are important sources of survey data about public opinion and the attitudes of various elite groups that influence policy formation; they analyze and report on various political and social developments; they advise on corporate decisions that have external-affairs implications (e.g., the acquisition of a local firm with strong national identification); and they assist ICs in influencing decision makers through lobbying and introductions.

There are many other types of intermediaries that are used sporadically or regularly by multinational enterprises in their government relations. Thus, some *engineering firms* have experience cutting the red tape in obtaining various government permits. *CPA firms* are in constant contact with tax and finance authorities; and like banks, they can provide abundant information about foreign legal and fiscal systems and their evolution. There are also *expediters, lobbyists, door-openers*, and *advisers*—usually individuals with good connections based on social status and/or political or bureaucratic experience (e.g., former politicians, retired generals, and members of a royal family, but also moonlighting government officials).

Finally, there are various outsiders who assist ICs on account of business or institutional relationships: suppliers, customers, other American subsidiaries, local partners, other governmental units (city mayors, province governors, heads of public agencies), and even labor leaders (e.g., when the survival of the firm and thus of its employees depends on government help). Belonging to the right clubs—the Rotary is quite important in a number of countries—can also be of great assistance to general managers and external-affairs personnel in contacting the right people in government and in dealing with them effectively.

Personal Contacts. Previous sections have already stressed the importance of personal relations in obtaining access to, and better information and other forms of help from, knowledgeable and influential people in business and government— particularly when sensitive areas must be probed and interpreted, and an overall climate of trust must be created so that valuable and credible information may be exchanged and influence in policy formation be accepted.

In general, it is easier for large ICs to develop such personal contacts because such firms matter more and can readily mobilize the resources (e.g., the services of "door-openers") needed for developing good relations. Still, some smaller international companies have been very effective in developing fruitful personal contacts abroad when their investment has assumed the character of a "showcase." Thus, the general manager of the Belgian subsidiary of a medium-sized manufacturer of sporting goods has developed extremely cordial and fruitful relations with economic-affairs ministers in Belgium because this plant has been extremely successful, and it is therefore often shown by government officials to prospective investors. The same situation obtains for an ITT subsidiary in Johannesburg, where exemplary policies have been adopted for improving conditions for the Bantus.

Yet such examples should not obscure the fact that most top American executives abroad are not temperamentally disposed to develop such personal contacts at high levels, and are not greatly concerned that this task be picked up by their subordinates who are more disposed to it.

Parent-Company Intelligence

One must distinguish throughout this section between *foreign* and *domestic* policy developments, because the parent IC is on its own territory when it comes to U.S. policies, while it is removed both physically and mentally from foreign ones. The parent company must keep track of and appraise both domestic and foreign policies through its own intelligence network besides monitoring what the foreign affiliates are doing in this area. Invariably, a number of sources—private and public, domestic and foreign—are used to appraise prospects and current conditions.

U.S. Government Sources. The general gauging of foreign-investment climates is not centered on U.S. government agencies at home or abroad. The recent search for sociopolitical indicators and political-risk indices has been the work of private companies (e.g., DuPont), service firms (e.g., Business International), and academic institutions (e.g., the Haner report at the University of Maryland), since State and Commerce do not publish anything of the sort on the basis of the information that they receive from the field. Nor would it be reasonable to expect a governmental agency to assess publicly the political stability or future of a foreign country (witness the uproar about the Camelot Project).

There are, of course, numerous government publications providing analyses of foreign countries for investment purposes (e.g., the *Overseas Business Reports* of the Bureau of International Commerce), but these are fairly general and of irregular publication. Country desks in the State and Commerce departments provide more specific and up-to-date unclassified information, but this kind of intelligence tends to be used more when a firm plans to enter a foreign country than during its operations there or at the time of its exit.

Needless to say, companies vary a great deal in their awareness and ingenuity in obtaining whatever U.S. government information is available. Actually, higher hierarchical levels are often more active than lower or specialized ones (including the external-affairs department of ICs) in tapping such intelligence sources, because the chief executive officers of international companies frequently interact with U.S. secretaries and undersecretaries in the context of testimonies, committees, and conferences where they exchange information about major foreign developments.

This is not to argue, however, that the information they receive from such highly placed officials is any better than what could be obtained from the civil servants who are in daily contact with the intelligence system. It is more likely that there is an aura of authority surrounding information exchanges at high levels, but their usefulness is highly colored by the elliptical character of such exchanges—assertions strong enough to be relied upon but vague enough to be meaningless for specific decisions by business. (These comments, however, do not apply to dialogues on specific issues facing companies, but to the conversations occurring in various forums.)

Washington Representatives. Only a score of international companies have a Washington representative/international (WRI). In the case of IBM World Trade, this position was created following the problems that company had when the State Department turned down a request in the early 1960s for selling a computer to the French government for military-research (nuclear) purposes. Other companies have done it simply because their regular Washington representative is already burdened by domestic matters while major bills (e.g., Mills and Hartke-Burke) and other events (e.g., foreign expropriations) increasingly deal with international-business topics.

The role of the WRI does not fundamentally differ from that of his domestic counterpart: gathering general intelligence and information; furnishing information to government agencies; expediting government action in such matters as export licenses; arranging meetings between top IC executives and government officials and congressmen; and transmitting the IC's viewpoint to legislators and civil servants.[5] The latter, actually, is not as common as it may seem, since it is largely done by line executives and company experts (e.g., the legal counsel) who testify before congressional committees and executive commissions, participate in conferences with assorted officials and legislators, and approach the latter with various requests. The exchange of high-level personnel between business and government as well as common elite backgrounds often facilitates these meetings and establishes a common basis for understanding.

Some WRIs are also involved in selling to foreign governments through their embassies and other missions and in checking foreign investment opportunities that surface in Washington on account of U.S.-government (e.g., AID), foreign-government, and international-organization (e.g., the World Bank) activities, but this further detracts from the time they can spend on intelligence work.

Altogether, their function is a facilitative rather than a representative or policy-making one, as they focus on building up and maintaining contacts, discovering and reporting what is going on, and handling various sales and administrative details. They are mainly intermediaries, with the business executive responsible for a particular area doing his own information-gathering outside of the regular reporting of legislative and regulatory developments, which is left to the WRI as well as to various business associations and special intelligence firms (e.g., International Business-Government Counsellors, Inc. and the International Economic Policy Association).

Their effectiveness depends largely on the strength of their personal relationships to headquarters. Here, however, very few companies have seen fit to place the Washington representative in the policy councils of the company. Those that have an effective arrangement have assigned top-level officials to the task, and they have relied on his former position and expertise to strengthen his voice. He is also expected to come back into the head office, in time, at a still higher level. Such a pattern is decidedly an exception to the rule that the Washington representative is a "distant staff" position.

Associations. U.S. International companies have mixed feelings about the use of business associations for governmental relations—a posture that carries abroad.

Still, ICs usually support a number of them to complement their own intelligence and negotiation efforts.

Some associations are domestically oriented, but with an interest in such international-business matters as imports (e.g., the Iron and Steel and the Petroleum institutes). This is also true of such capstone organizations as the National Association of Manufacturers and the Chamber of Commerce of the United States, which are predominantly domestic, although they have their "international committees" to deal with U.S. government policies affecting international operations. With increasing foreign involvement, this orientation may change somewhat.[6]

Other groups have more direct international orientations such as the National Foreign Trade Council (NFTC), the United States Council of the International Chamber of Commerce, the Committee for a National Trade Policy, the Emergency Committee on American Trade (ECAT), the Council of the Americas, and the Committee for Economic Development (CED). There is much overlap among these organizations in terms of membership and efforts,[a] but this duplication is not as significant as the fact that the members remain divided within these organizations on the issues of free trade and foreign investment.

Some ICs are very active in smaller associations such as the Council of the Americas, the Business Council for International Understanding (BCIU), the Committee on Economic Development, and the Council on Foreign Relations, which provide opportunities for business, governmental, and academic elites to interact regularly and to discuss various U.S. and foreign developments with visiting dignitaries and experts. These forums strengthen the contacts between business and government by providing personal familiarity and a better understanding of the interests and problems of others.

Another relevant group is the more personal and influential Business (Advisory) Council (BAC), which quarterly gathers some one hundred top business executives with cabinet members and assorted high-level government officials for mutual briefing. Some of these same business leaders chair or sit on select committees appointed by the President of the United States and by department secretaries in order to advise government but also to enlist business support for the administration's policies. Such privileged contacts are obvious sources of information and influence for chief executives—well above and apart from what their external-affairs department and Washington representatives manage to achieve in this area.[7]

There is no worldwide association of multinational companies, although the International Chamber of Commerce (ICC), the Business and Industry Advisory Council of the OECD, and the meetings of CIOS (Scientific Management Association) come close to providing some such representation;[8] and the ICC

---

[a]While he served as Assistant Secretary of Commerce, the senior author strongly urged the merger of three different business groups dealing with Latin America, since they were contradicting or weakening each other's efforts and draining the time of governmental officials, although they had the same company memberships.

has been very active in the matter of investment codes. All others having such claims are regional- or sector-specific, as occurs when national associations in a given industry meet on a regional basis (e.g., in the context of influencing the EEC authorities through UNICE). Still, such organizations provide useful if dispersed and overlapping sources of intelligence to the parent company.

Consultants. It appears that very few ICs use outside consultants to report on policy developments abroad *on a regular basis.* There are oil experts who are used for that purpose by petroleum ICs; and the largest investment banks and Washington law firms have roving ambassadors and advisers-at-large who report about major political developments at home and overseas. In general, outside consultants are brought in at critical points, as when a firm contemplates a new investment or faces expropriation abroad, but also when major policy developments are in the making—such as the conditions for foreign investment, and the taxation of foreign revenue. Such consultants are typically former political appointees (e.g., undersecretaries), civil servants, and business executives or researchers whose usefulness rests on their overseas experience and network of contacts.

There are also media consultants, which advise on methods for external affairs, including *broad* approaches on governmental issues. And some companies reinforce their use of public media by buying clipping services on specific issues. This move occurs most frequently when a new plant is announced or opened, when strikes occur, or when pressure is put on the company (or industry) from some quarter. Recourse to clipping services for *continuing* political information appears to be rarely practiced by any company, but the international-business press fills a much-needed role here.

Foreign Embassies. American ICs do not use the embassies of foreign countries in the United States and abroad to the same extent that European international companies do. Much of the contact with embassies by the parent company is of a commercial nature in the context of obtaining orders, permissions, and subsidies from foreign governments—especially in the case of socialist and totalitarian states. Still, such rapports (mostly through international Washington representatives, when such a post exists) provide opportunities for learning about political and regulatory developments in host countries; and foreign ambassadors are contacted in the context of major crises (for example, the contacts between various ICs and the Chilean ambassador in recent years).

In general, embassies in Washington are not considered major sources of in-depth intelligence about foreign policy developments, because of the reticence of foreign-service personnel, and their inability to keep track of numerous legislative and regulatory developments in their own country. Still, some ICs obtain good interpretations from such sources on account of well-developed contacts.

Personal Contacts. Some parent ICs are very strong in terms of personal diplomacy. The head of the international division of a major manufacturer of heavy industrial equipment visited the presidents of seven Latin American republics in one month; and people like David Rockefeller and Henry Ford II have better entrées in many countries than the U.S. ambassador. The vast majority of IC executives, however, shun such personal relations, limiting themselves to perfunctory contacts with government officials when they are abroad. Fortunately, executives who have served abroad are now increasingly filling toop positions in the parent company and have thus had the opportunity of developing fruitful relationships overseas, which remain useful at later dates for themselves and other executives.

Personal relations also matter very much *within* the firm. International companies like IBM send many people to the U.S. and overseas for training and operational assignments, and they organize frequent visits and conferences among their line and staff personnel, so that they may know each other well. This makes for speedier and more reliable exchange and interpretation of information inside and outside formal channels of communication.

A number of ICs, on the other hand, suffer from the isolation of international personnel from the rest of the organization, and from the appointment of amateurs who hide their incompetence by insulating themselves from their counterparts and subordinates overseas. Here again, the growing accession of former international business executives to top positions in the parent company is helping to remedy this situation.

Another source of personal contacts is visitors from overseas such as major customers, suppliers, experts and consultants, ministers, and civil servants. It is not uncommon for these foreigners to ask the overseas affiliates to arrange their business visits to the United States, although vacations and even stays in American hospitals may also be involved. When properly briefed by the foreign affiliate about the background of the visitors and the purpose of their visit, the U.S. headquarters does derive good intelligence as well as fruitful personal relations with them, besides earning Brownie points for the affiliate.

Processing and Transmission

The handling of international intelligence about foreign policies is still primitive in most international companies, as evidenced by the state of their reporting structures, criteria of assessment, and processing techniques.

Reporting Structures

It was seen in the previous chapter that the government-relations/external-affairs staff reports directly to the line management of the affiliate (the same is true at the regional and world levels), rather than to the corresponding GR/EA staff at higher levels. This situation introduces some delay in the intelligence network as well as an additional filter of what it is considered appropriate to report to other affiliates and/or the regional and world headquarters.

The existence of the regional management center permits collation of information from various countries, but also makes communication from it to local governments difficult simply because of distances. The distance problem is magnified in the case of management centers for Africa, because most such centers are located in London or on the European Continent since communications and travel are easier between Europe and African states than among the latter.

However, this hierarchical requirement is usually complemented by "dotted-line" relationships among GR/EA staffs at various locations and levels. That is, higher GR/EA levels advise and otherwise assist lower GR/EA levels, besides counseling their own superiors about directing, guiding, and reviewing the performance of those line and staff executives who are responsible for GR/EA activities in their country or region at lower levels.

A more complex reporting system exists in the form of general executive meetings. Thus, ITT-Europe regularly gathers executives and staffers from all over that continent and from the United States in order to review the performance of its European affiliates. Such meetings allow them to learn about what is happening in other countries—a type of briefing that provides for better interpretation of the news and reports emanating from there. Similarly, Caterpillar and IBM Corporation have held board-of-directors and executive-committee meetings abroad for their enlightenment regarding international decisions.

Besides, large ICs with complex organization structures combining geographic, product, and functional levels are appointing a member of the executive committee (various names are used to refer to such a group of major policy makers and reviewers) to act as a "contact man" for government relations and external affairs. Thus, a major oil company has a management committee made up of senior vice-presidents, each of whom supervises one or more companywide staffs, operating divisions, and regional companies: one such vice-president represents the finance and GR/EA staffs, while others direct the activities in major regions of the world. Relevant information is likely to appear before that management committee from several sources who have weighed it from different standpoints, permitting cross-checking of accuracy and relevance.

Besides, an increasing number of international companies such as Exxon and Westinghouse are adding prominent foreigners to the board of directors in order to tap their environmental knowledge, to interpret whatever information they already have, and to gain access to other elites in host countries—besides these foreigners' symbolic value in "internationalizing" the international company. Other ICs, such as the Chase Manhattan Bank, are achieving this result by setting up a prestigious advisory body of foreign leaders.

In addition, much informal gathering, interpretation, and transmission of GR/EA intelligence is achieved through travel, correspondence, telephoning, and gatherings outside of the formal reporting channels. An extreme case here is that of company chairman such as David Rockefeller (Chase Manhattan Bank) and Henry Ford II (Ford Motor Company), who meet with elites all over the world and are thus able to gather all sorts of information and interpretations, which can then be communicated to executives and staffers, as well as used to appraise their effectiveness. They are usually accompanied by aides who assure that certain data and impressions are transmitted. However, the "debriefing" of such peripatetic chairmen appears to be unsystematic in international companies; and much information therefore remains fallow for lack of means of transmittal and assessment.

Less prestigious executives and high-level staffers also have opportunities to learn about GR/EA developments through travel and informal networks with friends, former colleagues, and local elites. Still, there are real problems connected with appraising and communicating the information thus obtained, and with using it at headquarters level.

One major electronic firm combines both formal and informal approaches quite effectively as its various geographical executives and the relevant staffers are brought together through committee meetings, travel, the consultation of foreign personnel assigned to headquarters, correspondence, and telephoning, so that in the case of major issues (e.g., the Hartke-Burke bill), "all the viewpoints will have been examined," all the way up to the top-level management committee, which meets weekly. In addition, its national GR/EA staffs will have contacted key ministers, civil servants, and parliamentarians in order to keep on top of the situation; its European-wide external affairs working group meets regularly to discuss developments and affiliate responses in the various countries; and the European EA staff keeps in touch with the various directorates of, and national delegations to, the European Communities.

The previous chapter mentioned the ongoing concentration of GR/EA activities at the point where capability exists or where other factors justify it. Thus, an affiliate that is too small to do any in-depth intelligence work of its own leaves it to a larger national affiliate or to the regional headquarters—as in the case of petrochemicals such as Esso Chemicals, leaving it largely to the Esso petroleum firm in the appropriate countries and regions.

Locational factors also affect the allocation of GR/EA responsibility, as when the Belgian subsidiary is charged with following up EEC developments, since the EEC Commission is located in that country. Places like London and New York are very important listening posts regarding financial controls everywhere, because major international banks are located there and keep abreast of relevant regulations and conditions all over the world.

Finally, there is relatively little *formal* transmission of the intelligence gathered by U.S. international companies to American embassies outside of:

(1) small underdeveloped countries where personal relations among Americans and U.S. firms are tighter on account of greater isolation and lack of good external information sources; and (2) crisis situations where the U.S. embassy is often dragged in if major issues are involved (e.g., the violation of a treaty of establishment or some case of blatant discrimination). The factors explaining such distancing have already been presented above.

Loci and Criteria of Assessment

The general principle that decisions should be made where the facts are available and understood militates against much reporting to higher levels where such ability does not exist. However, international companies qualify this principle in a number of ways.

First, higher levels have to be kept *informed* of these decisions even if they did not participate in them, in order to: (1) appraise the effectiveness of government relations and external affairs at lower levels—particularly of those overseas executives and staffs who have been "caught by surprise" by political and regulatory changes that might have been anticipated; (2) evaluate the adequacy of the budgets requested and obtained for that function; and (3) form an impression about trends in policies and regulations in their region or in the world at large—something for which the national affiliate usually lacks perspective.

Second, reporting systems vary also according to the *types of external events covered and of required company responses.* Some governmental policies are beyond the control of higher levels, and are only *ultimately reported* to them for information's sake and/or in order to justify certain actions and performances of the affiliates (e.g., to explain why the subsidiary could not avoid a price freeze in a foreign country). The affiliate may protest such a freeze individually or collectively (e.g., through its trade association), and it may also try to obtain some exemption from it. However, there is usually little that higher levels can do to influence the host government's decision. Of course, the parent can instruct the affiliate to circumvent the price ceiling by exporting its production instead of selling it locally, or by shifting to products with higher margins—but these are not GR/EA decisions of the type analyzed here. The point is that promptness in reporting such a new regulation is not crucial, because the appropriate riposte can usually be decided by the local management.

Other local policy developments, however, may have more serious implications for the rest of the international company, and therefore require *immediate reporting.* An example would be stricter controls on capital movements in and out of a foreign country. Since the financial function is typically centralized in true multinational enterprises, the regional and world levels want to know of such a regulation or of its imminence right away because it has to shift funds around, alter financial plans, or make other decisions. It is also a kind of development where international treaties and special agreements between the parent company and the host government may be relevant, and therefore invite representation by the firm or the U.S. government if some violation or discrimination is involved.

This example involves a tactical response, but the parent company may also need to know of regulatory developments for *strategic purposes*. For example, the banning of cyclamates in food is a type of policy change that affiliates would report promptly, because it may require dropping an entire line of products and stepping up research efforts to come up with substitutes. It is also a regulation likely to be adopted by other countries, since concern with protecting the health of the consumer is widespread; and an IC may want to stop using such an ingredient in other countries even before it is obliged to do so. Another example is that of East-West trade, where new export opportunities may be first developed abroad, but the headquarters company has to make policy for all such trade under the constraints of U.S. policy.

The distinction made above is between what is urgent and must be immediately reported, what must be ultimately known, and what is of marginal or no interest to higher levels and should be left out of intelligence channels, which may be already overburdened. This sorting-out process is not always obvious but must be inculcated and implemented through company directives, conferences, reviews, and other means—a requirement that most ICs are only beginning to figure out.

Such a classification, however, does not hinge on the distinction between "good" and "bad" developments, because some restrictions may be of purely local import, while others may interest *other affiliates*. Thus, the EEC directive allowing some manufactured goods from underdeveloped nations to enter member countries duty free (up to a certain volume) made it possible for the Brazilian subsidiary of a U.S. international company to export more parts to EEC countries at a lower cost. Yet none of its subsidiaries in Europe thought of reporting this directive to the U.S. headquarters, which discovered this opportunity by itself.

One can observe here that good news often does not travel as readily as bad news, because overseas affiliates are not eager to be asked to do something more or to change procedures because some regulation has been removed or modified. Bad news, on the other hand, provides handy excuses for not meeting some assigned goals. In addition, perceiving new opportunities requires thinking changes through, but few affiliates have been staffed with that kind of managerial and staff talent.

Still, *crisis developments* tend to move very quickly up the organizational hierarchy. This is a reflection of the fundamental principle of "management by exception" whereby higher levels concern themselves with "exceptional" problems—especially when the amounts involved and the possible implications for other parts of the international company are significant and assume "policy" dimensions. Furthermore, difficult transactions with foreign governments bring about "escalation" in order to impress the latter with the fact that the international company has alternatives in other countries and must reconcile its national obligations with international ones. Finally, higher levels are usually brought in to remove the pressure from the national manager—especially if the affiliate is small and its manager a native of the country, because local managers are much more vulnerable to governmental pressures (including physical ones), while foreigners at least are somewhat protected by their embassy and bilateral treaties.

For example, Procter and Gamble people from headquarters were on the spot in London in the mid-sixties when the British Monopolies Commission investigated that company (as well as Unilever) about the impact of advertising on competitive structures and prices. There were real dangers that any strong antiadvertising decision would have struck very responsive chords in other countries. This situation is also a reflection of the fact that there is often more relevant experience about the prevention or mitigation of such threats in the United States than in the foreign countries.

Third, the assessment of intelligence also varies according to the *types of international companies* discussed in Chapter 2. The international holding company with loosely connected foreign affiliates is much more likely to let them process their own intelligence, decide accordingly, and simply keep the parent company informed than the true "multinational" firm bent on controlling its subsidiaries rather tightly.

Thus, some chemical ICs have let their subsidiaries decide about their own position regarding international negotiations (such as the Kennedy and Nixon rounds), about nontariff trade barriers (e.g., the matter of the American selling price), and about the protectionist Mills and Hartke-Burke bills. On the other hand, one major electronics firm carefully checks with its national and regional affiliates before major testimonies are presented by its executives before U.S. congressional committees; and the European headquarters of a large oil company is frequently represented when a national affiliate approaches a foreign government or the European Communities.

Fourth, it is well to keep in mind the *respective competences of field and headquarters.* The former, through its closer association with operations, is more attuned to local developments and remains aware of obstacles and of unpredictables, even though it is also susceptible to that complacency of those who feel that they are doing the right thing because they are the local experts. Headquarters, on the other hand, is often better at detecting the uncommon which may be better perceived from a distance; but it suffers from a deficiency in understanding the proper importance of such exceptional developments.

Finally, *advisers and decision makers* do occasionally disagree about the interpretation of their information and about alternative courses of action. Thus, in ITT's Chilean affair, there was a very extensive network of informants, advisers, and decision makers that could not agree on the risks involved and the actions indicated. On the company's side, there were members of the board of directors, the president of the company, its GR/EA staffs in New York, Washington, and Latin America, and the legal department. They also discussed the matter with Chilean political candidates and advisers, President Allende of Chile, and the Chilean ambassador, as well as with various U.S. government officials on the White House staff and in the State Department, the Central Intelligence Agency, and the American embassy. Yet, for all that information, there were two inside factions vying for the attention of the president of ITT, there was disagreement about the risks associated with intervention in Chilean politics and economics, and there was a lack of coordination of actions vis-à-vis the outside world:[9] Such a situation is obviously not conducive to effective government relations in policy formation.

Techniques

GR/EA reports from affiliates have to be *condensed* and integrated with other subjects in the short summaries prepared for higher levels. What may have started as a twenty-page analysis written by the GR/EA Director in France ends up as a one- or two-page component in the more general report of the French general manager to the European headquarters, which itself condenses France to a paragraph or two in the European report going to New York, where the worldwide analysis finally reduces it to a couple of lines. It is extremely difficult for anyone at that level to act meaningfully on such scanty information.

Besides, the *timing* of intelligence is frequently faulty. Most overseas subsidiaries do not catch problems at the incipient stage. Later on, they remain optimistic that things will work out because they have in the past. Therefore, they usually fail to communicate detailed information and forecasts about such developments. When events finally become unmanageable, they provide handy excuses for no longer performing satisfactorily. However, the matter of urgency should not be overstated to the extent that major policy developments are slow in coming; and there is usually time to obtain whatever information is available. Instead, the problem usually lies in that many ICs are not very well organized to gather and analyze such intelligence and to report it in a timely and useful fashion.

This difficulty is compounded by the fact that there is *little contingency planning* embodied in GR/EA reports. That is, affiliates very seldom report developments in a format outlining what is likely to happen (with various probabilities) and what alternative courses of action are open regarding each possible outcome. Instead, their reports aim at presenting some overall appraisal of the state of the environment, and at reassuring the parent company that the situation is being carefully followed up.

Part II
Government-Business
Dialogues

Introduction to Part II

The prior section is addressed to the problems of formation and use of a governmental relations function within the international company. Once the company has prepared itself appropriately and has adequate information concerning a given problem abroad, it still faces the decision of whether to call upon the U.S. government for assistance, to merely inform the U.S. Embassy or the Department of State of any problem arising, to approach the host government directly, or to let the matter drop. Decisions to adopt any one of these approaches will be taken in the light of the presumed effectiveness of intervention and the significance of the problem itself.

The significance of the problem, of course, depends on the particular circumstances, but if the State Department or the U.S. Embassy is to be asked for assistance, the conclusion will be that the problem is too big, complex, or serious in its impact to be handled alone. Or, the embassy will be called upon if it is deemed that it has a capacity to alter the solution favorably, which the company does not. (What the company perceives in terms of embassy capacity or willingness may not always match its actual capacity or willingness, however.)

A decision merely to inform the embassy (or the State Department) will derive from a conclusion that the company, while not needing assistance now, may desire help in the future and should prepare the way by involving the embassy at least to the extent of informing it of developments. There is an assumption that the embassy can and will be of help later, if needed.

A decision to approach the host government directly will be made when the effectiveness of the embassy is considered to be low compared to that of the company officials, or when the problem is so insignificant as not to bother embassy officials. Alternatively, of course, the issue may be highly significant and of such a critical nature that the company does not want to identify itself with the U.S. government in any way, and thus deals directly with the host government.

Finally, a decision not to engage in any kind of dialogue concerning an issue means that the company considers the outcome proposed by the host government as inevitable; or that it cannot influence the outcome by any reasonable action on its part, nor can the U.S. Embassy; or that the matter is too insignificant to spend any time on.

No one decision need be final; it can be reversed at any time within the duration of a given problem if significance or effectiveness changes.

Conversely, the host government must make decisions as to how to handle a particular issue between itself and an international company, and whether to involve or permit involvement of the embassy. The alternatives facing a government agency or official are to accept embassy representation, to accept an offer of mediation by the embassy, to accept or reject company representation directly, to warn the embassy of its action vis-à-vis an American company, or in quite special cases to mediate between the U.S. government and the American company over an issue affecting the national interest of the host government. Again, any one decision as to the approach to take can be reversed if the significance or effectiveness of a problem is altered.

The decision by a host government to accept or reject a direct approach by a foreign-owned affiliate is dependent on the underlying feelings of nationalism (threat to national sovereignty) posed by the dialogue with the company, and this feeling in turn depends on the nature of the problem itself and on the general setting or ambiance toward foreign investors within the country. If there is no feeling of threat or distrust of the foreigner, dialogues can take place readily at all levels; but if there is a general distrust and fear, any dialogue takes on the coloration of "imperialistic intervention."

A host government will decide to call on the embassy for help (or accept its representations) when it considers that it is highly advantageous to keep good will with the U.S. government, when it wants to attract and keep U.S. investors, or when it considers (whether true or not) that further assistance from the U.S. government is dependent on its treatment of foreign investors. (A signal that this last condition is important was made by the U.S. Congress in both the Hickenlooper and Gonsalez amendments to the aid programs.) Despite the significance of the issues, the host government may permit involvement of the embassy when it considers that its participation will bring a more efficacious solution (i.e., it would make the negotiations more efficient).

Similar considerations would militate in favor of accepting an offer of mediation by the U.S. Embassy, especially when it was clear that the embassy (and the U.S.) had no special interest in the outcome. (However, the host government almost invariably feels that U.S. government interests are more directly related to those of the IC than to those of the host government.)

The host government would find it desirable to warn the embassy of impending action when it considered that the embassy might wish to get involved or when it thought that mediation by it would be feasible. Alternatively, as with the company, it could merely prepare the way for future requests for involvement by passing information at an early stage.

Finally, the host government has a mediation role to play of its own—this time between the U.S. government and the U.S.-owned affiliate. Situations arise in which the U.S. government commands performance of one type or another (capital flows, technology transfers, exports and imports, competition policy, taxation, etc.) by the affiliate despite the interests of the host government. The affiliate would probably be quite happy to follow local customs and laws, rather than those of the U.S. The host government may add its weight to that of the company by insisting on the fulfillment of local laws or on the protection of local interests—despite the laws of the U.S. It will not always be in the interest of the host country to press this issue, but there are times in which it will not harm its own interests and would, over the longer run, tend to loosen the ties of the local affiliate with the U.S. government (or the parent company). However, the host government is not likely to enter this dispute unless the problem is quite significant, and it can be effective in altering U.S. policy (as with the case of the trucks to be sold by American-owned affiliates to Cuba in Argentina).

The third actor, the embassy, has alternatives of its own: it can support the company position in a given issue; it can support an overall policy agreed upon with the host government, within which the given problem falls (though the precise outcome may not be what the company wishes); it can opt out of the discussion entirely, leaving bilateral negotiations between the host government and the company; it can support the governmental position in the host country; it can warn the host government of a potential violation of its laws, customs, or morality so as to reduce future conflicts; it can become an intermediary in disputes between the host government and companies without taking or having a direct interest; and it can react to initiatives by the State Department or Congress in the U.S. that push it into the dialogue between the host government and the company.

Each of these approaches will be adopted, again, according to the significance of the issue and the probability of the action being effective, with the decision being reviewed as conditions change. Each of these decisions alters the triangular relationship of the company, the host government, and the U.S. government. They may be depicted as follows, reflecting the seven approaches noted above, and are likely to be perceived by the host government in a quite different fashion than that intended:

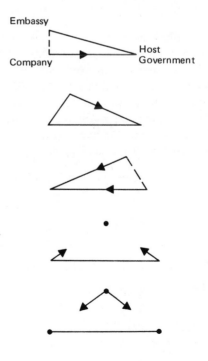

(a) Siding with U.S. company-affiliate—perceived as imperialism by company:

(b) Maintaining consistency in economic policies—perceived as imposition of foreign rules:

(c) Siding with host government—perceived as third-party conciliation:

(d) Opting out of the situation entirely—perceived as impotence or lack of interest, or ignorance of what is going on:

(e) Warning of host government or company—perceived as "boy-scout" syndrome or as a potential threat:

(f) Mediation between company and government—perceived as emphasizing importance of local interests:

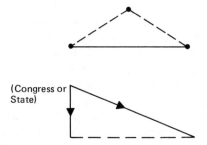

(g) Representation of unilateral position of U.S. Government or Congress—perceived as governmental imperialism:

   (Congress or State)

The decision to adopt any one of the seven approaches will depend greatly on the given situation, on the past relations between the host government and the U.S. government, on the perceived significance of the particular outcomes sought (including their setting a precedent for actions in other countries), and on the perceived negotiation (power) positions of the various actors which would alter the embassy's effectiveness in making representations. There are times, therefore, in which it would be appropriate for the embassy to opt out entirely; but the lessons of this section seem to add up to the likelihood of this option being less available to the embassies in the future. Only if the international companies are progressively taken over through the processes of expropriation or localization or participations in joint ventures will the role of the embassy decline; during this process of attrition, it would be likely to rise, if the U.S. government determined that such creeping rejection of its foreign investors was contrary to its national interests. (This aspect of the decision is taken up in Part III.)

In the eyes of the host government, there are greater common interests between the U.S. government and the IC than between the U.S. government and the host government. In addition, the host government particularly in a developing country thinks that the IC can and does gain the support of the U.S. government on matters of dispute between the IC and the host government. Therefore, the *perception* of the relationship between the U.S. government and the IC on the part of the host government is often quite different from what is portrayed in the diagrams above.

4

Issues and Areas in the Influence Process

Introduction

How does the international company (IC) attempt to influence the host government and the U.S. government? The term "influence" permits several definitions. However, for our purposes it refers to situations where the IC (as a participant in international business transactions) persuades the host government and the U.S. government to adopt policies and programs that serve to promote or protect interests of the IC.

Influence is exercised in varying degrees of overtness. For example, by offering information on a particular subject or by introducing one person to another, an individual exercises influence; information can be offered publicly or to only one company. Influence is relatively open when the U.S. Embassy approaches the host government to inquire about its policies on foreign direct investment or on treatment of certain tax provisions. In this context, the host government readily recognizes that the embassy is making inquiries on behalf of ICs. A highly explicit act occurs when the IC alerts the host government of its plans to seek the assistance of the U.S. government in making representations to the host government on general matters relating to the IC.

The fundamental characteristic of the influence process is the perception of power of the IC in the eyes of the individuals/organizations it wishes to influence. And often the extent of power possessed in reality by the IC is different from the host government's perception of its power. The ICs rely on this perception as well as on their actual power.[1]

Influence also occurs through direct and indirect representations. For example, the IC might not deal directly with the host government, but through third parties. Influence is exercised either through specific statements on given issues or through general comments; the latter retains flexibility for subsequent dealings.

In short, influence occurs in a variety of ways, through a host of individuals representing a range of organizations and for an array of issues. Therefore, the effective exercise of influence is based not only on the "what" but also on the "how," "when," and "who."

The IC is accused of gaining collaboration of the U.S. government to influence a foreign government, and in many parts of the world, such collaboration is accepted as a fact. But to what extent is it true? A greater understanding of the areas and extent of influence of the IC on the host and home governments will provide a better basis of determining the nature of policies for the primary actors in international business. Otherwise, erroneous perceptions lead to bad policies. The policy implications of influence by ICs on the U.S. government are significantly different from a situation of little or no influence.

Extensive reference is made to specific case situations to illustrate the points made in this chapter. To understand the nature of the influence process, it is important to develop a feel for the dynamics of the process, which a mere recitation of the facts cannot convey. A case situation is referred to in several different contexts to illustrate different dimensions of the influence process.

The Wider Perspective

While specific circumstances require a particular approach, there are several characteristics that determine the extent to which the IC seeks assistance of the embassy. First, large companies seek embassy assistance to a far lesser extent than is the case with relatively smaller companies. Second, companies with international business experience (which are typically the large companies) interact less frequently with the embassy than smaller companies. Third, companies with extensive experience in a particular country have limited reason for seeking the assistance of the embassy, as they are capable of handling problems on their own. Fourth, the particular orientation of an executive in a country has a bearing on the extent and areas in which he seeks assistance of the embassy. In addition, the orientation of the embassy personnel (especially the ambassador and the economic/commercial counselor) influences the extent and areas of interaction with the IC. Fifth, a unique, special, and highly publicized situation (such as a divestment or expropriation) with an obvious effect on U.S. government interests results in the need for interaction. (However, a mere handful of projects fall in this category.) Sixth, certain sectors such as extractive industries often involve situations where the interests of the IC and the U.S. government are interconnected to a significant extent, as reflected most recently in the oil crisis in the U.S.A. Seventh, the perception of an executive of the embassy's influence with the host government has a bearing on the nature and extent of interaction between the embassy and the IC. In general, however, the greater the experience of the IC in a country, the lesser is its tendency to seek assistance of the embassy.

The IC and the embassy interact on a range of issues (discussed below). However, it must be noted that for every example where assistance was sought, there are several more examples where assistance of the embassy was *not* sought by the IC. The IC has this attitude largely because it has not found the embassy to be of meaningful assistance and/or has preferred to tackle the situation on its own.

This chapter discusses the areas on which the IC interacts with the embassy, and the type of themes used by the IC to influence the host government.

Areas of Interaction with
U.S. Embassy

What are the areas on which the IC interacts with the embassy? The IC has various needs as it participates in international business ranging from favorable attitude of governments to clear procedures for customs clearance. The embassy serves as *one* source of information and know-how for the IC.[2]

Identification of the areas of interaction will permit comment on the extent to which companies seek and the embassies provide assistance to the IC. This will offer the basis for comparison with what the IC feels should be the role of the embassy vis-à-vis the IC in the coming years. Finally, the areas of interaction offer information that will throw some light on the extent to which bilateral bargains are used. (Trade-offs are discussed separately in Chapter 5.)

The areas of interaction between the IC and the embassy are divided into two broad categories. The first category includes *service* functions such as information, introductions, interpretation/advice, intelligence, and personal safety. The second category is of *complaints* on the part of the IC largely against the host government on areas such as procedures, regulations, discrimination, contract violation, legislation, impasse, and credibility. An assessment is offered at the end of the discussion of each issue through the following question: Did assistance of the embassy facilitate the IC's efforts to exercise influence over the host government?

Service

Information.[a] The embassy is one source of information for the IC on areas such as macrocharacteristics of a country, terms and conditions of foreign investment, characteristics of specific industries, rules and regulations for importing, lists and evaluations of possible suppliers, agents, and distributors, the "real" thinking within the inner circles of the host government, and policies of the U.S. government vis-à-vis the host country. (The IC invariably uses several different sources of information to check the prospects in a particular country. Views and interpretations of different groups—private and governmental, formal and informal—are sought in order to develop a balanced perspective on a given situation.)

---

[a]The areas of information, interpretation, and intelligence cannot be seen in watertight categories, for they obviously overlap with each other. One distinction between these areas is the extent to which assistance provided is specifically related to the needs of a company. Information tends to fall more in the category of general service, while interpretation and intelligence would relate more to specific needs of a company. However, embassy services specifically for a company might not be used by the company in attempting to influence the host government. Moreover, information is relatively general and publicly available (macroeconomic data, sources of information, etc.). Interpretation and especially intelligence are far less public in nature.

Typically the IC seeks information from the embassy when it first enters a country. For example, a chemical company had extensive discussions with the embassy in South Korea when it was seriously considering an investment in the country. It realized that the U.S. government was a major source of economic assistance to South Korea, the embassy maintained a large and highly qualified staff, and in the company's opinion the ambassador was well informed of developments within the host government.

Bechtel Corporation interacted extensively with the embassy in India when it first considered the idea of manufacturing a million tons of fertilizer per year. Given the uniqueness of the concept, the implications for U.S.-Indian relations, and the need for financial resources which would require U.S. government guarantees, Bechtel wished to ascertain the views of the embassy.[3]

The IC seeks assistance of the embassy to gain rapid access to major policy declarations of the host government, which often take a long time before being made public. In 1971, a law was passed which specified a new relationship between Pertamina (government-owned oil monopoly) and the government of Indonesia, and as a consequence between Pertamina and foreign oil companies operating in the country. The embassy secured a copy of the law, had it translated, and gave it to U.S. affiliates, who in turn transmitted it to headquarters for further study and analysis.

An official of the embassy often gains access to certain host government officials, which might not be possible for an individual in a private capacity, including former embassy and AID officials. However, unlike embassy officials, the American businessman is not limited by requirements of protocol and diplomacy in order to gain access to host government officials who are important at any given moment.

In Indonesia, the embassy became aware of plans of the host government to establish a steel complex. However, U.S. companies were ill-informed about this possibility, while the Germans and the Japanese were actively pursuing the proposal. The embassy played a role (along with selected U.S. companies) in organizing a consortium of U.S. steel-manufacturing and financing organizations for an on-the-spot survey of the prospects. In this way, the U.S. companies were brought into competition for the project.

The IC needs information and at times the embassy possesses the information but the two parties are ignorant of each other's needs and resources. However, if the information does become available, at times, it serves a highly useful purpose for the IC. For example, a large petrochemical company in Thailand was reviewing its plans for additional investments in agribusiness in the country. However, the country manager was concerned about the extent to which the host government was willing to offer credit to farmers, which was one of the major reasons for inadequate use of scientific inputs in agriculture. The existing rates were exorbitant, and the Thai government was not placing any pressure on the local banking community to extend preferential low-interest loans to the farmer. At a luncheon meeting with the agricultural attaché at the embassy, the conversation drifted toward credit needs of the Thai farmer. The attaché noted that he had just completed a major study which would be submitted to the Thai government making strong recommendations for sweeping improvements in this area backed by aid from the U.S. government. Of course, the country manager was delighted with this information, as it strengthened his argument with the corporate level and also offered him access to free and well-documented information directly related to his needs.

The IC offers information to the embassy in order to keep it informed of developments in an industry or in a country. The major oil companies in Japan have kept the embassy informed of important developments in the industry, as they affect Japan, and the general stand adopted by the companies on supplies to Japan. In Brazil, U.S. companies kept close watch over sentiment in the business community relative to governmental policies, and helped prepare documentation for the 1971 visit of Governor Rockefeller.

The government-relations executive in the European headquarters of a U.S. oil company is a former foreign service officer, and he deliberately keeps U.S. embassies informed of the company's major policies and moves—either through his own visits (facilitated by his former job) or through his correspondents in the national subsidiaries.

On broad issues of a "class action" or precedent-setting nature, ICs make it a point to inform the embassy. Thus, U.S. lawyers in Belgium drew the attention of the embassy to a new Belgian policy not to grant work permits for replacements coming from U.S. headquarters. In addition, the lawyers alerted the embassy of new and stricter limitations that could spell the decline if not the demise of U.S. law firms in Belgium.

Conversely, in Spain the U.S. companies provided the embassy with a translation of a new regulation of sales of pharmaceuticals to the government, under which preference would be given to companies with majority local ownership.

The U.S. government seeks views of American companies in particular foreign countries. For example, the embassy in Japan assisted senior trade negotiators of the U.S. government in securing the views of U.S. companies in Japan on specific examples of discrimination practiced by the Japanese government against American companies. The U.S. government wished to negotiate with the Japanese government on case situations that would force the Japanese to respond specifically instead of offering vague and general statements. American banks in Japan are contacted by representatives of the federal government to learn if the Japanese government is being unfair to them. This information presumably becomes part of the federal government's decision on applications of Japanese banks for operations in the U.S.

In the Philippines, American companies in an individual capacity and as members of the AmCham have expressed their views to the embassy on the preferred terms of a new treaty to replace the Laurel-Langley Agreement. A similar approach has been pursued in Thailand on the issue of alien decrees. The AmCham in Mexico not only discussed its views on the new foreign investment law with the embassy, but its officials were also given audience by the Mexican government on the effects of specific provisions.

The IC informs the embassy of major developments that might result in questions being directed at the embassy. In this way, the IC hopes to avoid embarrassment to the embassy. A Japanese bank made a major loan to a large American company in London. The terms of the loan were not in keeping with normal commercial banking practices, and were a sign of the immaturity and overeagerness of the Japanese banking community to rapidly achieve a position in the international banking community. A large American bank in Tokyo was alerted to the terms of financing offered by the Japanese bank. It informed the Bank of Japan of the implications of such terms for the image of Japan, acceptance into the international banking community, and possible charges of dumping of funds. (The Japanese government has already been criticized for dumping of products by Japanese companies, and is particularly sensitive to this charge.) The manager of the American Bank in Japan called the U.S. ambassador to inform him of the bank's initiatives with the Japanese government in case there was any publicity or questions from the Japanese government to the embassy.

Bechtel's proposal for fertilizer manufacturing was quickly identified in the Indian press as a venture with the strong and direct support of the embassy. Therefore, the company was particularly careful to keep the embassy briefed at all stages of negotiation with the Indian government.

The seriousness of an issue for a company and in its view for the embassy, the orientation of the executive involved, and the degree of sensitivity of relations between the U.S. and the host country concerned are among the considerations that influence the IC's approach to informing the embassy. For example, a pharmaceutical company is faced with a seriously deteriorating situation in India, with the distinct possibility of divestment, partly due to the curtailment of U.S. aid and to the poor relationships between the U.S. and Indian governments. Under these circumstances the company has been in close touch with the embassy. Similarly, in Kenya, a U.S. manufacturing company came under sharp criticism from customers and then the parliament, since it had a virtual monopoly, and turned to the embassy for support and advice.

The exchange of information is a two-way flow between the IC and the embassy. The embassy discovers what the IC is doing, which permits it to be briefed on specific developments and at the same time place other situations that have come to its attention in a comparative context. The IC, on its side, hopes to discover who else is faced with a situation similar to its own, or what precedents exist that might be useful to the IC in its particular situation. The embassy tends to be viewed as a reasonably confidential repository of such information, which might be of value to one or more companies.

In all countries, there is some form of a regular program through which the embassy and the American business community interact with each other. Monthly, quarterly, biannual, and annual meetings, informal contacts at sporting and social events—these serve as some of the methods for exchange of information between the IC and the embassy.

Access to better, more accurate and timely information is a source of power in the influence process. Does the information provided by the embassy to the IC assist it in influencing the host government? The answer to this question is largely determined by the extent of knowledge of a particular country on the part of the IC. At the initial stage, the IC might be more inclined to seek information from the embassy *as one of several sources of information used by the IC.* Over time, as the IC develops its own sources and seeks project-related information, it has limited reason for approaching the embassy as a source of information. However, to the extent that the IC approaches the embassy for information especially at the initial stages of market exploration, the embassy probably has some influence on the IC.

The IC also influences the embassy as it possesses greater information, greater experience, and a greater range of relationships within the host country. The IC can provide the embassy critical information, however, especially after the IC has proceeded beyond the stage of initial exploration of a country market. Conversely, the embassy is used and relied upon comparatively *less* frequently as a source of information by the IC than are banks, other companies, and private consulting organizations.

Introductions. The embassy has a continued and established presence in a country which permits cultivation of relationships with individuals in the host society. In addition, the power and the prestige of the U.S. offers access to certain members of the host country which might not be available to the IC, especially one that is just beginning to gain entry into a market.

In many countries, introductions are a necessity; otherwise, one does not get through the maze of appointments. For example, in Kenya, it is not unusual for an executive to be kept waiting for a week or more to meet the appropriate officials.

Key executives from the regional and parent level are introduced to the embassy. The chairman of a large pharmaceutical company was visiting Japan and the country level manager arranged for a meeting with the U.S. ambassador to Japan. This pattern also applies to other countries. At times, dinners are organized by the embassy where selected host government officials and local businessmen are invited to meet with one or more American businessmen.

The IC seeks introductions with host government officials or local businessmen through the embassy generally at the initial stages of exploring entry into a market. Thereafter, the IC develops its own relationships and sources of introductions through other American businessmen, local partners, and banks.

The introductions offered by the embassy to the American businessman in the host country are almost invariably at the senior levels of the government and the local business community. Such introductions are helpful especially on broad policy matters or general approach to interpretation of policies. However, on specific details of implementation and problems of operations, the needs of the IC are for introductions at relatively lower levels of the host government. The IC develops introductions at these levels largely through its own contacts and resources once it goes beyond the stage of initial exploration of a market. Of course, more often than not, the IC does not seek introductions by the embassy especially to host government officials, as it might create the wrong impression in the eyes of the host government that the IC was closely affiliated with the U.S. government.

The embassy exerts some influence on the IC through its selection of officials and local businessmen introduced to the IC. More often than not, the embassy's contacts are with officials and businessmen who are favorably inclined toward the U.S. and American companies. However, this source of influence when it exists is limited to the initial stages of market exploration by a company.

The ICs already operating in a country are the ones called upon by the embassy to advise and inform the visiting executives. In this way, the extent of the influence exercised by the embassy is further restricted than would be the case if the contacts were limited to the embassy.

In general, the embassy's influence through power of introductions is largely limited to the initial market-exploration stage. However, even at this stage the IC meets other American companies, specifically American banks. In addition, as a matter of policy, the IC does not rely on any one source of introduction, but uses several sources.

Interpretation/Advice. The embassy is one source of interpretation and advice for the IC. The IC might seek the views of the embassy on specific programs of action being considered by the company. For example, faced with excessively large profits that could expose them to adverse public reaction, some of the American oil companies in Indonesia are considering investments in areas deemed to be of high priority by the host government, such as rice estates. Some companies have presented their general plans to the embassy for reaction and comment on ways in which the resources of the U.S. government might be utilized; for example, in development of rice estates, U.S. AID might care to be involved. In this way, U.S. companies gain a general assessment of the views of the embassy, which can then be encouraged to explore the idea in general terms with appropriate members of the host government without identifying the individual companies. (The embassy therefore has a chance to influence company policy.) Direct explorations with the host government at the initial stages would tend to bind the companies to a preliminary proposal if the host government expressed interest in it.

In the case of the fertilizer program in India, Bechtel Corporation approached the embassy at all stages for advice and interpretation on what was likely to be the response of powerful government officials to certain terms and conditions of investment. Similarly, in Kenya, sponsorship by an interested or key minister can be critical in approvals by the investment committee.

The IC seeks the assistance of the embassy for gaining clarification of policies of the host government on various aspects of foreign investments. In Thailand, American companies have sought the views of the embassy on interpretation of alien decrees in the light of the existing treaty between the U.S. and Thailand. In the Philippines, the embassy has received a flurry of questions from American companies on implications of the termination of the Laurel-Langley Agreement, and the new treaty being negotiated between the U.S. and Filipino governments. In Egypt, American companies are seeking embassy interpretation of meaning and likely continuity of recently promulgated laws on foreign investment.

An American company was considering a joint venture in Iran for the manufacture of cables and wires, but the host government refused to regard these products as high technology meriting royalty payments. After considerable discussion with the host government, the company alerted the embassy. The embassy was well versed with the host government's emphasis on attracting high-technology industries, and knew that it had approved royalty payments for a joint venture for assembling air conditioners in Iran. The technology involved in the manufacture of cables and wires was surely of a far higher order. The embassy informally inquired of the host government regarding its policy on royalty payments for high-technology industries, and whether certain industries were deemed to be high technology. The government responded informally, and its reaction was transmitted to the American company, which then made another effort at gaining approval from the host government.

A host of problems have arisen in various countries requiring clarification of policy on areas such as acquiring and/or renting land, use of foreign technicians, labor laws and regulations, and tax provisions. The IC has sought the assistance of the embassy as one source of gaining clarification of policies from the host government.

The IC seeks advice of the embassy in negotiations especially for initial entry into a country. A chemical company was negotiating a major plant in Iran. The host government insisted on imposing a requirement on the company that it would export a certain percentage of production. The company was reluctant to accept such a demand. Having kept the embassy informed from the beginning of its negotiations with the host government, the company turned to the embassy for advice. The embassy suggested that the company make sure that the host government did not require an unreasonably high level of exports, and that the company might offer some general assurances on exports, but only after some period of time after the plant became operational in Iran. The company followed the embassy's suggestion (which was similar to recommendations by other ICs and consultants operating in Iran) and settled for an agreement to export under 5 percent of production after five years of commercial operations. (However, the company does not expect to export at all, because of the high domestic demand.)

The IC also seeks the interpretation of the embassy on developments within the U.S. The Hartke-Burke bill and the deliberations over a new trade bill are examples of the areas on which information is sought. A few farsighted companies are beginning to question the embassy as to what their stand would be once U.S. Congressional hearings critical of the American IC started and were reported in the local media in a foreign country. Would the embassy take a particular stand on comments and accusations against the IC made in the U.S. by a senator, congressman, or committee?

The degree of advice and interpretation offered by the embassy is influenced by the priority or preference of a particular proposal from the standpoint of the embassy and/or the U.S. government. For example, the embassy in Taiwan was extremely helpful to a large company in the initial stages of a proposal for a telecommunication system for the country. However, another company entered the picture and the embassy let it be known to the initial bidder that it was more sympathetic to the proposal of the new bidder. The reason was that the new bidder did not have the controversial image of the original bidder, and was planning on importing a far greater value from the U.S. than was the case with the original bidder; in addition, the embassy was uncertain whether the original bidder would supply from the U.S. or only from a European subsidiary.

Another example of definite discouragement of one U.S. bidder in favor of another is reflected in the case of the concurrent negotiations of the Indian government with Standard Oil Company of Indiana (AIOC) and the Bechtel Corporation for the Madras fertilizer project award. The embassy in India warned AIOC that it favored the fulfillment of the one-million-ton-a-year fertilizer project being proposed by Bechtel, and AIOC's proposal for a refinery and a fertilizer project was interfering with the fulfillment of a larger objective. Therefore, it preferred to have AIOC become part of the overall program offered by Bechtel to the Indian government. When AIOC balked at the idea, the embassy let it be known to Amoco that it would not be favorably inclined to recommend AIOC's project to U.S. AID for guarantees or loans. Nor would it encourage the Indian government to proceed with the project. AIOC was highly dubious about the prospects of success of the Bechtel proposal. It knew that once the Bechtel proposal was rejected both the embassy and the GOI would turn to AIOC to salvage something out of a bad situation.

The IC approaches the embassy as *one* of the sources of information on broad developments within the host government that might have an effect on the IC. In Bangladesh, a pharmaceutical company sought the views of the U.S. ambassador on the probable pattern of relations between the U.S. and Bangladesh and the resultant role of U.S. investments. A large chemical company in South Korea sought views of the embassy on the long-term stability of the government because of increasing political opposition to the Korean president. The current developments in the Middle East are strongly influenced by political considerations, including U.S. government policies in the Middle East. Therefore, American companies are keeping abreast of these developments by reference to the embassies in the region as a source of interpretation of events.

To the extent that the IC seeks interpretation/advice from the embassy, the embassy has an opportunity to influence the IC. However, the IC seeks this form of assistance generally when it first enters a market, when it is faced with an unusual situation, or when it has reached an impasse with the host government in resolving a matter. Moreover, the embassy is only one of several sources (banks, other American companies, local and international accounting and law firms, etc.) of interpretation/advice used by the IC.

The ICs also influence the embassy through greater experience and a broader and more diverse range of contacts in the host country. Nationals who are employees, senior executives, and board members offer the IC access to sources of interpretation that are likely to include a broad cross-section of the local decision-making groups in a country.

Intelligence. Intelligence refers to cultivating and utilizing sources of information on relatively sensitive and delicate areas—such as internal politics—in order to position the enterprise favorably in a country or to permit it to act more effectively. Intelligence differs from information in that it is more specific, related to particular events or persons, and aids directly in specific actions by the IC. The IC turns to the embassy as one source of intelligence on the host country. The responsibilities of the embassy extend far beyond matters of business and economics into questions of internal politics, regional relations, international implications of developments and the emerging lines of thinking within the key members of the host government and opposing political groups. All these and other areas have a direct bearing on the manner in which a company interprets the foreign investment climate and analyzes the environment for its impact on a specific industry and project.

In Iran, a large oil company had poor relations with some key members of the host government originating during an episode when the company refused to succumb to certain terms being demanded by these officials. The controversy achieved some publicity resulting in loss of face by the host government officials. The embassy gathered from its sources that the managing director of the company was in the process of being declared persona non grata and would be allowed only a very short period of time to leave the country. The embassy alerted the company of the developments within the host government in order for the company to have some advance warning to formulate a course of action.

To the extent that the embassy is used as a source of intelligence by the IC, it possesses the opportunity to exercise influence on the IC. The typical pattern, however, is for the IC to develop its own intelligence sources, especially after it moves beyond the stage of initial exploration of a country. Moreover, as a matter of policy, the IC seeks intelligence from several different sources. As in the context of other types of services discussed, the IC has an influence on the embassy through its sources of intelligence on host-country developments.

Personal Safety. The IC seeks protection from the embassy where personal safety of the executives and their families is involved. In South America (and of late in Argentina in particular) kidnapping of U.S. executives has become a serious problem, requiring close coordination between the ICs and the embassy. Outbreak of local violence in a country results in inquiries to the embassy on whether U.S. citizens are in any particular danger. For example, the violence in Indonesia preceding Sukarno's overthrow, racial violence in Malaysia, the student demonstrations in Thailand and South Korea, the imposition of martial law in the Philippines, and the India-Pakistan war over Bangladesh are situations when the embassy advised U.S. citizens on the state of law and order.

Complaints

Procedures. The embassy is one source of assistance to the IC in understanding the often vague and complex procedures and in working through them to save time. A large chemical company had received official approval for a project in Japan. However, another permit for implementation of the approval was not secured, and the corporate level insisted on securing it before proceeding. The country manager approached the embassy for assistance in obtaining the permit. In Belgium, representations were made by the embassy on behalf of U.S. lawyers whose work permits were being delayed. In this case, the embassy was also testing the Belgian government's promise to remove newly introduced restrictions.

In Thailand, immigration procedures have been complex, cumbersome, and prone to extensive graft, and American companies have faced serious problems as a result. Individual American companies and the American Chamber of Commerce have brought this situation to the attention of the embassy, including the ambassador. Finally, the embassy played a role in developing procedures and gaining acceptance of them by the host government which greatly reduced the complexity involved in securing the necessary visas. Similar efforts have been made in other countries (e.g., Ivory Coast) to break through a preference for European technicians and personnel. Throughout the world, the embassies have been most active in getting governments to comply with their own regulations and agreements on import licenses. Governments often renege, and embassy officials see this as a violation of an agreement which they can rapidly protest.

Smuggling from PX stores in Thailand had reached massive proportions. Sales of American companies were affected because of the much lower price on the open market for smuggled goods. Individual companies and the American Chamber of Commerce conveyed their displeasure to the U.S. ambassador (and to higher U.S. government levels in Washington), who instructed the chief of security to institute tight measures to prevent smuggling from PX stores. (The situation was a delicate one. High Thai officials were involved in the smuggling, and the U.S. ambassador did not wish to handle this "hot potato.")

The embassy might get involved on procedural matters on behalf of ICs with the host government, provided that the embassy is approached by a number of ICs on the same issue (import procedures, tax issues, etc.). Where an American Chamber of Commerce exists, the representation is made to the embassy by the AmCham on behalf of the member ICs. Typically, representation by the embassy to the host government is as a result of pressure brought on the embassy by the AmCham.

The relative role (including initiative) of the embassy in changing procedures of the host government is limited. The ICs go through AmChams for seeking changes. Often, the IC seeks favorable interpretation as against changes in stated procedures which satisfy its particular needs.

Regulations. The stated regulations of countries are often considerably different from the actual intent or practice of the host government. Administrative discretion often permits individual decision makers in the government to interpret regulations in keeping with their personal viewpoints. A country might liberalize foreign investments through issuance of regulations while in reality it imposes different types of restrictions on the inflow of investments. For example, the Ivory Coast is cited as being the most open and receptive to foreign investment. But this is true only if one comes in on a fifty-fifty basis; otherwise approvals are hard to obtain. The embassy is a source of assistance to the IC on matters of regulations of the host government, which include areas such as import restrictions, labeling requirements, and taxation.

In Japan, a large chewing-gum manufacturing company approached the embassy for representations to the Japanese government for a reduction or removal of tariffs on the import of chewing gum. A large chemical company with long-established operations in Japan sought the assistance of the embassy on regulations that prohibited the company from importing finished as against semifinished film. In Japan a considerable percentage of representations to the embassy are in areas of import restrictions imposed by the host government with the balance being for restrictions on existing operations, particularly expansion of operations.

Thai law requires that the labels of all goods entering Thailand should be in the Thai language for inspection and clearance at customs. This was a serious problem for companies as it would require printing and labeling of products prior to shipment to Thailand. The embassy, along with the AmCham, played a role in working out a requirement with the host government whereby only a sample of a shipment would be labeled in the Thai language upon arrival and the sample would be subject to customs inspection. Thereafter, the goods would be released to be fully labeled in the Thai language prior to distribution.

Tax regulations of countries have presented an area of considerable confusion to the IC that has sought the assistance of the embassy. Tax rules change or are given new interpretations with retroactive features which cause considerable discomfort to the IC. Adequate court appeals might not exist, encouraging companies to refer to the embassy. In Iran and Indonesia several companies are faced with ad hoc interpretation of tax regulations by the host government. The companies have discussed their tax situations directly with host governments, but have also alerted the embassies of the growing problem. The embassies have been encouraged to explore the matter with the host governments, as it is creating a negative climate for foreign investments.

The embassy might be approached for assistance on regulations by ICs. However, such assistance if it is sought generally occurs after the American Chamber of Commerce has formulated a stand and entered into a dialogue with the host government. Often the IC makes direct representation to selected host government officials, not for a change of regulations but an interpretation of regulations favorable to an industry or a company. Also, the embassy is only one of several sources used by the IC to change or seek favorable interpretation of regulations by the host country. The embassy's role is limited and relates largely to stages when the host government is formulating regulations.

Discrimination. American companies at times feel discriminated against by the host government in favor of indigenous or other foreign companies. In such situations, they might seek the assistance of the embassy, besides using other means.

A large electrical company in Japan felt that the Japanese shipbuilders were discriminating against use of non-Japanese turbines. It approached the embassy to make representations to the Japanese government to correct the situation. Informal inquiries by the embassy indicated that the Japanese shipbuilders in fact had imported several turbines from Sweden, with the result that the American company's charge was incorrect.

In Iran, an American company had bid for a communication system in competition to a Japanese bidder for the forthcoming Asian games in Iran. The contract was awarded to the Japanese company and the American company informed the embassy that it felt it was being discriminated against. The embassy made inquiries within the host government and discovered the reason for the success of the Japanese bid. The Japanese company promised to install a portable communication system at its own cost for the Asian games in case the larger system required under the terms of the bid was not completed. Given the importance being attached to these games by the Iranian government, the Japanese were preferred over the Americans.

In West Germany, the embassy was asked by the AmCham to protest new proposed features that were considered as discriminatory against the IC. The embassy studied the German bill and discussed it with various officials, and concluded that the host government was simply proposing to remove features that discriminated in favor of such companies. Hence, the embassy refused to make representation on such matters.

The IC that is a newcomer to a country might seek embassy assistance as against the IC with experience in a country. As the newcomer develops knowledge of the local context, its dependence on the embassy as a source of representation to the host government is greatly reduced. The IC prefers to work directly with the host government. Where anonymity and group representation is sought, the IC almost always works through the American Chamber of Commerce.

Contract Violation. Policies of many countries on foreign investments are vague more often than not; legislation is always subject to change, and administrative discretion plays a major role in interpretation of policies and legislation. The local administrative and judicial review process does not always offer a reasonable method of resolving differences. The embassy is one source of assistance for the IC in situations of contract violation.

One type of violation is the clear-cut nonfulfillment of contract terms. An Indonesian coffee explorer failed to fulfill terms of his contract causing financial loss to the American importer. The importer asked the embassy to encourage the Indonesian government to make good his loss. The embassy informed the appropriate host government officials of the importer's grievance. Similar disputes arise with government officials who have agreed to limit imports of competing products—as one company obtained from the three members of the East African Community, but found the agreement inoperative when the community broke up and the country of location also did not honor the commitment. The ambassador or economic/commercial officer are usually quite willing to take up such a matter—so long as the issue is clear.

An American company established a cement manufacturing plant in West Java on the condition that the host government would not permit the establishment of another cement plant within West Java for a period of five years from the date of commercial operations of the original cement plant. Shortly after the plant was being erected, the American company discovered that the host government had approved another plant in West Java which involved powerful local interests. The manager of the American company alerted the embassy of developments partly as a means of protecting the OPIC insurance carried by the company.

A more typical situation is modification of terms of contract once a company has started operations. For example, a company was given the right to import duty free into Indonesia certain types of products required in the overall manufacturing process. Once operations started, the host government refused to permit imports, on the grounds that the terms of entry did not apply in the light of new regulations of the government. The IC alerted the embassy of the development.

A pharmaceutical company had been granted protection against imports in South Korea under the terms of agreement for entry into the country. However, subsequently the host government changed its policies, causing significant discomfort to the U.S. company, which proceeded to alert the embassy.

Differences of interpretation have arisen over the meaning of certain clauses. The IC has informed the embassy as these problems have arisen. A large timber company in Indonesia was granted certain tax concessions for operations outside of Jakarta. However, these provisions were never firmly stated, at least in the eyes of the host government, resulting in conflicts between the government and the company. The company proceeded to inform the embassy of the merits of the case. In another case, the embassy has been informed regularly of the ongoing conflict between the Indonesian government and a U.S. company over the intent and interpretation of a contract clause regarding which party is to administer and collect payment for communication services from overseas users. In India, Standard Oil Company of Indiana and the Indian government disagreed over the terms of contract calling for the establishment of a separate unit for manufacture of sulphur as against the import of sulphur. The company held to imports, while the Indian government insisted on local manufacture. The U.S. AID sided with the Indian government, on the grounds that if the contract term was as important to the American company as it claimed, then it should not have kept the clause vague, but should have been far more precise and specific.

The IC informs the embassy of contract violations where it is required to do so (as in the case of OPIC guarantees) or where it deems it wise to do so in case the problem becomes severe at a later stage. However, the typical pattern is for the IC to deal directly with the host government to achieve reconciliation. This approach is deemed more effective than seeking involvement of the embassy. In general, the embassy seldom wishes to become involved. And, particularly in developing countries, embassy involvement ruffles the feathers of the host government, which results in worsening the position of the IC.

Legislation. Legislation affecting the IC is at times vague, hard to interpret, conflicts with other legislation of the home or host country, and imposes certain reporting requirements. The embassy is one source of assistance to the IC on matters of legislation.

U.S. laws require companies in certain industries to report sales to the U.S. government. For example, companies engaged in the atomic energy field have to maintain close relations with the Atomic Energy Commission and with the liaison officer for the AEC at the embassy. The same relationship applies in selling defense-related equipment requiring clearance and approval of the U.S. government.

The IC interacts heavily with the embassy, especially when forthcoming legislation might reduce the privileges of the business community. The pharmaceutical companies encouraged the embassy in the Philippines to dispatch a representative to the public hearing scheduled by the host government on the question of a new bill for patents. The issue of a new treaty to replace Laurel-Langley has resulted in intensive and extensive discussions between the American business community and the embassy. The ICs sought the involvement of the embassy in making representations to the Indian government against the proposed patent bill. In Spain, the pharmaceutical companies urged the embassy officials to enter the dialogue on regulations giving preference to local companies, but the embassy demurred because it did not consider that the positions of the companies were at that time sufficiently firm and unified.

The IC also leans on the embassy in cases where new local legislation that is adverse to the foreign company is in violation of existing treaty obligations that are favorable to U.S. companies. In Thailand, the promulgation of alien decrees resulted in extensive and intensive interaction between the business community and the embassy; similarly, ICs interacted with the embassy in Belgium regarding the pending law on economic expansion (which originally treated non-EEC firms differently) and on procedures for work permits to U.S. lawyers. In these cases, the new measures of the host country violated international treaty arrangements with the U.S.

On matters of host-country legislation, if the embassy does get involved it is only on issues of interest to the American business community in general. While it varies by orientation of specific people, embassy personnel generally attach greater importance to the formulation and passage of legislation by the host country than to the interpretation of legislation. The IC typically works through the AmCham for representations to the host government. And more often than not, the AmCham exerts pressure on the embassy to adopt a certain course of action vis-à-vis the host government. Also, unlike the embassy, individual executives place as much if not greater weight on the interpretation rather than formulation or passage of legislation.

In general, the embassy plays a limited role in the IC's process of influencing the host government on matters of legislation. Bilateral treaties such as Laurel Langley and alien decrees, however, result in a dramatically increased involvement of the embassy.

Impasse. The IC is more likely to interact with the embassy when it has reached an impasse with the host government on some issue of importance to the IC. It then seeks to inform the embassy and determine if the embassy can and will assist the IC.

In South Korea, a leading American bank became exposed to the wrath of certain elements of the South Korean government, which proceeded to cause labor unrest and to arrest one of the officers of the bank. The bank first initiated action on its own to resolve the situation. But when an officer was arrested on trumped-up charges by the Korean CIA, the bank sought the assistance of the embassy. In Pakistan the same bank was unable to encourage the Pakistan government to honor the terms of purchase of certain cement plants from the Indian government with the bank serving as an intermediary. The reputation of the bank was at stake, and it would have paid the monies from its own resources to protect its name. In this case, after exhausting all avenues of direct settlement, the bank turned to the embassy for assistance. The examples cited in earlier sections on discrimination and contract violation are often referred to the embassy only after companies have exhausted other means at their command to resolve the issue.

An impasse indicates a stage when the IC is most likely to inform the embassy of its difficulties. Of course, for every one IC that informs the embassy, there are several more that attempt to solve their problems without embassy involvement. In informing the embassy of an impasse, moreover, the IC does not necessarily seek representation to the host government by the embassy. The typical pattern is for the IC to seek several sources of influence to resolve an impasse, and the embassy is only one source that might be contacted by the IC. In fact, the embassy plays a relatively minor role in IC representations on matters of impasse because: it is generally against such involvement; its involvement typically arouses strongly adverse reaction against the company on the part of the host government; and it is not inclined to develop a solution immediately, which is what is needed by the IC.

Credibility. The embassy has knowledge of many dimensions of the host country that influence the foreign investment climate, and therefore can assist in a company's assessment of a country. The corporate level at times feels reassured when reports from the country level (especially from the developing countries) include comments and observations of the embassy. The IC interacts with the embassy, therefore, also for achieving greater credibility to the reports submitted to the senior levels of corporate management. In this way, the embassy can influence the company.

For example, the regional vice-president of a large pharmaceutical company attaches little significance to the views of the embassy or of the U.S. ambassador to a particular country. However, he makes it a point to visit the ambassador in order to be able to refer to such a visit in his report to the headquarters level. A large automotive company was in the midst of negotiations in the Philippines when martial law was declared in September 1972. The corporate level was seriously concerned about what was happening in the country and the long-term implications of the change in government policies. The country manager submitted his report and attached an assessment of the situation from the embassy. He also requested the embassy to ask members of the State Department to contact headquarter executives. A similar situation occurred in October 1973 when the students forced a change of government in Thailand. Embassy reports analyzing the situation were submitted by managers in their reports to the regional and headquarters levels. The Bechtel Corporation was able to convince other companies to join its proposal for fertilizer manufacturing in India partly as a result of the strong support of the idea by the embassy. In Belgium, the embassy's interpretation of how the government would apply the new linguistic law requiring use of the native language in dealing with employees (including the American manager's communication with his Belgian secretary!) was of some help to U.S. companies, which could thereby assure the legal counsel at headquarters that no strict application of this requirement was intended or expected.

To the extent that the embassy's views are inserted in a report to the corporate level, the areas on which the views are stressed are local political developments and the emerging patterns of relationship of the U.S. with the particular country. The views are generally on political and not economic/business matters.

The foregoing discussion permits some general observations on the areas of interaction between the embassy and the IC.

1. The IC and the embassy interact on a range of issues, from simple search for information to changes in legislation by the host government and specific support of company interests.

2. The IC often seeks embassy representation to the host government only when it has reached an impasse.

3. Major changes in relationships between the U.S. government and the host government cause significant increase in interaction between the IC and the embassy.

4. Individual characteristics of the IC executives and embassy officials have a major bearing on the extent and areas of interaction between them.

5. In general, the embassy's assistance plays a limited role in the IC's efforts to influence the host government.

Areas of Discussion with Host Government

This section discusses the major issues which are the subject of dialogues between the IC and the host government. (Chapter 5 discusses who is involved in the dialogues.)

The IC attempts to influence the host government by arguments that include effect on foreign investment climate, including the implications of divestment; economic benefit or loss to the host country, including effect on domestic investment climate; and use of trade-offs. These arguments are economic in nature, and indicate that the IC views its contributions to the host country to be essentially economic in nature.

Foreign Investment Climate

A favorable investment climate in a country results in the inflow of resources possessed by the IC, such as technology, organization capacities, foreign exchange, and access to international markets. Conversely, an unfavorable investment climate results in reducing the inflow of such resources, thereby hindering the country's plans for development. In addition, poor investment climate might be viewed unfavorably by donor/lending countries and by international organizations which stress the role of foreign investment in the development programs of a country.

In Iran, the ICs have informed the host government (often through the embassy and the American Chamber of Commerce) that its approach to taxes, customs, visa procedures, delays in decision making, and discriminatory treatment of American companies is not favorable to promoting greater inflow of foreign direct investments. The embassy was an intermediary in the settlement of the expropriations of ITT telephone properties in Brazil in the 1960s, representing the U.S. government's interest to the Brazilian government in having a prompt, adequate, and effective settlement so as not to damage future prospects for foreign investment. This aspect of climate was acute enough to be included in the final communiqué on the settlement, with the company publicly declaring that it had received fair treatment. In the case of the attempted acquisition of Jeumont-Schneider by Westinghouse, this was a major theme of embassy representation to the French government, namely, that allowing such an acquisition would provide proof of a more favorable French attitude toward U.S. investors following the advent of the new Pompidou/Chaban-Delmas government.

The manager of an American company in Indonesia was able to gain the support of the Indonesian government in stopping serious patent infringements. He alerted the host government that if it did not correct the situation, corporate management was threatening to complain vigorously to various bodies of the U.S. government and to major U.S. companies with investments in Indonesia. In the Philippines, a lumber company informed the host government (directly and through the embassy and the AmCham) that its inaction over gross contract violations was highly detrimental to promoting foreign investments in the country. During the initial stages of the Bechtel proposal, the Indian government was anxious to demonstrate to the international investing community (private and government) that it welcomed foreign investments and was creating a favorable climate in the country.

Representations by groups of American companies (such as AmChams and industry associations) place particularly strong emphasis on the theme of foreign investment climate in attempting to influence the host government. In Japan, the AmCham stressed the need for a rapid pace of capital liberalization to the Japanese government in order to create a positive image and to avoid possible retaliatory moves by the U.S. government. The joint venture proposal between Mitsubishi and Chrysler was viewed as a test of the intent of the Japanese government to actually implement terms of capital liberalization.

In Thailand the AmCham has been particularly emphatic in stressing to the host government the negative effects of the alien decrees on foreign investments. The same approach has been used by the AmCham in the Philippines in making representations to the host government on the need for protecting the economic interests of U.S. companies in a new treaty between the U.S. and Filipino governments in order to attract foreign investments. The host government is anxious to attract foreign public and private resources as a sign of confidence of the international community in the New Society and to achieve concrete demonstrations of economic development to retain the support of Filipino power groups. These considerations suggest that it will attach importance to the effect on foreign investment climate, though not necessarily investment climate as viewed only by American companies.

Moves to change patent laws in India, Thailand, the Philippines, Peru, and Indonesia have resulted in strong representations by ICs against provisions that might reduce protection for the ICs' proprietary rights. The major argument used by the ICs was that restrictive provisions would greatly reduce the inflow of foreign investments.

The IC places strong emphasis on the need for a positive foreign investment climate in its representations to the U.S. government. The official policy of the U.S. government is to encourage American companies to invest in the developing countries, partly as a way of making up for a decreasing level of official aid to these countries. Also, host countries have typically sought foreign investments, which makes it simpler for the U.S. government to promote the idea as it is in keeping with the wishes of host governments. The argument of adverse effect on foreign investment climate has been by far the predominant one in the cases we have examined where the American company has either informed or sought representations to the host government by the embassy to resolve its problems.

By assisting in promoting a positive investment climate of a country, the IC hopes to exercise some influence over the host government.[4] Benefits to the IC, however, typically occur over a period of time, and management cannot expect returns over the short term. A few examples illustrate the types of assistance of the IC to the host government: a large U.S. bank has assisted in training Indonesians and establishing financial institutions in Indonesia in the hope of payoffs occurring at a later date; a pharmaceutical company has offered know-how for establishing the Asian Heart Institute, a pet project of the First Lady of the Philippines; an oil company has assisted the Singapore government in publicizing the benefits of Jurong industrial estate; U.S. banks assist in organizing seminars for visiting government officials and often publicize their participation in consortia to finance projects in a particular country.

In general, the effectiveness of the foreign investment climate argument varies by country, and is based on two considerations. First, it depends on the importance attached by the host country to attracting foreign investments. For example, in the mid-1960s, when Singapore was first beginning to seek foreign investments, it was willing to bend over backwards to create an investment climate sought by the IC. However, having been successful in attracting ICs, at present Singapore feels it can continue to attract ICs without having to offer the same incentives as it did originally. Egypt at present is highly desirous of attracting foreign investments, and therefore is attaching particular importance to what ICs consider to be a favorable investment climate.

Conversely, the Indian government attaches limited importance to foreign investments, preferring to depend upon indigenous development; therefore, it attaches limited weight to foreign-investment-climate arguments. Similarly, Peru has developed policies on foreign investment with minimal weight to what is considered to be a favorable investment climate by U.S. companies.

The second consideration is the importance attached by the IC to a particular country. If a country is considered attractive, the IC will accept terms and conditions that otherwise it would consider as unattractive. For example, Iran is viewed as a highly attractive country for investments because of its ability to buy and its potentially large internal market. Yet the IC is faced with many problems of restrictions on foreign ownership and management control, government red tape, serious lack of trained people. Again, the appeal of the Japanese market has been strong enough for U.S. companies to accept severe restrictions on terms of entry and operations.

The effect on foreign-investment climate is among the more powerful arguments available to the IC. However, it is not as powerful as ICs would like to think it is. Often it is not presented effectively. For example, the IC places stress on the international image effects on a country, though this might be of limited consideration to a government decision maker, especially a politician who is concerned with the political impact on himself of certain economic decisions. Also, the argument loses weight where the IC is viewed as seeking special concessions as a condition of staying in a country.

Divestment by a company is viewed as having a particularly negative effect on the foreign-investment climate of a country. Divestments are voluntary (corporate decision to withdraw from a product line) and forced (host country actions forcing divestments). The image effect is negative in both cases except that, in the forced type, the potential conflict between the IC and the host country is greater and applies to a range of issues. For example, Esso decided to divest from its fertilizer operations in the Philippines and to significantly reduce its presence in India; both these decisions are within the category of voluntary decisions. Conversely, in some of the Andean Common Market countries the ICs are being forced to divest as a condition of continued operations.

Divestments of a forced nature create greater publicity, are characterized by conflicts which extend over a period of time, and in one way or another typically result in some form of involvement of the U.S. government. These and other characteristics have a negative effect on the foreign-investment climate of one or more South American countries in the eyes of the American IC.

However, the effectiveness of the argument by ICs that "forced divestment will create a poor foreign-investment climate" is influenced by two main considerations. First, if the threat is made openly and publicly by the IC it is likely to force the host government to "call their bluff" (if it is that), for reasons of national pride. Second, the extent to which the host country has access to alternative sources of supply of the needed resources will determine the weight attached to the threat of divestment.[5] However, both the IC and the host country recognize that the act of divestment represents in many ways the ultimate threat by either party. And for it to be meaningful and effective it must be used sparingly, and more by subtle hints than by specific statement.

Economic Benefit/Loss

In undertaking an investment in a country, the IC has a direct and indirect economic effect on the host country. The direct effect is in the form of the resources provided by the IC. The indirect effect, or the multiplier effect, is in the form of activating a series of indigenous resources. For example, an investment to manufacture pottery in a Southeast Asian country has created the following related operations: a packaging operation, a printing plant, a uniform business, and a plant for manufacturing transfers. Several other related projects are being considered. The pottery plant (the nucleus) has spawned several satellite operations. Therefore, actions by the host government that adversely affect the pottery operation will also have an adverse effect on the satellite operations, which are almost exclusively owned and managed by nationals. Such indirect economic effects, when effectively documented and presented, are a powerful means available to the IC for influencing host government officials.

American ICs account for the significant majority of foreign direct investments in certain countries, such as the Philippines. Therefore, host government actions that are deemed unfavorable by the primary source of foreign investment could have potentially serious economic consequences on the host country. This argument has been stressed by the American Chamber of Commerce to the Filipino government in the negotiations for a treaty to succeed the Laurel-Langley Agreement. The AmCham in Spain has produced a study by the Stanford Research Institute on the impact of foreign investments on the host economy, pointing up its many contributions.

At times, American ICs account for a major share of output, employment, and exports in a particular industry such as electronics in some Asian countries. The host country is keenly conscious of the fact that the ICs can move to another country if its actions are viewed as being unfavorable.

However, as often as not, the IC does not sufficiently analyze and document its position on an issue to convince the host government. For example, the American business community has warned the Thai government of the seriously negative consequences of the alien decrees on foreign direct investments. However, it has not been able to offer concrete evidence to the government that shows, to the satisfaction of the government, that the inflow of investments by American companies has been reduced as a result of the decrees. Similarly, the AmCham in the Philippines has warned the host government of the seriously negative effect on U.S. investments in the country if certain provisions of Laurel-Langley are not retained in a revised treaty with the U.S. However, U.S. companies have failed to demonstrate to the satisfaction of the host government that there has been or is likely to be a significant exodus of U.S. companies from the Philippines; or that other countries in the region offer more attractive terms than those contemplated by the Filipino government upon termination of Laurel-Langley; or that non-U.S. investors, especially the Japanese, are deterred by terms of investment that are being labeled detrimental by U.S. companies.

In some countries, American ICs promote themselves as an alternative source of investment in order to diversify the foreign investment base of the host country. The Japanese account for the significant majority of foreign investments in Thailand and Indonesia and the host countries are anxious to diversify their sources of investment. American ICs are viewed as a desirable alternative.

In general, two considerations determine the extent to which the economic benefit/loss argument is a source of influence on the host government. First, the relative importance attached to foreign investment by the host government influences the related argument of economic benefit/loss. However, even in countries that attach limited importance to foreign-investment-climate argument, the ability of the IC to demonstrate the economic benefit/loss from existing investments is a useful argument with the host government, as it relates to benefits derived by indigenous groups in the host society. Second, the economic benefit/loss argument does not change the basic attitudes toward the role of public and private enterprise (including the role of foreign investment) in the development of a country. These attitudes are based on long traditions and outlooks extending over several decades, if not centuries, and cannot be significantly influenced by argument of economic benefit/loss.[6] However, operational modifications in licensing terms, use of foreign technicians, and import procedures are aspects that can be influenced through this argument.

The economic benefit/loss argument would carry more weight if the ICs were to develop information demonstrating the effect of foreign investments on a country. At present the vast majority of ICs have done very little systematic analysis, or for that matter even planning, along these lines.[7]

Bilateral Bargains

The IC, the host government, and the U.S. government possess certain resources (finance, technology, organization, markets, etc.) that are sought by the others.

For example, the IC possesses desired technology, organizational skills, and access to international markets of the type sought by the host country. Conversely, the host country possesses the power to grant or deny access to local markets to the IC. The U.S. government has the power to offer or deny loans and guarantees in addition to other tangible and intangible means of facilitating or impeding an IC's investments in a particular country. In brief, the IC, the host government, and the U.S. government engage in bargaining: they have common interests (something to negotiate for), conflicting interests (something to negotiate about), and the use of trade-offs (a give and take on terms). (The potential influence of the U.S. government on the IC and vice versa is strongly perceived by the host government, and this perception is used by the IC in negotiating with the host government. This dimension of trade-offs is discussed in greater detail in Chapter 5.) A few examples illustrate the use of bargaining.[8]

The Japanese government approved a joint-venture application of a large U.S. chemical company for manufacture of magnetic tapes in Japan, provided that the U.S. company licensed another product from its line to a different Japanese company. A U.S. conglomerate is seeking several investments in Indonesia, but the host government is declining to discuss them until the conglomerate reaches agreement with the government on an existing dispute. A company with several years of manufacturing experience in Iran is being forced by the host government to terminate a clause in its original agreement calling for payment of 3 percent of sales as technical fees in perpetuity. The government has refused to discuss the company's plans for expansion until it terminates the clause. The Indian government offered Standard Oil Company of Indiana favorable crude oil supply terms if it undertook both a refinery and a fertilizer complex.

The concern over ownership is reflected in the new foreign-investment code of Mexico, in the Andean code, in the Mercantile bank case in Canada, and in other countries ranging from Japan to India. Though governments would like to promote greater local ownership and activities, reflected also in the requirements for local content of production in countries ranging from Canada to Argentina and from Mexico east to the Philippines, they are not eager to see the money paid out in reverse takeovers or expropriations leave the country. In the case of the expropriation of ITT in Brazil, the company agreed to reinvest a substantial amount of the funds in the Brazilian economy, thereby easing the drain on foreign exchange. Mexico, despite its desire for local content, has been willing to increase imports of some items in exchange to force exports of some components produced in Mexico. Trade-offs are possible, therefore, regardless of the restrictions imposed, and the embassies should be in a position to advise on the feasibility of particular trade-offs.

In the eyes of the host government, the IC has access to the influence of the U.S. government with the host government. The IC knows that such a perception exists and, where appropriate, attempts to capitalize on the perception (or reality) in attempting to influence the host government. Such influence is feasible in one circumstance but not in another. For example, it appeared for a time to be useful in the IPC case in Peru, certainly was in ITT

5

Actors in the Influence Process

Once companies have information relevant to governmental policies, decisions are taken as to whether and how to use it in affecting those policies. The actors in the process of using information are sometimes the same as those gathering or supplying it, but often different. This chapter provides illustrations of the actors involved and the dialogues undertaken.[1]

Channels

The IC has access to different groups that can be used to influence the host government. Each group has its particular strengths and limitations, and the extent to which any one group is used depends upon the nature of the situation, the characteristics of the host government, and the orientation of the decision makers involved. In general, the groups that could be used by the IC to influence the host government include the U.S. government, particularly the embassy, various levels of the host government (central, state, and municipal), chambers of commerce and associations, individuals at different levels of the IC (parent, regional, local partner), plus a variety of other groups and influential individuals.[2]

New associations and groupings of countries are beginning to develop and will serve as a channel of influence to and from a government. The Organization of Petroleum Exporting Countries (OPEC) has demonstrated its power by negotiating as a group with the major industrial/military powers of the world. Other raw-material-producing countries are likely to move in a similar direction to form groups. Regional groups such as the Andean Common market are negotiating on a group basis with large ICs and their governments, and such groupings are likely to spread before long to Asia and eventually to Africa.[3]

A strong and growing anxiety about large ICs, regardless of their country of origin, pervades almost all developing and several developed countries. This anxiety is beginning to find expression in the form of study groups (such as the United Nations group), which become channels of influence particularly on the developing countries.

In brief, increasingly in the future, the ICs' process of influencing host and home governments will include the types of industry, commodity, regional, and common-cause-oriented groups, which will gain in numbers and importance in the future.

The U.S. Government

The IC has two levels of the U.S. government through which it can act to affect policies abroad—that in Washington and the embassies.

ICs in Washington. The IC seeks assistance in Washington at several levels of the government. In the negotiations for a new treaty to succeed the Laurel-Langley Agreement, ICs have made it a point to seek out, individually and as members of business associations, various decision makers in the U.S. government. In addition, ICs have planned a major program of lobbying and publicity if the new treaty does not contain provisions being sought by the U.S. business community. These representations are made not only to exert influence at the policy-making levels in Washington but also to alert the negotiators in the Philippines (both Americans and Filipinos) that ICs have access to senior levels of the U.S. government. A similar pattern of representation has been used by ICs regarding the alien decrees in Thailand. Similar evidence was adduced by the company in the International Petroleum Company (IPC) case in Peru, which seemed to be effective for a while.

The American business community has actively lobbied with the U.S. government for a rapid pace of capital liberalization by Japan. The business community of each country is fully aware that the other has access to top governmental officials. Access to key decision makers was a point that was not lost on Chrysler and Mitsubishi as they sought the approval of the Japanese government for their joint venture.

A timber company in the Philippines faced with serious problems with the host government seriously considered seeking the assistance of its senator, who in turn would be asked to make strong representations to the State Department, which would eventually filter down to the country level. However, the company decided against this approach because it would not be able to control events once the senator started to act. Another timber company in Indonesia succeeded in having the difficulties of its project discussed at the IGGI meeting, courtesy of the company's home-state senator. A pharmaceutical company faced with a serious violation of contract terms in South Korea sent the manager from South Korea to brief two U.S. senators who were particularly interested in Korean affairs.

The prestige of a higher level of the U.S. government is sometimes brought to bear in an ongoing negotiation for initial entry into a country. For example, a senior State Department official on a visit to Tokyo during the Mitsubishi-Chrysler negotiations made it a point to inform the Japanese government that the U.S. government was favorably inclined toward the proposal and hoped that the Japanese government shared its view. Similarly, during the ill-fated Bechtel consortium negotiations, the U.S. ambassador-at-large visited India and was asked by the embassy to stress to the host government that the U.S. government attached importance to a favorable treatment of the proposal.

The U.S. government was also induced to send high-level intermediaries and officials to Jamaica in the bauxite disputes, to Peru in the case of IPC, and to Argentina in the rupture of petroleum contracts in the early 1960s and during negotiations of oil companies with OPEC in 1970. The results were by no means felicitous. During the recent controversy over the treatment of U.S. lawyers in Belgium, a senior officer in the legal department of the State Department made a special trip to Brussels to discuss this matter with Belgian government officials in order to stress the U.S. government's interest and concern in this matter, which bore on the substance of the bilateral treaty between the two countries and forbade such discriminations against U.S. lawyers and law offices in Belgium.

Through the Embassy. The embassy is on the spot, has an understanding of the local context, knows the personalities involved, and feels a greater sense of involvement than is the case for U.S. government officials sitting several thousand miles away in Washington. The IC seeks the assistance of the embassy for representations to the host government.

As discussed in Chapter 4, the IC seeks assistance of the U.S. Embassy in representations to the host government. Often a company seeks embassy assistance through its business associations for changes or clarification of the host country's policies. It achieves almost the same benefit (without any risks) if the embassy takes up the matter on behalf of other companies. Such indirect efforts have produced direct negotiations for a company, even when it took no initiative, as in Iran when all pharmaceutical companies were summoned by a minister as a result of representations through the embassy to the host government made by one American company.

Embassies Other than U.S. An IC maintains operations in several countries, which permits the use of more than one embassy in making representations to the host government. A conglomerate in Iran has referred certain matters to the British Embassy because a British subsidiary is partly involved in the proposed venture. Management feels that the British Embassy might be willing to make a more forceful presentation for the project to the host government. An automotive company involved the Australian High Commissioner to the Philippines because the company's operations in Australia would play a major role in establishing operations in the Philippines. An American company established a tripartite venture in the Philippines by offering a relatively small equity interest to a Japanese firm, which was then encouraged to seek the support of the Japanese Embassy in promoting the venture with the host government.

Though the American IC does, on occasion, seek information and other forms of assistance from an embassy other than the American, in the vast majority of cases, the IC relies solely on the U.S. Embassy for representations to the host government on its behalf. This characteristic attests to the strong sense of affiliation of the IC to the U.S. government.

Through the Host Government

The host government is not a monolith, but is composed of many diverse and conflicting interests that are for, against, or indifferent to the IC. Often the IC has to influence one interest of the host government in order to influence another within the same government. This occurs within and across ministries, and within and across organizational levels of the host government.

At Central Government Level. Within the central government there are many different interests; the IC must choose among them, gaining the support of one or more powerful interests.[4] In Japan, Chrysler and Mitsubishi recognized the conflicting interests of the MITI and the Ministry of Finance, and the important role of the Japan Automobile Manufacturers Association in any decision of the host government on the proposed joint venture. In the beginning, Bechtel Corporation stressed interacting with the Ministry of Finance, which was willing to take the initiative in having the Indian government consider the fertilizer manufacturing proposal. When the original proposal was rejected, Bechtel shifted its attention to the Ministry of Petroleum and Chemicals, which as the operative ministry would be blamed for inadequate indigenous fertilizer manufacturing, and therefore, would be more receptive to revised proposals by Bechtel. In the Philippines, Esso recognized that the Sugar Producers Cooperative Marketing Association was the logical buyer for its fertilizer plant, because SPCMA had the power to influence the host government for concessions that could not be attained by any other local group. A timber company in the Philippines has developed new ways to influence the host government as a result of martial law; for example, use of legislators is greatly deemphasized in favor of technocrats. In Kenya, it makes a difference which ministry an IC goes through to get a proposal to and through the Investment Committee.

In Thailand the Ministry of Foreign Affairs was largely responsible for negotiating the Treaty of Amity and Commerce with the U.S., while the Ministry of Commerce and Industry was largely responsible for drafting and promoting the alien decrees. Yet the provisions of the treaty and the decrees were in conflict, mainly due to lack of coordination and communication between the two ministries. The American business community strongly encouraged the Ministry of Foreign Affairs to inform Commerce and Industry that the decrees violated the rights of Americans under the treaty, and that the treaty was a higher order of law than the decrees. American companies sought to influence by promoting greater communication and coordination within the host government. Such a role in varying degrees of intensity is often required of the IC. For example, in the case of capital liberalization in Japan, interpretation of the new foreign-investment laws in Egypt, tax provisions in Iran, development programs in Saudi Arabia and Iraq, and foreign-investment policies of the Andean Common Market countries the IC has sought to promote dialogue between host government ministries to achieve a clearer policy or one that favors the IC.

In the U.S. lawyers case in Belgium, new regulations were issued by the Ministry of the Middle Classes covering professional work permits. The U.S. law offices and the embassy sought the support of Economic Affairs, Finance, and Foreign Affairs (particularly interested in the application of the FEN treaty) against Middle Classes, because these other ministries were much more interested in a favorable investment climate for U.S. investors.

In its search for good local partners in Indonesia, a company sought suggestions from the minister of the operative ministry, who suggested that the company consider a joint venture with an organization established by retired officials of the ministry. The American company was not enthusiastic about the suggestion. It developed a list of several potential candidates who were "pure" Indonesians, known for their honesty, and not associated with any of the established political and business interests in the country—criteria strongly emphasized by the Indonesian government, the local press, and the student leaders in the development of Indonesian entrepreneurs. The minister did not object to this approach. In this situation, by referring to the larger objective (developing entrepreneurs) established and supported by powerful Indonesian groups, the company was able not to offend the minister.

The key theme reflected in the foregoing examples is that the most important source of influence for the IC with the host government in fact lies *through* other officials of the host government. Knowledge of the personalities, characteristics, and power structures within the host government coupled with the art of effective cultivation of powerful decision makers is essential in the efforts of the IC in influencing the host government. This characteristic holds for all countries from Algeria to Zaire.

State and Municipal Levels. Influence is needed at more than one level of the host government, because several levels are involved in the range of approvals required for implementation of a project. A chemical company had to seek intervention of the central government to buy land for a factory in a prefecture in Japan. The prefectural authorities had never heard of the foreign company (which made it suspect), and the nature of the product (chemicals) would create problems of pollution. Gaining clear title to a site is a problem area on which companies operating in the Far East typically seek the assistance of the state and central governments.

The state governments are also channels through which the IC exercises influence on the central government. As in Quebec, a foreign investment is a source of employment and general economic welfare for a community that wishes to strengthen its hand in bargaining with the central government. Similarly, cities in Colombia compete for plants, and municipalities in France are among the strongest supporters of a foreign-investment proposal being reviewed in Paris. Bechtel was approached by several states when its proposal was first publicized. In Belgium the rivalry among the Flemish and Walloon parts of the country typically results in equal (and high) incentives offered in each region to the investor, irrespective of the real needs.

Legislature. The legislature is another group through which the IC can attempt to influence the host government. However, it is used to a very limited extent. The developing countries with a colonial background are highly sensitive to any hint of foreign interference in the legislative processes. The IC recognizes this point. Furthermore, it does not concentrate on the phrasing of the legislation but the manner in which it will be interpreted, which is largely in the hands of the executive branch of government, which is where the IC concentrates its efforts.

In parliamentary democracies of Western Europe, significant legislation is initiated or shaped by the executive branch of government, although opposition groups can create awkward situations on the floor of parliament.

Often the IC prefers legislation that is general in phrasing, since it permits greater latitude of interpretation. However, disagreements arise on the interpretation of general terms. The American Chamber of Commerce and the embassy in the Philippines are in conflict on this point. The Chamber insists that the embassy should spell out the specific terms of operations (such as ownership and management control) in order to protect the interests of the companies. The embassy, on the other hand, maintains that such specification will reduce the flexibility for host government officials responsible for interpreting the treaty, and consequently reduce the freedom available to American companies. (Serious differences often exist between the country and the corporate level on the degree of specification of terms of investment from the host government. The country level typically prefers host-government statements that permit flexibility of interpretation for the host government and the IC. Corporate management seeks a more specific and precise statement of terms on the part of the host government.)

Some companies go through members of parliament or congress to influence the government. For example, before martial law, congressmen in the Philippines maintained law offices (often retained by the ICs) which served as a means of gaining influence with the executive branch through congressmen. In addition, questions could be directed at the executive branch in Congress (or parliament) designed to solicit information or embarrass the executive. Relatives of congressmen (and other members of government) are hired by companies for the sake of access to the decision maker. In one case a large company rented jeeps and helicopters for local politicians in an election in India. Arranging plant visits for electioneers is practiced by a number of U.S. subsidiaries in Europe as a way of making or helping friends who welcome the opportunity of shaking many hands in factories and offices.

Through Chambers or Associations

U.S.-Based Associations. The type of issue, the need for anonymity, and access to information are some of the considerations for use of U.S.-based associations and chambers of commerce by the IC in seeking to influence host governments. The U.S. Pharmaceutical Manufacturers Association (PMA) in response to interest of its members has asked the State Department to encourage the Japanese government to recognize U.S. FDA registration of products in Japan. The PMA has offered information to U.S. companies in challenging the Indian and Filipino patent bills.

American Chambers of Commerce in a foreign country seek the assistance of apex bodies in the U.S. for representations to the U.S. government on issues such as alien decrees in Thailand, capital liberalization in Japan, and the new treaty to succeed Laurel-Langley Agreement in the Philippines, which affect the entire American business community.

Throughout Latin America the AmChams have formed a coordinating group called the Association of American Chambers of Commerce in Latin America (AACCLA) to strengthen the work of each member and explain better to governments the role of private enterprise. (A similar group exists in Asia.)

Visiting foreign dignitaries are exposed to the views of the U.S. business community and the U.S. government through organizations such as The Asia Society, Council of the Americas, and the Far East-America Council.

American Chambers of Commerce. AmChams provide information, a place for a two-way opportunity for influence between businessmen and government officials, and perhaps most important of all anonymity to a company in expressing its views. The AmCham in Japan is well organized for these functions and has presented the views of its membership on a range of subjects, including capital liberalization, correction of discrepancies in import, duties and assisting the U.S. government in collecting information on specific charges of discrimination experienced by U.S. companies in Japan.

The AmCham in Thailand has taken the lead to challenge and clarify implications of alien decrees for U.S. companies through actions such as representations to the host government, development of position papers, and exertion of pressure on the embassy for stronger complaints. Similarly, the AmCham in the Philippines has been actively presenting the views of its membership to the host government and to the U.S. government on a treaty to succeed Laurel-Langley.

In Europe AmChams have been generally quieter, for lack of major conflictual issues and sometimes for lack of strong leadership, but they are very active in Spain and West Germany. Everywhere they monitor developments and keep good contacts with the embassy.

The AmChams attempt to influence the governments (especially the host, but also the U.S. government) on behalf of their members, through direct and indirect representations on issues of interest to the larger membership. In addition, they offer anonymity to U.S. companies in representations to governments.

Host Country Associations. The use of host country associations to influence the host government often reduces the adverse reaction of local companies against foreign companies and conveys to the host government that the entire industry (domestic and foreign) is for or against a particular position. In certain countries, such as Japan, industry associations have an important role in government policy making and implementation, as reflected in the Mitsubishi-Chrysler proposal.[5] Another example is of a large electrical manufacturer in Japan who felt that Japanese shipbuilders were discriminating against foreign-made turbines in Japanese ships. In response to an informal representation by the embassy, the host government refused to take any action until the appropriate association had explored the charge and had failed to resolve it on its own.

U.S. auto companies in Brazil, in an effort to obtain support for a complementation agreement with other countries, worked through the industry association ("sindicatos"); in this case they were stymied because other foreign companies (e.g. Volkswagen) did not have plants in third countries in Latin America through which they could form integrated operations.

While American firms typically do not play a leading role in trade and industry associations, such leadership is unavoidable in some cases (e.g., automobiles in the U.K., where three of the four major firms are American). In a few cases such as pharmaceuticals in the United Kingdom, it is a U.S. firm which strengthened the weak association to become an effective negotiating tool with the government.

Associations in LDCs are particularly active in making representations to the host government on industry-wide issues. For example, the pharmaceutical industry associations in Iran, India, Thailand, and the Philippines made representations to the host governments on price increases and patent legislation.

Intergovernmental (Regional and Multinational) Organizations. Regional organizations (such as the Asian Development Bank, the Inter-American Development Bank, and international organizations such as The World Bank and the Organization for Economic Cooperation and Development) influence countries because of their prestige and influence with major donor and lending countries. Moreover, countries are less inclined to react negatively to suggestions by such organizations than to suggestions by a foreign government.

Assistance is also sought of governmental consortia which offer aid to particular countries. Such consortia are extremely influential with the recipient countries. A lumber company in Indonesia secured representations of its interests with the Indonesian government through the IGGI. Bechtel sought the assistance of the members of the Aid India Consortium for a favorable treatment of its proposal by the Indian government. The embassy in the U.K. sought unsuccessfully to have the OECD object to a British Treasury ruling discriminating against non-EEC-owned or -controlled firms, since this was a desirable way of elevating the issue and investigating similar discriminations in other member countries.

Directly by IC to Host Government

Much of the dialogue of ICs with host governments is direct, rather than through any intermediary. But these direct contacts are made by officials at different levels within the company.

Parent to Host Government. The parent usually becomes directly involved in negotiating with the host government only on critical issues. It normally engages in general exploratory discussions with key decision makers in the host government for purposes of business development.

Personal relations with senior policy makers in host governments offer one means of exploration of ideas and the exercise of influence. The chairman of Ford Motor Company has a personal friendship with the Shah of Iran, which has obviously included discussions on the role of the company in Iran. Again, the Ford family is friendly with the family of President Marcos of the Philippines. This fact was recognized by executives of General Motors as they negotiated for a project in the Philippines.

The IC parent need not engage in any overt act, but merely rely on its image in order to obtain desired treatment. Ford Motor Company at one time was to be offered preferential access to Indonesia because of the respect and admiration of President Soeharto for its founder. Conversely, an unfavorable image makes the enterprise suspect.

However, access through the parent level to the most senior levels of host government officials does not mean that the IC is structured to follow through with the host government for effective representation of views. For example, the chairman of a large conglomerate is known to have had several discussions with the Shah of Iran on the role of the conglomerate in Iran. The country manager of the conglomerate in Iran is largely ignorant of the nature, content, and direction of the discussions between his chairman and the Shah which might guide him in following up for specific projects with the host government.

Regional, and a growing number of parent, executives have contacts at senior governmental levels, especially in countries where they served before achieving their current positions. Such executives are used for representations to the host government for a particular project or position. A senior executive who had spent almost two decades in India before being promoted to the corporate level played an important role in helping to convince the Indian government that the fishing project being recommended by his company was in the best interests of India. The former managing director of a large oil company in Southeast Asia has maintained his contacts and credibility in the host country. Therefore, in particularly sensitive issues he is asked to present his company's position (a situation that is beginning to erode his credibility with the host government). A pharmaceutical company faced with serious problems with the South Korean government enlisted the support of one of the parent company board members who was a retired general and had played a major role in the defense of South Korea and the development of South Korean forces. The general had access to all levels of the Korean government, especially vital at a time when the Koreans were refusing to see any "white" representatives of the pharmaceutical company.

In general, the parent level is involved in deliberations with the host government only to a limited and carefully controlled extent. The parent level is involved especially when a company is entering into a country for the first time in a relatively large investment. The most senior levels of Chrysler management visited Japan at various stages of the negotiation of the joint venture with Mitsubishi. A key objective of these visits was to convince the Japanese government of the sincerity of Chrysler, and to offer assurances that Chrysler would not attempt to take over the joint-venture company. In the Bechtel proposal, Steven Bechtel, Chairman of Bechtel Corporation, and General Lucius Clay, senior partner of Lehman Brothers, visited India at the initial stages to convince the host government of the sincerity of their effort.

The parent level is also involved in matters of extreme urgency. Members of the corporate level directly contacted the host government when a bank's officer was jailed in South Korea and when the Pakistan government refused to honor its financial commitments to the bank. Top management was directly involved in the IPC case, though the president of Standard Oil Company of New Jersey apparently made no visit to Peru. Geneen of ITT was willing to visit Brazil if that was deemed desirable; Wriston of Citibank was in direct contact with major participants in the Mercantile Bank case in Canada; Firestone sent top officials to Kenya; and the presidents of several companies went to South Africa under the urgings of U.S. groups to examine the effects of apartheid.

Corporate executives are also used for protocol and expression of interest. An American bank that has been seeking a branch in Kobe for several years asks visiting senior corporate executives to reiterate the bank's interest in establishing a branch in Kobe in the process of discussions with government officials. They do so, which permits a representation of their position without formal negotiations with the host government. Senior executives from the parent company are thus frequently used to indicate the "symbolic" value of the negotiations at their outset. They are also often present at the conclusion, for example, at the "ribbon cutting" with the appropriate minister.

Involvement of the corporate-level executive in influencing host government officials also has a negative effect. A large conglomerate operating in Indonesia dispatched a brilliant lawyer to settle some areas of conflict in the contract with the Indonesian government. The lawyer refused to listen to the country manager on the art and process of dealing with the host government in Indonesia. At a meeting with the minister concerned, he displayed his ignorance of how to deal with government officials by saying: "Call me Joe. What's your first name?"

In Iran, an American company is faced with serious problems with the local partner, who has close political connections. One group of executives at the country level is warning the local partner that he is not essential to the venture, and in the process gaining some support from the technocrats in the government. However, concurrently and unknown to the country managers, the corporate level has entered into correspondence with the local partner suggesting that he should consider an additional venture in a related product. Of course, this has seriously damaged the credibility of the country managers with the host government technocrats.

Regional Management Center to Host Government. Being higher than the country level, the regional level basically adds additional weight on behalf of the country level in dealing with the host government. In general, the decision on extent and areas of interaction of the regional level with the host government are determined by the country level, except when the national subsidiaries are young and weak.

The regional executives of pharmaceutical companies have assisted the country-level managers on representations to the host governments on matters of pricing and patents. When the country level and the host government are at an impasse, the regional level might be invited by the country manager as a way of breaking the impasse. The regional level is involved in recommendations made by the country level to the parent for actions to influence the host government.

Local Partner. An important method of attempting to influence the host government is through the local partner of the IC. Sharing in nationality with host government officials, knowing the system of government, recognizing the personalities involved, being able to be more bold in representations to the government—for these and other reasons the local partner plays a major role in influencing the host government.

In Chrysler's efforts for a joint venture in Japan, the task of influencing the host government was left almost entirely in the hands of Mitsubishi. The same approach was followed by another U.S. automobile company in negotiating with the Japanese government.

In almost all developing countries, the role of the local partner remains important in dealing with the host government. Joint ventures in Spain and Mexico are recognized as an effective means of obtaining audience with government officials. However, using the partner to influence the government is a double-edged sword, for if he can influence the host government in favor of the IC he can also influence it against the IC. For this reason, some companies prefer to use the local partner sparingly, to keep him in check. In Iran, a pharmaceutical company seeks the influence of the local partner with the host government only when the American executive has reached an impasse in settling the matter through direct dealings with the government.

Other Organizations or Individuals

The IC uses several additional organizations and individuals to influence the host government. Some organizations (law firms, banks, accounting firms) represent professional expertise along with knowledge of and influence with host government officials. Selected individuals often present themselves (alleged members of the royal family, close cousins of an influential politician) largely as influence peddlers. The IC typically uses established organizations such as banks and law firms, and adopts a cautious and selective approach toward the use of influence peddlers in interacting with the host government.

Law firms (international and local) offer contacts with host government officials, especially in countries such as the Philippines where legislators also maintain law firms which provide preferential access and consideration by the host government. At times, the IC has a policy of using more than one local law firm, for the reason that law firms serve as the breeding grounds of future politicians, and, as in Spain, each has its own set of personal contacts in the government. In the Philippines, a pharmaceutical company wanted to secure the views of a senior cabinet member of the host government regarding the study of multinational corporations being conducted by the United Nations. The senior partner of a law firm retained by the company is the son-in-law of the cabinet member concerned. A copy of the statement presented by the chairman of the parent company to the UN study group was forwarded through the son-in-law to the cabinet member for the latter's reactions. Law firms also offer a means of testing ideas with the host government without identifying the company.

Banks (international and local) play a role similar to law firms in offering contacts to host government officials, particularly to the central bank and the ministry of finance.

Influential individuals are used on the board of directors of a company or as employees. They are also retained for specific assignments. A large chemical company retained a distant member of the Iranian royal family for representations to the host government while negotiating the terms of a major project. A few American companies have started to retain retired government officials, especially from the ministries of finance and the MITI in Japan. These officials have preferential access to their former colleagues within the government. Relatives of influential figures are often employed solely for the purpose of gaining access to the influential figure. These contacts are not always productive, however. One of the reasons for failure in the IPC case was that the company lost the support of the old oligarchy, which in turn has lost much of its influence with the government and the Congress.

A few observations are suggested by the foregoing discussion on who is used by the IC to influence the host government.

1. The IC does not use a single source, but relies on several sources of influence.

2. If the IC seeks direct assistance of the embassy with the host government, it is generally when the IC is faced with an impasse and has exhausted means of correction at its disposal.

3. The most important source of influence for the IC on the host government is through local officials sympathetic to the IC. Nonhost-government officials (indigenous and foreign) might be considered as parties who facilitate this process.

4. The critical determinant of who is used by the IC is whether the IC can control the individual once he becomes involved; for this reason, primary reliance is placed on direct contact by company officials.

Agency or Official Influenced

The IC undertakes many actions involving several people and organizations in order to influence the host government. However, influence is more effectively exerted if the IC knows who is ultimately to be influenced. But as often as not, it is difficult to specify who in the host government is to be influenced. This section discusses the question of who is influenced by reference to the nature of host-government decision making, the nature of the issue (general and specific), the personal interest of key decision makers, and the importance attached to an issue. Comments are also offered on who is influenced by the IC within the embassy, and in other organizations such as chambers of commerce.

Within Host Government

Host-Government Decision Making. More often than not, the decision-making characteristics of the host government make it difficult for the IC to specify individuals or organizations that are to be influenced. Authority might be highly concentrated in the hands of a few officials, as in the case of Iran and Indonesia. This simplifies the task of identifying the key sources of power, and therefore the parties who need to be influenced. However, confusion arises when the extent and areas or responsibilities of the parties in power are loosely defined and subject to change. Therefore, the IC might not know who is the real source of power in a given situation within the host government. For example, because of shifting power relationships within the Indian government Bechtel had to influence a series of officials in different parts of the government. Changes in cabinet and senior secretariat levels cause important power realignments within the government.

In some countries, the existence of expatriate advisers to local governmental bodies makes negotiation more complex. The interests of these advisers, whose strength and influence vary greatly, are not always those of the host government officials. Yet their competence means that proposals of ICs are likely to be more fully understood. In the Ivory Coast, the pervasive presence of French advisers gives one the impression that it would be difficult to obtain approval of anything that was "un-French." In Zambia, British advisers are equally omnipresent in some agencies (Mindeco, over mining, for example) but do not seem to have the policy influence felt in the Ivory Coast.

In terms of organization structure, the decision-making centers of the host government might be well identified. However, certain situations result in conflicting policy preferences by powerful interests in the host government, and the IC has to know which are more powerful than others. Mitsubishi and Chrysler recognized from the very beginning that the key source of power for their joint venture would be the prime minister's office, with the support of the ministry of finance. This coalition would have to overcome the objections of the MITI and the JAMA. Therefore, the companies concentrated their efforts at the initial stages of the idea in influencing the groups who were favorable to them.

The need to influence government officials is not limited to any one level, but extends vertically as well. Bechtel was also seeking to influence leaders of important states in India in order to influence the central government. A timber company discovered the hard way that the fact of gaining approval in Jakarta from the central government still required gaining acceptance of the contract from a provincial governor (a military general).

Changing power relations between groups in a country creates uncertainty for administrators, who then adopt the safe approach of not making any decisions on their own. Consequently, the IC has to influence a more diverse group of officials. For example, the recent set of events in Thailand resulting in a change of government through student demonstrations has created a vacuum of leadership and rules of behavior for the administrators causing them to adopt a very cautious approach to decision making.

The policies that guide the decision rules are vague, and the decision rules simply cannot accommodate the range of diverse situations that arise. Therefore, the administrators possess a great deal of administrative discretion in the interpretation of policies. This is reflected in the cases of the alien decrees in Thailand, tax rulings in Iran, shifting interpretations of contract terms in Indonesia, varying meaning of the terms of capital liberalization to different

Japanese ministries, national interpretations of the Andean code on foreign investments, the role of foreign investments in India's development program, and the provisions of the new Egyptian foreign-investment laws. Those who make the decision rules refer to the policy makers as the ultimate source of power, and more often than not the policy makers state that the original source from which they derive their own power is inherent in the broad pronouncements of their leaders. The implication is that the IC cannot specify any single individual or group as the entity to be influenced, but has to cast a wider net, hoping to include a meaningful range of decision makers.

Certain governments possess decision-making characteristics that are unique to them, such as the consensus (*ringi*) approach to decision making in Japan. Consensus requires that over time and through extensive decision and debate all parties reach consensus on a given policy or program of action. The *ringi* system is based on a decision-making approach, where the initiative for a particular course of action originates from the lower levels of management and officialdom, while the senior levels play the role of coordinating and maintaining harmony. However, under consensus and *ringi*, a large range of interests and individuals is involved. This means that the IC must attempt to influence more than one individual or interest without having anybody lose face, as reflected in the case of the Mitsubishi-Chrysler joint venture. A modified pattern of consensus approach also exists in Indonesia and Malaysia.

Nature of Issue—General and Specific. A general issue, such as alien decrees or Laurel-Langley, covers many interests and therefore involves a large range of ministries and individuals whose views have to be recognized. Therefore, the IC cannot limit its representations to any single individual or group, though it can assign priorities to such representations. A few illustrations demonstrate the different types of general issues that exist.

In the attempted acquisition of Jeumont-Schneider by Westinghouse, it was not very clear where the preponderant influence existed: in the ministry of finance, which is generally very powerful and handles foreign applications; or in the ministry of industry, which stresses restructuring of French industry and generally prefers "French" solutions; or in the president's office, since the decision had implications for the general investment climate in France. Fortunately, all three could be approached without creating ill will with the others.

In the case of hastening Japan's capital liberalization program, various sources of influence were activated, such as the U.S. government, the OECD, International Monetary Fund, U.S. and European trade and industry associations, and Japanese groups in favor of rapid liberalization. The ICs could engage in a fairly obvious display of influence, because capital liberalization even in major precedent-setting projects such as Mitsubishi-Chrysler did not cause significant domestic political agitation.

Conversely, in the Philippines, the termination of Laurel-Langley has been a highly emotional issue, and the new treaty under negotiation is considered as a way of expressing the Filipinos' sense of equality with the Americans. The use of publicized influence by the IC would be seriously detrimental, because of the strong feeling of nationalism in the country. A similar situation exists regarding the alien decrees in Thailand. However, the concentration of decision making within the government since martial law makes it simpler for the IC to identify the key members of the government who need to be influenced.

Conversely, in Thailand the change from a military junta type of government to a civilian government lacking strong leadership has dispersed power, making it difficult to specify any one individual or group to be influenced by the IC. Priorities can only be established subject to change in the shifting power relationships within the host government. Promoting tax reform in Iran is made complex because of shifting power relationships of concerned ministers.

On issues that are specific to a company, the question of who is to be influenced is less complex. The IC identifies the individuals within and outside of the government who can influence the key decision makers. This approach was pursued by Mitsubishi in Japan, Bechtel in India, a conglomerate in Indonesia, a timber company in the Philippines, and a pharmaceutical company in Iran. Even in the case of company issues, the IC needs to influence more than one person, in several agencies and at different levels of the government.

Importance of an Issue. The importance of an issue for the operations of the IC will partly determine the answer to the question of who is influenced. In general, the situations faced by the IC in a foreign country might be presented in three categories: critical, serious, and operational. The primary groups to be influenced for each type of situation vary, though they are not mutually exclusive.

An American flagship plane was allowed to land at Teheran airport after the airline's station manager contacted the embassy, which in turn contacted the airport manager. (The Iranian government was displeased with the ongoing negotiations with the U.S. government on landing rights.) The airport official was not involved in the larger negotiations on U.S.-Iran civil aviation agreement. Yet he was the person with the authority and ability to correct the immediate operational problem.

Serious problems include changes in policies or major reinterpretation of policies such as alien decrees, successor agreement to Laurel-Langley, capital liberalization, patent bill, restrictions on use of foreigners, and tax laws. The IC handles such issues on two levels. The first level is that of direct interaction with the nonpolicy levels of the host government, to get an idea of implications for daily operations. The second is of policy implications, including the intent of the government, and reasons and long-term consequences of such moves for overall foreign investment climate. These are handled with officials at the policy levels.

Operational problems include questions of customs procedures, visa formalities, and procedures for securing raw materials and import licenses. To the extent that these issues become major operational problems, the IC raises them with policy makers in the host government. Otherwise, they are largely relegated to discussions and informal influences with the implementing levels of the host government.

Personal Interest. Who is to be influenced by the IC is also based on who in the government is interested in a project or proposal. Bechtel knew that senior officials in the ministry of finance were interested in the project; Mitsubishi knew of the interest of the prime minister's office in accelerating capital liberalization.

Often the IC prefers to deal with technocrats in the host government, especially when they are in powerful policy-making positions. Unlike political appointees, technocrats tend to take strong personal interest in the professional treatment of an issue. A significant shift from the politically oriented approach to a professional approach of senior government officials is reflected in the Philippines since martial law and in Egypt under President Sadat.

Host-government officials often expect personal gains from the transaction in the form of bribes, share of the enterprise, or some form of commission payment on sales generated, or job for a relative or for an official approaching retirement. In such cases, the IC possesses access to one or more individuals within the host government who are influenced and who in turn attempt to influence other government officials.

Personal Relations. Who is to be influenced is answered to some extent by the related question—whom does the IC know? Executives especially at the country and regional levels have relationships developed with host-government officials that are utilized in attempting to understand the inner thinking of the government on policy matters and specific proposals. These relationships are used for introductions and informal and discreet inquiries, and as a source of guidance on who should be approached by the IC.

Within Embassy

Unlike the host government, there is relatively far greater specificity about who the IC attempts to influence within the embassy in a particular country. Personal relations, expressed interest, shared background, problem-solving orientation, and importance of an issue are some of the determinants of the ICs decision on who in the embassy should be influenced on a given issue.

Personal Relations. At times, an executive develops personal relations with members of the embassy, generally within the economic/commercial counselor's section, whom he tends to influence. The presence of a senior and successful businessman from the American business establishment as ambassador to Japan has presented an opportunity to other business leaders who know the ambassador personally to attempt to influence him toward their particular way of thinking.

Personal Interest. Often the IC attempts to influence the embassy official who shows an interest in the enterprise's issue and is willing to get something accomplished as against engaging in bureaucratic dodging. In Indonesia, the IC typically seeks to influence the office of the economic/commercial counselor, because of the personal interest displayed by members of the section. In Taiwan, American banks concentrated in gaining the support of an official in the commercial section who displayed strong personal interest in solving the difficulties of the banks with the host government. In India, the commercial counselor at the time of the Bechtel proposal had made a vow to attract at least $1 billion in new American investment into India before completing his tour of duty. Understandably, Bechtel Corporation concentrated on gaining the support of the commercial counselor.

Shared Background. The executive feels more comfortable in seeking the support of an official with a business background. Where such a person is present, the IC often seeks his support, hoping that he will then fight its battles within the embassy. However, at times, the IC has false expectations of the power of a former businessman turned embassy official. In fact, such a person operates within a structured environment that strongly limits him from acting alone to get things accomplished. However, the businessman does not understand the broader context in which his former colleague operates, and therefore feels that the former businessman has been brainwashed and is not of much use to the business community. This requires concentrating on some other member of the embassy.

Problem-Solving Orientation. The IC interacts with the embassy especially when it has a problem it wants to have solved. The official who displays a problem-solving attitude is the one sought by the IC. In the Philippines, the American business community wanted to discuss the provisions of the draft of a treaty to succeed the Laurel-Langley Agreement which was to be presented by the embassy to the host government. The economic/commercial counselor decided to do this with selected representatives of the business community, and alerted the State Department after the fact. Some other examples include: securing a permit in Japan, clarifying import and licensing procedures in Indonesia, and reducing smuggling from PX stores in Thailand.

Policy Orientation of an Issue. The relative nature and importance of an issue and the speed at which settlement is sought are some of the additional determinants of who the IC attempts to influence in the embassy. Issues might be viewed at three levels—procedural and operational, operational with policy orientation, and largely policy. On the first type (import restrictions and procedures, tax regulations, contract violations, etc.), the IC typically attempts to gain the support of the commercial counselor. The issues call for a certain amount of action being taken in a relatively short period of time to correct an existing situation. The second type (operational with policy orientation) includes questions of tax reform, visa regulations, and customs requirements for product labeling. Again, the commercial counselor's office is involved, but with referrals of the issue to other levels of the embassy, including the ambassador. The third type is largely policy-related matters that have operational implications, such as the alien decrees in Thailand and the termination of Laurel-Langley in the Philippines. In this type, the IC seeks to influence the commercial and economic counselors and through them and directly the U.S. ambassador.

In brief, the IC does not seek to cultivate influence with a single element of the embassy, though by structure, orientation, and responsibility it is almost entirely in the economic/commercial counselor's office. The IC attempts to cultivate influence where the power lies within the embassy—power to act or power to influence others who possess the power to act. And this often includes the office of the U.S. ambassador.

The foregoing discussion suggests some general observations on the question of who is influenced by the IC.

1. The IC generally does not know who exactly within the host government needs to be influenced. Therefore, specification of the target is as much ad hoc as it is planned.

2. The IC draws a distinction on who is to be influenced on matters that are largely of a policy nature versus those of essentially an operational nature.

3. A general identification of host-government officials is based on personal relations and a general understanding of the circumstances and cast of characters in the host government at any given moment on any particular issue.

4. The central theme, however, of the IC is to influence directly the key decision makers (of the host government or the embassy) on a given issue. If this is not possible, then the IC attempts to influence those who have access to or influence over the key decision makers.

5. Direct access to decision makers in the embassy is far greater for the IC than is the case in its efforts to influence decision makers in the host government.

Assumption of Initiative

Who takes the initiative—the IC, embassy, or host government—in seeking/offering assistance to the IC? The party taking the initiative is the one most directly affected and seeking to correct the situation. Some general comments are made on the flow of initiative followed by a discussion of selected determinants of initiative.

General Comments

In almost all cases the initiative has been taken by the IC in seeking from the embassy information, advice/interpretation, intelligence, or request for representation to the host government. The embassy hardly ever takes the initiative in interacting with the IC, except through the published information it develops and disseminates.

A few exceptions exist, such as the time the embassy took the initiative to advise an American oil company in Iran that its senior executive was about to be declared persona non grata. Or a case in Jakarta where the economic/commercial counselor acted vigorously to develop a consortium of U.S. companies to consider a steel complex. (In general, it appears that embassies began taking greater initiative during the Nixon administration.)

The host government seldom takes the initiative in initiating interaction with the IC. (This excludes the normal reporting requirements.) In the formulation of policies there is limited effort to seek the views of the IC. The IC almost always initiates action with the host government. The lowly status and distrust of businessmen, preoccupation of officials with various matters, fear of being charged by local interests as being partial to the IC—these and other considerations account for lack of initiative on the part of the host government to interact with the IC.

In Belgium, however, government officials expressed interest in having a liaison committee with U.S. lawyers when the problem of work permits became acute. Besides, some ministers and civil servants have regular contacts with selected U.S. subsidiaries, embassy officers, and U.S. lawyers, so that they pick up quickly what problems are emerging.

Initiative by the parent and regional levels for direct interaction with the host government occurs infrequently, and is almost always with the prior knowledge, participation and, approval of the country level. Conversely, the country level seeks the approval of the regional and parent levels for representations by it to the U.S. government at the Washington level. The parent and regional levels are more likely to take initiative even on a country-related issue (such as a patent bill) if it has larger regional and global implications.

Within the IC, more often than not the exact source and at times even the level at which the initiative is taken on a particular issue is hard to specify, and often impossible. This is largely due to the wide range of individuals with varying and often overlapping responsibilities who are involved in a particular project at the parent, regional, and country levels. For example, the country coordinator for a large conglomerate assists the electrical, hotel, communication, and defense groups who are members of the conglomerate and are operating in Iran. He does not even know how many other members of the conglomerate are considering activities in Iran. Therefore, matters that develop within the hotel group are not referred through him unless the line executive wishes to do so.

Determinants of Initiative

A direct and discernible effect of an action on the responsibility, reward, and penalty of an individual is the key determinant of initiative. The IC executive experiences a far greater effect than is the case for host government or U.S. government officials.

In general, the IC's initiative is first directed at the host government, especially on issues that pertain largely or solely to the company. Initiative by the IC toward the embassy and the American Chamber of Commerce for representations to the host government typically occurs on general issues such as the alien decrees and Laurel-Langley. A major reason for this pattern is that the embassy and the American Chamber offer anonymity to the IC.

Use of Trade-offs: Reality
and Perception

To what extent, if any, does the U.S. government engage in trade-off negotiation with the host government to protect and promote the economic interests of one or more ICs?[6] The discussion in the preceding sections of Chapters 4 and 5 has commented on this question indirectly, and this section will focus on it.

There are a few examples where trade-offs were used by the U.S. government with a host government, as in the case of petroleum. Some observers are of the view that a trade-off was threatened by the U.S. government on food imports if the Indian government did not permit a greater role to foreign investors in the Indian fertilizer industry. The U.S. government ultimately authorized a (modified) licensing agreement between SNECMA (a French government-owned aircraft-engine manufacturer) and General Electric, in return—among other things—for an understanding from the French government that it would not seek or support new tariffs against U.S. aircraft (and parts) imports into the EEC. It should be noted that these are a handful of fairly remarkable cases, and the vast majority of IC activities do not have these characteristics.

The Reality

The reality of the use of trade-offs by the U.S. government is considered from the respective viewpoints of the U.S. Embassy, the IC, the American Chamber of Commerce, and the host government.

The embassies interviewed for this study maintain that they have not and do not know of any example of explicit use of trade-offs by the U.S. government with the host government on behalf of one or more U.S. companies. However, especially in developing countries, U.S. embassies suggest that an implicit effect of trade-off does exist. In time, a country has usually received varying amounts of aid and other assistance that could be interpreted as IOUs from the U.S. to the host country. At some stage the U.S. government might wish to collect on some of the IOUs. The collection does not take the form of explicitly saying, "We gave you so much aid, now you need to give preference to an American company," or "You need to modify legislation that is detrimental to American companies." The implicit nature of the IOUs tends to be reflected largely in the form of ease of access to government officials, faster access to policy pronouncements, preference for an American project over a non-American one (all other things being equal), and the benefits of understanding and shared experiences that accrue as a result of joint programs conducted over a period of time. These characteristics, however, are determined by the nature of individuals involved rather than official aid policies.

There are several reasons why trade-offs are rarely used by the U.S. government on behalf of the ICs. (1) The objectives of the U.S. government go far beyond the economic and commercial to include regional and international political and security considerations. (2) Moreover, meaningful long-term relations with foreign countries, especially the developing ones with strong nationalism, require that they be treated as equals, especially by the larger powers. (3) Inability to control the IC further discourages the U.S. government in engaging in trade-off negotiations with foreign governments for the IC. (4) The U.S. government historically has had a policy of maintaining a distance from the IC.

In the vast majority of cases, the IC does not seek U.S. government influence, strongly preferring to have the host government view it as an independent entity. This approach has been adopted by the IC because it has not found the U.S. government particularly helpful in dealing with host governments, because of their different and at times conflicting objectives and the different orientation and ways of thinking of government officials and business executives.

The AmChams do not know of any example of use of trade-off by the U.S. government. In Thailand, the Chamber maintains that instead of assisting the ICs, the embassy has acted in a manner that is contrary to the interests of the business community. In the Philippines, obvious areas of disagreement exist between the U.S. government and the IC on the broader framework of considerations to be included on a new treaty of amity and commerce with the Philippines. The reasons for the distance between the U.S. government and the IC offered by Chambers are the same as those provided by the ICs.

Host-government officials maintain that implicit trade-offs are used by the U.S. government with them on behalf of U.S. companies. But they could not offer any explicit examples. In addition, the term "implicit" appears to apply largely to examples where the embassy made an inquiry or a representation on an ongoing negotiation of an IC with the host government.

The Perception

The host governments believe that the ICs possess sufficient influence over the U.S. government to have it engage in trade-off negotiations with a host government to promote and protect the interests of the ICs. An implicit and indirect (as against an explicit and direct) use of such influence serves the IC's purpose. For example, instead of a direct threat of reduction of U.S. aid to a country, the IC might encourage one or more members of Congress to make a speech suggesting the need for a review of aid and assistance to that country. The host government would then be encouraged to adopt a more accommodating attitude toward the ICs. Other opinion-forming elites in the developing countries (students, journalists, educators, professionals) subscribe to the foregoing interpretation of IC influence over the U.S. government.

This attitude exists for several reasons. (1) The experience of colonization demonstrated the close relationship of economics and politics, and the developing countries remember the experience. (2) Trade-offs between economic and political interests are used in the host countries; therefore, they are more inclined to believe that a similar situation exists in other countries, including the U.S. (3) The greater economic-commercial orientation of U.S. embassies overseas suggests to the host governments that the trade-off dimension will gain in importance, and indicates the influence of the IC over the U.S. government. (4) The close relationship between the Japanese government and Japanese companies and the use of fairly explicit trade-offs has made host governments, especially in Asia, extremely sensitive and cautious on this point with all foreign investors and their respective home governments.

The host governments' perception of the close liaison between the IC and the U.S. government is quite different from the reality. The implication of this reality/perception gap is that the policies of governments (both host and home) and the ICs are affected—not necessarily in conformity with their interests. It would probably be better for all if the reality were more fully understood. How the U.S. government might alter its behavior is the subject of Chapter 7.

Part III
Improving Government-Business Relations

6

Criteria of Success of Government-Business Relations

If recommendations are to be made that government-business communication and consultation should be closer and that U.S. embassies or companies should adopt particular methods to achieve this end, there should be some criteria for determination of success.[a] And while it is not difficult to delineate such criteria, it is difficult to measure their attainment. As in advertising, no one is quite sure what the effects are, but everyone is sure that the effort should be made. Not only is it difficult to determine the precise result from any given effort, but long-run results differ from short-run results; and while continuous efforts may not pay off in the short run, they may very well in the long run. In addition, the continuation of similar efforts over any length of time may produce quite different results, as conditions change or receptivity changes with different governments. Also, the effort of any group of companies can be thwarted or made ineffective by the noncooperation or contrary action of any one company. The case of company dialogues with the Venezuelan government over oil policies is illustrative. After difficult but quiet negotiations, a group of the companies had convinced the government officials that certain provisions in a bill should be changed. One company, not in the group, made a public announcement that it was "now ready" to negotiate with the government on the bill, making it impossible for the government to change anything without appearing to capitulate to the oil companies. The bill passed in its original uncompromising form.

In the mid-sixties, the action by Remington Rand in closing a French plant was cited throughout Europe as evidence of "irresponsible behavior of American companies," despite the fact that no other case could be cited.

Finally, despite continued and rather sophisticated efforts on the part of either government or business, external factors may be introduced that make the situation worse than it was before. It is therefore not possible to demonstrate that the efforts were ineffective, because the situation could well have been worse without them.

The criteria of success of government-business relations will differ according to *what* is done, *how*, *when*, and *by whom*, and how each of these aspects is

[a]It is, of course, arguable that government-business ties should be loosened, separating their activities clearly and distinctly. This view would fit with a neoclassical world in which governments set the rules and the market dictated company actions. Whether the world ought to be ordered in this fashion is not argued here—rather, we see the problems that are emerging in the present setting as requiring closer government-business ties to attain mutual objectives under market and nonmarket criteria and activities.

perceived. For example, *what* one company official did abroad was quite unacceptable: he offered to give the host government information it desired on the company's activities *if* it would give the company twenty-four-hour notice of an impending devaluation of the currency. *What* is done in one country with a given government official may be unacceptable in or with another. *How* it is done relates to covert or overt activities, and whether they are institutionalized or ad hoc, private or public, and at national or international levels. *When* it is done relates to the particular stage or phase of an investment activity in a country-from entry, through operations, to termination (or expropriation). *Who* does it relates to the level of the communication—ministerial or technical within the host government and parent-company or affiliate officials.

Not all parties to a situation will see the same methods as desirable at the same time. Not only will the criteria as to the desired content of the communication differ, but one may want it to take place at top levels and the other at technical levels—as discussed in this chapter. But also each party may have institutionalized or organized the communication, in uncoordinated ways, which directly affect the content of the subject of the dialogue (as is discussed in Chapter 7).

Since the criteria of success applied by one or more actors will not be the same, there will probably never be a time in which the structure and subject matters of government-business relations can be considered fixed or resolved. Continuous and changing efforts will be required on the part of all concerned; particular efforts are less important than that there be *continuity*. Continuity will not necessarily produce the best results, by itself, but without it, it will be hard to create an atmosphere that can produce the most desirable results when specific problems arise.

One of the reasons that continuity is so important is that the representations of both business and government must be believable. If the efforts of each to persuade the other occur only infrequently and are related to only the most critical issues, each will see the other as attempting to make a case for its viewpoint in the particular situation and, therefore, as not having provided full information on the issue. Lack of credibility has plagued the representation by the international companies on both the balance-of-payments impacts in the U.S. and the employment impact. These companies were advised over ten years ago to begin to develop data on these impacts, but they were very reluctant to do so. Consequently, they have produced the data under the pressure of attack, and it has not been as believable as it would have been had the communication been continuous. The lack of timely delivery of evidence is notable in the arguments of American companies against the termination of privileges under the Laurel-Langley agreement in the Philippines and the alien decrees in Thailand; they have argued that the investment climate will be adversely affected, without offering evidence. Similarly, the NAM wrote the West German government in the 1960s that the passage of the codetermination law would retard U.S. investment in the country; no evidence was adduced, nor could there be.

It is not too difficult to demonstrate the problem areas in which business ought to be providing information and creating dialogues with governmental representatives. What is difficult to demonstrate is that the cost of doing so is worth the results. Just as public relations efforts are costly and do not produce a specific result that can be attributable to any given effort (and therefore budgets are frequently closely circumscribed), governmental relations efforts will probably be contained simply by budget cutting. But it can be argued cogently that without adequate government-business communications, the long-run profit of the companies will be greatly reduced because of the reduction of opportunities open to them—especially in the developing countries. A corporate executive in Asia made this point tellingly with the statement that effective communication with governments is not a question of choice but one of survival.

What is required is less of a cost-benefit analysis than a "declaration of faith" that the future requires and will be improved by closer government-business cooperation—which includes a fuller exchange of information concerning objectives and operations of both governments and business. It is only through a frank and open discussion that governments will understand the role of business and appreciate better what it can do, and that business will be induced to constrain its overeagerness for short-run returns and to dedicate itself to the longer-run objectives of social transformation and economic development in the less-developed countries. These goals are the primary responsibilities of governments, but their pursuit by the foreign investor provides the basic legitimacy for his presence. No investor would be accepted who proclaimed "I come to make a profit—the most I can—and to return it to my stockholders." Only by actual pursuit of host-country goals can he achieve legitimacy abroad.

Increasing pressures of shortages and the necessity to allocate resources and products even among the developed countries will also require closer communication of business and government, with ample evidence provided that companies do not receive excessive profits from the scarcity situations. Therefore, the dialogue must become wider, more open, and fuller.

The following sections relate to the criteria of success as seen from the viewpoints of the company, host governments, and the U.S. government. A final section provides some "objective" criteria based on factors common to these three.

Company Criteria

Taking the interests of U.S. business as illustrated by their behavior within the U.S. economy, one would conclude that their criterion of good business-government relations would be that of "being left alone" by government to carry out their activities as they see fit. The maxim, "That government is best which governs least" is oft repeated, and leads to a minimum of business-government interaction. However, there is increasing recognition, not only in the U.S. but certainly in the countries where foreign investment is taking place, that not only is government necessary, but it must expand its responsibilities. (Of course, larger government does not necessarily mean greater interference *in* business decisions, but it does mean a smaller range of decisions left to business, as government widens its operations and expands its rule-setting.)

The attitudes of U.S. business to host governments abroad has generally reflected those it holds towards the U.S. government—namely, it seeks a governmental policy in support of business objectives and a low business profile to avoid being interfered with by the government. But this approach will be modified abroad as national governments assume responsibilities pressed on them by the populace, which is dissatisfied with the way in which the benefits and costs of industrial growth are distributed. To recognize that governments are not only necessary but desirable and are pursuing objectives desired by the people is likely to change the orientation of business fundamentally.

Individual businesses will have to adopt an attitude of cooperation with other companies so that the reception of the entire private sector improves. American companies in India have realized only recently that they need to assist the overall private sector in presenting a more positive and vigorous image—not just that of foreign investment. The same realization has developed in Thailand and other countries of Southeast Asia as a result of the stigma attached to Japanese foreign investment and the likelihood that it will rub off on other investors. In Latin America, local entrepreneurs have become fearful that the antipathy to foreign investors will be directed at all private enterprise.

Although it might improve its own short-run-profit picture, no company can afford to act so irresponsibly as to damage the image of all business. Some companies will do so in any case, but what is needed on the part of the public and governments is a recognition that such action is an aberration, and not part of a generalized pattern. This recognition will be enhanced if the other companies are able to demonstrate that such action is unusual, and can put sufficient pressure on the company so that it does not act that way or is penalized for doing so. This is a difficult prescription to make, much less to have business follow, but it will become increasingly necessary as closer government-business relationships develop.

Companies have a variety of preferences vis-à-vis their reception by host governments. Basically, they seek *stability, certainty*, and *flexibility*: stability in the domestic economic and political scene; certainty in the rules of the game; and flexibility to adopt appropriate business policies as changes occur in the market and in desired technology.

Governmental postures range from prohibition and restriction through acceptance (under a favorable climate), through audience or listening to business viewpoints, or even to accepting them, to an eagerness to attract the foreign investor. Business criteria of success would involve a movement from restriction to attraction. Specific evidences of success would be multiplied considerably if one but listed all of the constraints on business, and stated that success would be the removal of such constraints. More realistically, the interviews with the companies held around the world indicate that the following results would indicate an acceptable degree of success from the standpoint of business:

1. Probably the most widely used criterion of satisfactory government relations would be the "achievement of performance targets" (denominated in sales or profits) set by the parent company for each of its affiliates abroad. This is not to say that shortfalls under the targets would mean that poor government relations existed. But if there were no external forces created by the government to affect adversely the achievement of the projections, then prima facie the relations with governments must be good—or at least as anticipated in the target planning.

Each affiliate, in negotiating the targets for the coming period, usually makes an assessment of government legislation, governmental policy changes, and political stability in the country—to avoid surprises. Where conditions appear to be changing adversely, actions will be prescribed if the company can have influence; and if not, adjustments are made in the target. This is still not to say that government-business relations could not be improved by some effort on the part of the company. It is only to say that the targeting should include a realistic assessment of the relationship between government and business, permitting the target to be fulfilled.

Of course, targets themselves can be unsatisfactory—in the sense that a given target might be a reduction of prior losses or a growth rate much less than anticipated at the time of initial investment. An improvement in government-business relations might make a substantial difference in targeting possibilities, jumping the projections from below the line to above it. The mere achievement of a target, therefore, is not an acceptable criterion for the long run, though it may be for the target period itself. Targets themselves need to be adjusted in accord with improved government-business relations, especially in developing countries.

2. A second criterion that seems to be adopted by many companies—especially for affiliates in developing countries—is that of not being the subject of any kind of governmental comment or criticism. This is a criterion that indicates that the company has been able to maintain a low profile. (A recent *Wall Street Journal* article (January 9, 1974) states that ITT is proud of its "low profile" in Europe.) This criterion is different from the old saw that the "least government is best." It says, rather however much the government wishes to interfere with others, it is desirable for the particular company not to be recognized in any way. This lack of recognition is buttressed at the governmental level through scant communication. Still, it is difficult in many developing countries to remain

outside of the purview of governmental decision makers, simply because of the sizable impact of the investment on the host economy and society. Therefore, a low profile and little communication will not necessarily *be* successful—witness the problems of the Japanese, who have sought a low profile in Asia but face eruptions and disturbances wherever they go. In the case of the Japanese, neither communication nor its absence will probably succeed.

Companies seeking a low profile would like to be able to "slip" into the host country through the normal procedures without raising visible problems. But they cannot avoid dialogue with the government (unless there is no authorization process), and will in all likelihood seek to gain preferences or incentives, especially in developing countries. Given the increasing desires for "localization" of ownership, not even the smallest selling operation is likely to escape governmental attention in developing countries—as is the case in Kenya currently.

But the policy of a low profile is most difficult for a company to follow if it is in the public's eye or has an international image—as with IBM and ITT, though both assert that they seek a "low profile." For a consumer-product company, it is quite difficult to expand sales through advertising (notice the large signs of auto and tire companies in Latin America) and still to maintain a low profile.

3. A more positive criterion of success, which is increasingly recognized as necessary from the standpoint of foreign investment, is the continuation of a favorable climate for all private-sector activity. This view considers that foreign investment is well treated only to the extent that local private investors are well treated. Government-business relations, therefore, should be aimed at improving the ambiance for all private enterprise. The success of such efforts would be indicated by the existence of a general agreement as to the role to be played by private enterprise in the economy, a clarity of rules concerning its behavior under statutes or regulations of the government, an equitable application of these rules between both domestic and foreign investors, and the absence of attacks by the governments on the private sector, in principle, or of its use as a political football.

This criterion does not require that governments sell off state-owned enterprises, reducing the extent of governmental activities and industry; nor does it necessarily require the government to remain static in its industrial activities. All it does require is that the role of the private sector be clearly delineated, and that the rules not be changed without substantial reason and extensive dialogue with the private sector, so that the understanding of the rules and any changes is adequate, thereby providing a positive motivation on the part of private investors.

This criterion of success of government-business relations is probably the easiest to describe, and the most significant. It would result in a condition in which private investors collectively and individually considered that future investment was desirable in and desired by that particular country, and one in which the government saw the objectives of business as being largely coincident with its own.

4. Related to the above criterion is one that asserts that success is achieved if companies are brought into a dialogue with government before new regulations or laws that adversely affect business operations are promulgated. This criterion would not necessarily require that the government incorporate the views of business into the laws of regulations—only that business be given the opportunity to demonstrate what the probable impacts of the new moves would be. Although business might complain about the laws that were finally passed—as with the patent bills in India, the new treaty to succeed the Laurel-Langley in the Philippines, and the recent Mexican investment code—they could not complain that their views were not heard.

5. Another criterion of successful government-business relations would be the existence of support for the views of the foreign business community by the local business community. (Of course, such support cannot be provided where there is virtually no local private business or no business associations—as in the less-developed countries.) This support could come in the form of a mutual representation to the government, or independent support by the local business community of initiatives taken by the foreign business community. Such support could also be shown in declarations by the local business community of the desirability of having foreign businesses within the country. Similarly, support could be shown by the local business community within the governmental party structure. In addition, support could be shown by the opposition political party, even if the party in power was pressing against the foreign business community. This criterion of success would indicate that, despite some pressure from the government in power, other groups—local business, the public, or the opposition party—did in fact support entrance of foreign investors and the objectives of the foreign business community.

6. The next criterion would be the absence of unacceptable changes in the regulations concerning foreign business. These regulations extend from the very first moment of negotiation about entry, through daily operations, to the final termination of the business relationship. What the international companies want most of all vis-à-vis regulations is not to have them changed in the middle of the game, and especially not to be imposed retroactively. Even changes in the rules for future behavior tend to be retroactive in some sense because of the projected plans for investment over five- to twenty-year periods. Such changes increase the uncertainty faced by companies, and therefore reduce the willingness to invest. If they could decrease the uncertainty of their future situation through effective government-business relations, it is clear that they would consider this a successful result.

Some responsibility for success in this regard rests with the company. It can, by closer communication, avoid surprises even if changes are made by the government. An early-warning system could be set up to provide sufficient notice. And the business organization could be set up to accommodate such changes. Two notable failures in this regard are the mining companies and pharmaceuticals. It was evident to many observers that the mining companies needed to change their policies long before it seemed to become apparent to them. And government officials are signaling the pharmaceutical companies, who seem equally unable to interpret these signals and prepare for a new relationship. Of course, one reason for not accommodating is that the company hopes it will not *have* to, as in the case of those oil companies that did not sell out to partners in Uganda despite the admonitions of the government and were not (later) required to do so by President Amin.

7. Successful government-business communications would exist under still another criterion if the host government would distinguish in its policies among different industries and companies. Treatment of all companies alike—as though they were all contributing or not contributing to the host country in the same way—or treatment of all industrial or nonindustrial companies the same way would be considered an undesirable result. One purpose of business-government relations, therefore, is to demonstrate that a common treatment of all companies or industries is likely to produce quite varied results—more or less desirable to the host government.

In addition, such activities would be directed at demonstrating that companies in general were "acting as good corporate citizens," thereby isolating any company that was acting in an undesirable fashion. The problem of the "bad actor" is critical in assessing the success of government-business relations. A well-planned, candid, and full communication by any group of companies can be upset by one that has not accepted the approach of the rest. Although such separate and distinct actions by a single company may be deemed advantageous to it, if its action plays into the hands of dissident political groups within the host country, the rest of the business community may be seriously harmed. And the results may not be good for the host country itself. It is, therefore, impossible to assess the probable impact of government-business communications without some assessment of the probability of a recalcitrant company upsetting the applecart. This situation has occurred often enough to make it a serious problem in government-business relations. The remedy is in better intrabusiness communications and agreement as to the objectives of government-business relations.

8. The above criteria of success are applicable to the entire foreign business community, not just to particular companies. There are some criteria of success for particular companies, however, that relate to special restrictions toward a company under the process of "localization" or expropriation. The application of "Africanization" or "Mexicanization" to some companies and not to others would shift the criterion of successful government-business relations to that of avoiding being "localized." Or, similarly, the lack of being expropriated, when others in its sector were, could be a signal of singular success.

In the event of expropriation, the criterion of successful communications shifts to that of achieving "prompt, adequate, and effective" compensation for the expropriated properties. The conditions of settlement that would fulfill these criteria are seldom the same in the view of the company or the government involved. Still, a company might consider that it was quite successful if it came out of such a negotiation relatively satisfied. The degree of satisfaction is itself dependent on what others got in a similar event. For example, Kennecott held a much better position in Chile than did Anaconda in terms of negotiation of their settlement.[1] Kennecott might, therefore, consider that its government-business relations were considerably better than those of Anaconda, despite the fact that the prior image of the two companies was the reverse. Before the expropriation, Anaconda was generally considered to have the more forthcoming attitude toward the problems of the government. Though Kennecott obtained a better settlement, it is not at all clear that the government provided such a settlement because it felt that Kennecott was more cooperative. On the contrary, it was probably a result of the fact that Kennecott had made a better bargain with the government in anticipation of future expropriation. Anaconda failed to protect itself adequately in the event that expropriation occurred by a succeeding government. This particular experience demonstrates the difficulty of assessing the success of government-business relations. It shows the complexity of trying to meet the pressures from governments, which are themselves being pressed by their various political groups, and also the difficulty of assessing the impacts of changes in the government itself. The criteria of successful government-business relations as seen by the companies, therefore, change as governments change and as other relevant conditions change. What was eventually seen as "successful" by the companies in an expropriation settlement would not have been considered even satisfactory five years earlier, when expropriation was not envisaged. And the actions that would have been necessary five years earlier to prevent expropriation would not have been seen then as satisfactory.

9. The criteria for good government-business relations between the international companies and the U.S. government are seen somewhat differently. First, the companies would like the government to see their activities as important enough to gather appropriate information concerning the political and economic situation of the host countries to assist them in their decisions on investments and operations. Second, they would like to have adequate channels of communication between the embassy and the companies in general and individually to transfer that information at appropriate times. Third, they would like to have assistance on particular problems of each company, such as obtaining import privileges or quotas, imports of technicians, and other day-to-day problems. Fourth, they would like to have the assistance of the embassy in making representations to the host government on changes in its regulations and laws that adversely affect direct investment. And finally, they would see as a successful set of relationships one that included assistance from the U.S.

government in settling any major disputes, such as expropriation, taking the initiative in representations to host governments.

Each of these relationships already exists (as will be seen in Chapter 7), but the quality and quantity leaves much to be desired, as many companies see it. No argument against these relationships is made by embassy officials, in principle; but their relative significance and specific application is in dispute among posts abroad and within the State Department. There are no general principles, however, by which one can determine beforehand how much of each should be provided at all posts abroad.

Some companies feel that these relationships go a bit too far. They would prefer not to have involvement of the U.S. Embassy in dispute situations, because they are trying to identify themselves wholly with the host country. Even in the case of some major disputes, as with Ford in South Africa and AMAX in Zambia, the companies sometimes see it as better for host-government-business relations that the U.S. Embassy stand aside. This stance is taken to achieve a separate identity—from any government. The company does not want to be seen as influenced by the U.S. government or as subservient to the whims of any one administration in a host country where governments change frequently.

Host-Country Criteria

Similar to the "noninterference" criterion of the companies, host countries would see as eminently successful a pattern of government-business relations that produced an automatic pursuit by the companies of the national interest; that is, that companies voluntarily heeded the interests (and representations) of the government, actively supporting its objectives. Government officials emphasize that this would include an expansion of exports by foreign-owned affiliates, a transfer of appropriate technology from the parent to the affiliate, the establishment of local research-and-development laboratories, a minimization of capital outflows to the parent or other affiliates, expansion of employment opportunities, increased participation of local citizens in managerial and technical positions in the company, greater participation of locals in ownership, the rationalization of industrial activity, and integration of the foreign company with local industrial development. These and other activities are included in what governments mean by "good corporate citizenship," as illustrated in the "codes" promulgated by both Canada and Mexico for foreign investors. Although many companies feel that they are already complying with these criteria, there is sufficient continued discussion of the desirability of such codes to indicate that governments feel that they have not yet been successful in persuading companies to act voluntarily in pursuit of governmental interests.

Some governments would be satisfied if they could merely be certain that companies obeyed their laws. Even if all companies did so, however, it is not at all clear that the problem of government-business relations would be solved—even from the viewpoint of governments. Governments are not concerned solely with the end results, but desire also that the means by which government-business relations are carried on reflect their sovereignty. The satisfaction of these demands would not preclude host governments from escalating them in the future, as with the Arabian countries; it appears that "a satisfied need motivates no one."

1. One of the most important criteria of success in the viewpoint of host governments is noninterference in its policies by the U.S. government. Conversely, at times, host governments would like interference by the U.S. government on their behalf—for example, representations of the U.S. government in the Bechtel case were well received by the Indian government as long as they were in its favor; they were ill received if otherwise. Similarly, U.S. government representations in the Chrysler-Mitsubishi negotiations were well received as long as they moved in the direction of Japanese interests. There is a strong feeling on the part of many of the developing countries, at least, that the U.S. government can and will take an initiative to interfere in local governmental affairs through and on behalf of the international companies if it suits its interests. This view, however poorly supported by the facts, is argued strongly by those who have an ideological revulsion against "capitalistic imperialism."

In addition, many governments do not appreciate American companies calling on the U.S. government for protection or assistance in negotiation with the host country.[b] They have frequently asserted that this is "poor" government-business relations. This view is held especially strongly in Latin America, where the Calvo doctrine is upheld and is written into agreements under which companies come into the host countries. This doctrine states that the companies will agree to place all disputes before the national courts of the host country, and not call upon the U.S. government for assistance in disputes within that country. Not all companies have abided by this agreement. They have, especially, called upon the U.S. government when they found they could not get an appropriate settlement within the host country, at least in their view. And the U.S. government has responded when it thought desirable, stating to the host countries that it cannot stand aside when its interests are in jeopardy.

2. A second criterion is that of "full disclosure" of information to the government of the host country. Governments have a strong feeling that they are told only what the company wants to tell them—or that they are often given information that is either too extensive to be useful or analyzable, or only partial and therefore misleading. It is frequently the case that host countries do not have officials with sufficient expertise, or a sufficient number of such

---

[b]The degree of interference on behalf of U.S. companies in Europe is considerably less and therefore less resented. In addition, European governments represent interests of their companies abroad and understand a U.S. effort to do the same in their countries.

officials, to be able to ask appropriate questions to discern whether or not they have adequate answers. And even if adequate information was given them, they would still be suspicious that something had been withheld. Despite the importance of this criterion of successful relations, it is highly unlikely that governments will, for a long time, feel that they do have a "full (or adequate) disclosure."

A critical problem in such disclosure, however, is the opposition of local business interests to providing more information. In Europe and elsewhere, information is considered the basis for wider governmental control. The local community would not like to see the information flow extended, and certainly not by legislation that reached them also.

3. An additional criterion of success from the viewpoint of the host governments is that of restructuring the decision-making procedures of international companies so that they are able to carry out an effective dialogue with the managers at the local level. Host governments are dissatisfied with the business-government relationships because most of the important decisions are either made, vetoed, or approved by the headquarters company. This means that government officials are not in direct communication with the decision makers. An effective procedure for carrying out the dialogue would require that the manager at the local level be given greater authority. Such a shift of the locus of decision making would imply that governments seek to restructure the channels of authority within the companies; until that restructuring took place, they would not consider business-government relationships successful.

4. Since governments do frequently take an initiative to obtain information from companies on the effects of pending or existing governmental regulations, one measure of success would be their feeling that they had received objective replies and analysis. But not only should they see this information as objective (and not self-serving, from the viewpoint of the company) but also they should preferably receive it at a technical level to avoid embarrassment to the government, which does not want to be seen as subservient to the foreigner. This means that a continuing dialogue should be carried out between the companies and technicians within the government, so that critical information would be transferred along with regular exchanges of information, thereby not heating up a particular issue. It would be up to the ministers to determine when they should be included in the dialogue, rather than being pressed by the foreign companies to give them audience. In other words, the government would perceive itself as being in the position of taking the initiative in, and determining the level of, the dialogue.

5. Correlative to the above criterion would be the absence of demands for *special* treatment from any of the companies on matters of taxes, customs, import of technology, use of foreign technicians, or protocol. Governments tend to find it is embarrassing, and again an indication of weakness before the foreigner, to have to agree to special treatment, ranging from requests for special

tariff treatment to the reception of delegations from business by "high level" officials. This is not to say that there are not times in which it is highly desirable for such treatment be accorded. But they should be seen as rare exceptions from the normal pattern between the host government and the foreign investor.

6. In the event of an expropriation, good government-business relations in the view of the host government would include an acceptance by the foreign company of a settlement determined within the juridical system of the host country. That is, it would prefer not to have to face a negotiation with the U.S. government or to put the matter before international arbitration. For example, none of the Latin American governments has signed the agreement to use the International Center for Settlement of Investment Disputes under the World Bank. They consider that using ICSID would imply a loss of sovereignty; full respect for their sovereignty is a criterion of successful government-business relations.

7. In some countries, successful government-business relations are possible only through national associations that include local companies as members. Thus, it is not seen as desirable for the host government to have to deal with a separate chamber of commerce including only American (or other foreign) companies. Such a separation makes an undesirable distinction in government-business relationships. Conversely, some governments feel that the separation of foreign and domestic business associations is desirable, in that they do not face a single coordinated group; one group may be more ready and willing to follow the government's initiatives than another, thereby putting pressure on the recalcitrant group. The opportunity to "divide and conquer" is provided by the institutional structure of the business community.

8. Finally, a most important criterion for both the company and host government is for the company *not* to be *perceived* in the host country as a tool of, channel for, or protected by the U.S. government. Some companies seek this detachment so strongly as to avoid *any* relation with the U.S. Embassy. Even if it does socialize or maintain information contacts, a company will often handle *all* problems with the host government without reliance on the embassy in order to avoid this coloration. Of course, a joint venture with a local partner enhances the separation from U.S. influence.

It can be readily seen that these criteria do not coincide with those used by companies in judging their own activities. Further, they are not the same as are likely to be used by the U.S. government in assessing its relationships to U.S. international business.

U.S. Goverment Criteria

The criteria employed by the U.S. government in determining whether government-business relationships abroad are satisfactory come from the objectives of the embassies and the State Department. Similar to the ideal criteria of the host country or the companies, the U.S. government would like some contribution to U.S. goals abroad and no significant conflict arising abroad over the activities of U.S. business. In reality, of course, such a quiescent situation is highly unlikely. Therefore, the embassies and the State Department would likely accept less stringent criteria of success. Several such criteria can be outlined.

1. One of the most desirable situations would be that whatever conflicts arose between U.S. companies and host countries would not involve the U.S. Embassy. Successful business-government relationships, therefore, would mean that all of the problems were so small as not to require the concern of embassy personnel. The absence of official complaints by the host government over activities of U.S. business would imply that either there are no serious disagreements between business and the host country or that any disagreements were resolved without reliance on the U.S. Embassy.

Of course, it would not be acceptable to the U.S. government for the other two parties to resolve significant issues in ways contrary to U.S. interests, when those interests were strong. Therefore, the criterion relates more to the significance of the conflict than to the absence of embassy involvement. If all of the troubles are little ones, maybe the embassy can avoid involvement without significant cost to U.S. interests.

2. At a higher level, the same could be said of involvement of the State Department itself. Host government and U.S. business relationships might involve the embassy, but it is to be hoped that the issues could be small enough or routine enough to be handled by its personnel without requiring the involvement of State Department officials. Referring issues back to the State Department means that they are potentially significant enough to involve critical national interests of the U.S. For such a situation to arise means, of course, that business-government relations abroad have not been successful.

3. At still a higher level, a criterion of at least partial success would be that of not involving the president. It would be hoped that the issues would be small enough to be handled at either the embassy or the State Department level. Several conflicts between U.S. companies and host governments (such as ITT in Brazil and IPC in Peru) have involved the president directly, and in public situations, which he would have preferred not to have had to handle.

4. At any of the three levels above, a criterion of success in government-business relations from the viewpoint of the U.S. government would be that there would be no necessity to make a trade-off of any other policy toward the host country in favor of the interests of U.S. business. If, in order to settle the matter, the U.S. government is put in a position of having to expand foreign aid, recognize an extended two-hundred-mile limit of jurisdiction into the oceans, make military sales or grants, or other concessions, it will certainly not consider that government-business relations abroad were successful.

Although the U.S. government would like not to have to make trade-offs, they are made on occasion—as with the development of the petroleum companies in Arabia. But with few exceptions, they are not made, and they are probably not required to protect U.S. business.[c] It would be unrealistic to try to determine, in advance, a schedule of permissible trade-offs. One way to reduce situations that might involve trade-offs would be to eliminate calls for protection that arose from a company's own inappropriate behavior. The embassy might perceive in a request for entry by a U.S. company that the proposal would likely generate a situation leading to expropriation (or creeping expropriation) and a request for its assistance. It could, at that point, warn the company and require it to waive any "right to representation." Similarly, the embassy might withhold assistance if the company had withheld from it significant and relevant information affecting its representations to the host government. These comments point up the desirability of a full disclosure of relevant information in requests to the embassy for assistance, so that it can make reasoned judgments on the appropriateness of different tactics it could use.[d]

5. The U.S. Embassy is likely to consider business-government relations more successful if there is a *continuous* disclosure of company activities impending on the U.S. government interests in the host country—rather than an ad hoc disclosure. One of the fears of embassy personnel is that of becoming involved in representing a company position vis-à-vis the host country only to find out that there is relevant information not provided by the company which would affect the reasonableness of the U.S. government position. To be undercut by not having relevant information is certainly unacceptable; even if the matter were settled without such disclosure, there is an underlying problem of equity which might later embarrass the U.S. government. In order, therefore, for the U.S. government to feel good about government-business relations abroad, there is likely to have to be a larger flow of information on a continuous basis so that

[c]The evidence for this statement comes from numerous interviews at posts and with business and host government officials. However, the comments apply to *direct* trade-offs; no one can say that the act of representation does not affect indirectly (or directly in a covert way) other negotiations with or later policies of the host government, for example, the later promulgation of a foreign investment law or a later negotiation of an aid agreement. However, even indirect trade-offs may be dampened by the fact that not all representations by the embassy go through the foreign office of the host country. Given poor communication among ministries, a request at lower levels of the ministry of trade (or industry or economy) may be acted upon without any notification to other ministries. Therefore, no future reaction from the latter would be discernible.

[d]What is "all relevant information" cannot always be determined beforehand, and given the short institutional memories of all actors, some information may merely be forgotten. The criterion is simply that there be no withholding of information that each party *knows* to be relevant and would affect the action of the other directly. If support of the U.S. government is obtainable only by the company withholding damaging information (which is likely to come to light, to its embarrassment and that of the U.S. government), good business-government relations would mean not putting the government in such a tenuous position; the company should proceed on its own without such support. If the U.S. government is "sucked in" to represent a bad case, the cost will be much greater than the loss of this one case alone.

the embassy officials know what kinds of data to ask for and how to assess the adequacy and relevance of what they have when disputes arise and their representation is requested.

6. Given the fact that government-business relationships are a two-way street, the embassies and the State Department are likely to feel that their relationships with U.S. international companies are more successful the greater support that they have from the business community for the policy positions of the U.S. government. Such support can be given within the U.S. before Congress—for example, on trade, technology transfers, labor problems, etc.—but it cannot be given as easily on policy positions toward host countries. This later support involves the companies in a posture that demonstrates that they are essentially foreign companies bound to U.S. interests and unable to make the interests of the host country primary.

Yet it is difficult for the U.S. Embassy to support these companies if they go so far as to undercut the U.S. position in the host country. A situation involving a conflict of this type arose under "Operation Intercept," which was aimed at controlling the flow of drugs from Mexico across the U.S. border in illegal trade. The methods employed by the U.S. law-enforcement officers were so stringent as to create an emotional backlash in Mexico affecting the image of U.S. business. U.S. businesses in turn joined with Mexican business in complaining to the U.S. government both publically and privately, to the embarrassment of the U.S. Embassy in Mexico. Similarly, the Indo-American Chamber of Commerce cabled Nixon against the U.S. stand on the Indo-Pakistan war over Bangladesh.

7. In a similar vein, the embassies will handle more readily any cases that involve policy positions rather than exceptions to policies. The embassies are better prepared to take initiatives on policy matters (e.g., violations of the OECD Code of Liberalization of Capital Movements or of FCN treaties or double taxation treaties, or GATT, etc.) and can more readily see their "duty." In such cases, they are less representing the interests of the company than maintaining the integrity of agreements or treaties. If a specific problem is not covered by existing agreements, guidelines may not exist for how to handle it, and if it involves an exception to an agreement, embassy support is even more reluctantly given, if at all.

8. The embassies are also likely to see as successful a relationship that induces the U.S. business community to accept their suggestions on business behavior. Although no embassy official would consider that any single company should follow its advice on how to carry out its operations or to decide on investments or liquidation, the posture or behavior of the entire business community is another matter. It is especially important so as to reduce the problems of a "bad actor" who breaks the pattern of "good citizenship." If the local U.S. business community agrees with the posture recommended by the U.S. Embassy, bringing all major companies into line, the embassy is likely to count this as a criterion of success.

9. One of the more critical relationships between U.S. companies and the embassies is the process of reporting on intelligence-gathering by the companies. Not all embassies accomplish this task equally well, but where it is given a significant priority, the business community can and does provide an interpretation of news or developments and evidence of significant changes that embassy personnel might not otherwise obtain. When this information is gathered readily and transferred frankly and openly to the embassy by the U.S. business community, a rapport is established that makes both U.S. officials and company officials feel that these business-government relationships are proceeding on a firm foundation. But they also make host governments feel somewhat suspicious about their own relations with U.S. investors.

This intelligence-gathering is made more difficult by the fact that ambassadors are not kept at posts for lengthy stays; they hardly get familiar with the situation and the people involved before they are moved, making it difficult to know the various actors and their attitudes. This problem is accentuated by the fact that governmental counterparts in the host country are also moved in and out through governmental changes or shake-ups. This lack of familiarity is magnified by the fact that the institutional memory of the embassy is short, as a consequence of the shifting of personnel in all staff positions among posts.

There is no single criterion that can be suggested by which to guide the development of closer relations with business. No single set of interests is always involved, the time frames are different, the settings are different, the trade-offs are different, and the orientations and capabilities of officials are different. One cannot, therefore, prescribe a "rulebook" for "good government-business relations"; one can employ officials with a sensitivity and a sound judgment who are also willing and able to get at the relevant facts and to negotiate in good faith under broad policies laid down by the State Department. Nor is it clear what criteria the State Department might use to judge the success of its relationships with U.S. business. At one extreme are those who would wish that the companies would drop from sight, not interfering with the normal diplomatic relationships among the U.S. government and other countries; at the other are those who see in business activities abroad the very core of international relations, in that all political and security relationships are affected by—if not directly determined by—basic economic conditions and relations. With the reduction of the probability of the use of force around the world, it is clear that economic relations are increasingly important in determining the political relations among countries. The ability and willingness of countries to use their economic power to gain political and military ends is seen in the oil embargo by the Arab states, and in the potential for similar action by other raw-material producers. The importance of economic relations is seen also in the extensive expropriations in Cuba and Chile. It is not possible, therefore, to avoid involvement with the U.S. companies, nor is it permissible for them to dictate the underlying relationships with foreign government.

Yet it is not possible to establish a predetermined pattern for good government-business relations, as seen by the State Department, since there cannot be a clear, generalized delineation on the objectives which the Department would seek vis-à-vis particular U.S. company activities abroad. Each case is different and requires procedures adapted to the host country. The officials in State and the embassy operate on an ad hoc basis, relying somewhat on precedents of prior cases. The nuances depend not only on the situation of a particular case and the overall U.S. foreign policy objectives vis-à-vis the host country but also on who knows whom—not only abroad but between the U.S. government and the parent company. The handling of the Mercantile Bank case in Canada was undoubtedly influenced by the personal relationship of the Undersecretary of State and the president of Citibank—though the outcome was not visibly affected by this fact.[2] In the case of ITT's expropriation in Brazil, the ability of Geneen to get to high U.S. government officials did seem to intensify U.S. government effort, though the direct impact on the outcome was not visible.

The continued absence of a policy toward international business (as distinct from trade, technology transfer, antitrust, taxation, etc. as functionally separate activities) will hamper the determination of these criteria for embassy actions. It is not the purpose of this work to propose alternative policy positions for the U.S. government toward international business, but it is virtually impossible to determine the way in which the embassies should be organized or embassy personnel instructed until such policy positions are taken.[e] Even if the Department cannot establish a single, clear, and sufficiently extensive policy to cover all situations, at least position papers could be developed that recognize the complexities and proffer some tentative guidelines for action. Such papers would themselves demonstrate the extent to which dialogues are desirable between the parent companies and the State Department itself—as is being done in an early-warning committee concerned with situations likely to lead to expropriation of U.S.-owned companies abroad. The position papers should be developed not only within the State Department but in cooperation with the departments of Commerce, Treasury, Justice, and Defense, and the myriad of other agencies having responsibilities in international business activities. In the discussions it would become clear that there are a variety of channels of communication with business that need coordination within the government (as is discussed in Chapter 7), and that delineation of principles for all cases would not be possible. Watershed events, such as lack of application of the Hickenlooper amendment, alters policy positions so radically as to outdate specific

---

[e]Similarly, the stances of *each* of the actors—companies and governments—to the others cannot be institutionalized effectively until policy objectives of each are described. We are in a period presently in which past paradigms are not applicable or acceptable. Until new ones are found, existing institutional structures tend to behave in defense of past policies, giving rise to ever greater tensions. Once the tensions are sufficiently great, policies will be altered.

guidelines. However, there are some guidelines for embassy officials that could be laid down.

1. Seek all relevant information, and do not represent a case in which it appears that relevant information is withheld—i.e., behavior by the company which would alter the U.S. government position or representation.

2. Do undertake cases that support a principle agreed upon with the host government, and one violating a contractual relationship between the host government and the company, but only when it is clear that redress is not obtainable under local procedures.

3. Do not press a case under a principle that will not be adhered to or generally supported by the U.S. government—e.g., the principle of "prompt, equitable, and effective" compensation in expropriation.

4. Move into a case gradually, checking with State on information it has on the parent company.

5. Do not offer a trade-off unless national interests are clearly at stake—and only after checking with high State officials.

The criteria relevant to the U.S. government involve not only successful relationships between U.S. business and the host country but also between U.S. business and embassies abroad. The criteria for each are not the same, nor will all embassies place the same priority on relationships of different sorts with the U.S. business community. Each ambassador tends to impose his own set of priorities on the embassy, and the personnel tends to reflect his view on the importance of business-government relationships. The State Department will, at times, constrain the embassy from taking too forward a position on a given case (as with that of Krebs in Argentina), and at others will decide to give the ambassador a free hand (as with Korry in Chile).

Buffer Concept of Government
Relations for Companies

Over a decade ago, the chairman of Jersey Standard was quoted in *Fortune* to the effect that the company had its own foreign policy and that all international companies should have their own foreign policies. This statement implies also that there is a kind of company "foreign service" that would generate appropriate information and help pursue abroad the policies set out by the parent company. None of the companies interviewed appeared to have such a "foreign service" in being—not even Exxon—but some officials are attempting to carry the functions of a foreign service. Successful government-business relations, in fact, would require a company structure and orientation similar to a foreign service. It would perform a role similar to that of the ambassador of a country between his own country and another, a buffer, a conduit, and an initiator between the company and government. The government-relations function of a company is complicated by the fact that, frequently, multiple company units are involved as well as multiple representatives by the company in a given country. The increasing significance of joint ventures will also complicate this function. It is complicated still further by the fact that the companies have no "State Department" at headquarters but rather a staff or a series of staff positions that filter the representation from the field (as discussed in Chapter 2). Finally, company orientations are complicated by the priority given to short-run success as compared to long-run success of affiliate managers abroad.

Similarity to Ambassador

The basic justification for the existence of ambassadors is that meeting of heads of state would tend to raise somewhat minor difficulties to the highest level. The lack of such meetings keeps insignificant problems at lower levels; this fact of distance provides flexibility to each sovereign in that information is passed back and forth and positions can be changed in the interim. Further, the distance in both space and time tends to reduce tensions that might otherwise be raised to a high peak if there were frequent meetings. Conversely, of course, distance not closed by *any* representation through an intermediary could also lead to tensions. Therefore, the ambassador supplies the role of buffer as well as an intermediary.

The ambassador's role is successfully carried out only if he is capable of explaining each government to the other. He must help his own government understand the positions of the host government, yet at the same time press his own government's interests or position. He also has a substantial role in determining his own government's position toward the host country by providing careful analysis and by continuing to press for modifications that he considers appropriate. Once a position is taken, he still has the responsibility to pursue those objectives in ways in which he determines will produce a successful result. The more this role is undercut by specific and detailed instructions as to how to act or argue, coming from the State Department, the less capable is the ambassador in being a buffer.[f] Conversely, of course, his bargaining position is often strengthened by reference back to Washington—both for policy support or as a delaying tactic.

A successful government-relations function on the part of a company would adopt this description for those in its own foreign service. Of course, the

---

[f]The representations of an ambassador can be complicated further by a personal interest (involving a conflict of interest, even) of a U.S. government official in the case, or of a host government official so that objective representations are difficult if not impossible. The personal involvement of ministers or families of top officials is found frequently in developing countries.

company is not supposed to be a buffer between the U.S. government and the host government (though at times it may be asked by the U.S. Embassy to become one), but between the parent company, the host government, and the home government.

General Manager as a Representative

The general manager of an affiliate abroad is not simply the operating head of the company, but is also the representative (ambassador) of the parent company in that country. The success of the company, and the purpose of the government-relations function, lies in the creation of a *mutual* understanding between the parent company and the host government of the objectives of the affiliate and its methods of operation. This understanding is likely to be facilitated *only* through a full and frank disclosure of all *relevant* information on the part of each. The purpose of the company representative should be to see that this disclosure takes place. He should ferret out information within the host country concerning governmental attitudes and objectives, and he should be able to supply to the government information concerning his operations that are relevant to the national interest. The affiliate is a "guest in the house" of the host country, and its objectives and activities should be as circumspect as those of any guest. Where there is *any* question about the activities or motives of the guest a quick, frank, and full disclosure is required. Without it, suspicions are intensified and inappropriate policies result.

Representation does not have to occur through contacts at the "top level" of government. More successful communication often occurs when technicians are involved. It is often better that communication arise from an initiative by lower-level officials with civil servants rather than among top officials. In many developing countries, it is highly desirable to lower the level of communication and the probable exposure to press criticisms of undue influence on ministers. This does not argue that top-level contacts be severed, but merely that initiatives taken at lower levels can be just as much an evidence of success—if not more so—than initiatives taken at top levels of government.

Such disclosure is much more important for affiliates operating as part of a multinational enterprise than for those that are tied together under an international holding company. The latter operate much more independently and under criteria developed with reference to the host-country market; whereas the former are much more integrated with the parent and the other affiliates of the enterprise, and are therefore operating under criteria related to the welfare of worldwide enterprise.

The role of the representative is both complicated and eased by the existence of joint ventures, altering both the reality of the communication and the perception of business-government ties. The fact that a joint venture includes local citizens of the host country means that these individuals can supply the necessary personal and official connections with the host government and can interpret the company to the government and the government to the joint-venture partners. The same individual, however, is not necessarily capable of carrying the communication back to the parent company. Not only does a question of loyalties arise, but a lack of effective communication frequently occurs simply because of differences in language, customs, and traditions. Similarly, officials from the U.S. partner are able to be the buffer between the affiliate and the parent company and can provide to local partners a better understanding of parent company interests. But they are not as able to understand local government objectives or objections, since they are not in close contact with it. A reconciliation of divergent views tends to occur within the joint venture itself, in that the partners have to translate the positions of the host government and the company to each other and then seek an accommodation. This accommodation may not be the one desired by either the parent company or the host government. Third-party interests are introduced—those of the host country partner, which probably will have its own objectives vis-à-vis the affiliate and the host government; that is, the local partner is likely to have interests apart from the joint venture that it would not want to be upset by activities of the venture. Nor is it always the case that the local partner is attuned to the political pressures in the host government or to the needs of the country.

Headquarters GR Staff

The similarity between company government-relations functions and those of the ambassador ceases with the inclusion of a headquarters staff concerning government relations around the world. One might assume that such a staff would have functions similar to the State Department in the U.S. government, but this is not the case. The State Department has responsibility for *line* activity—not staff, being the direct operating arm of the president around the world. Although ambassadors are the direct representatives of the president, in practice, they report to the desk officers and the assistant secretary for the region in which they function.

Company GR staff are not yet sufficiently developed (budgeted or supported by line activity) to perform functions similar to a foreign service. If they were, they would be able to make trade-offs among countries as to the primary interest of the company, and to compromise a general principle in one country or another where it was desirable to do so. Being staffs, they do not have such authority; that is, such accommodations can generally be made only within the office of the presidency of the company.

In addition, it appears that the lines of influence are stronger from the presidency through the government-relations staff to the affiliates than vice versa. The government-relations staff is frequently looking at reports from the field and sending back instructions that tend to support the policies enunciated by the company president. If such GR staffs argue strongly for the position coming from the field, their loyalty or understanding of company policy may come in doubt. (Similar doubts have been expressed by various departments or interest groups in the U.S. vis-à-vis the Department of State, which has been seen as having foreign governments as its clients, rather than the interests of the U.S. itself.) Only if the principle of full and frank disclosure and discussion is adopted, can this staff be an effective instrument in meeting the problems that the companies face abroad. To date, few international companies are willing to devote the time, effort, or money necessary to accomplish the necessary degree of mutual understanding and accommodation of goals. In addition, what they have done reflects the primary attention to developed countries where little governmental relations are required, compared to developing countries, where greater communication is required.

Short-run vs. Long-run Criteria

One of the reasons companies are reluctant to expend the money and effort is the fact that success can generally be seen only in the longer run. Both company target-budgeting and managerial assignments abroad tend to be short term—three to five years. A manager's success is measured by his ability to meet targets, and his promotion depends on that success. Although companies do intend to stay in a country over a long term (usually seen as permanent), the criteria of successful operation tend to downgrade the long term in favor of the short term. Consequently, a representative of an international company will frequently seek to press the host government for conditions permitting it to achieve short-run objectives, despite the fact that repeated pressures of this sort by different managers are likely to build up a resentment and a backlash of restrictions in the long run. It is, of course, not to the interest of the international company to have short-run success bought at the price of long-run restrictions on its activities. However, governments in power also often have short-term goals that are matched by company goals—though both may be seen as unacceptable by a subsequent government, with dire consequences for the company.

Conversely, when the international company headquarters pays attention to longer-run impacts of a negotiation over a particular issue, it will frequently itself insist on a solution that will not set an adverse precedent for other countries and other affiliates around the world—despite the fact that such pressure may backfire not only in the long run in that country but even in the short run. This appears to have been some of the basis for the reasoning of the parent company in the IPC case in Peru, and for the results there.

It is not argued here that these trade-offs are easy to make. It is rather argued that they cannot be made readily by any one affiliate by itself; nor will the parent always make them in the most effective manner even with what is considered to be full information. In addition, the results of such decisions by the company will directly affect the image and position of the U.S. government vis-à-vis the host country.

Perception and Reality

Critical to the success of government-business relations is the creation of a reality that is acceptable to all participants and then of a perception that matches that reality. As Alfred North Whitehead wrote, the search for truth is the narrowing of the gap between perception and reality. The mere effort to alter perceptions without moving them in the direction of reality is cosmetics, and will backfire in the longer run.

The objective, therefore, should be to achieve agreement as to the acceptable responsiveness of the companies to both host and U.S. governments, and to act in such a way that these relations are perceived to exist. The only method of achieving such perception is open and frank exchange of information. Business problems are seldom so sensitive that they cannot stand such an exchange—even though not made public.

The understanding does not have to be codified either among several governments or between the U.S. and each host government. To formalize the understanding would raise a variety of issues that might never arise in practice. But what is necessary is a sufficiently open communication so that host governments realize that neither are the companies being used by the U.S. to interfere in national affairs nor is the U.S. government being used by the companies. Evidence that such interferences are rare is found in the hearings before the U.S. Senate Subcommittee on Multinational Corporations. The efforts by ITT in the Chilean case are quite exceptional. The mere fact of such investigations shows that there is no close tie between the U.S. companies and government, for no effort was made by the Executive Branch to quash the hearings. Rather, these hearings should prove that host governments' interests are being looked after (at least in part) by the U.S. Congress. In fact the hearings have proceeded even though there is a likelihood that the image of U.S. companies abroad will be tarnished by disclosures of some ill-considered policies.

Despite the problems of a "too close" relationship between the U.S. government and companies, host governments will recognize that legitimate U.S. interests will be the subject of diplomatic representations if necessary. Such representations will be perceived as evidence of precisely the close relationship that is feared. But efforts should be made to narrow the gap between perception and the reality of the wide separation of U.S. government and business attitudes and objectives. Discussion by embassy officials with host government counterparts would be a starting point—for example, distribution of the present study and its use in "seminars" between U.S. and host government officials should go a long way in clearing the air by surfacing the concerns of host governments, airing a variety of misconceptions, and permitting examination of the reality. Discussion of relationships arising in *other* countries would open up a frank exchange without increasing tensions over local problems.

7

U.S. Government Alternatives

The evidence of the previous chapters is that the State Department and embassies are involved in a variety of relationships with international companies and have, at times, extended considerable assistance. But the growth of international business is such that these contacts will undoubtedly increase, in both developing and advanced countries—raising the question of the readiness of the U.S. government to play an expanded role, if it decided from a policy standpoint to do so.

To play a more effective role in its relations with U.S. international business the State Department should adopt several measures, in stages or simultaneously. They include an improvement in the procedures of communication and attitudes of cooperation with business; a shift in the international economic priorities away from the postwar criteria and assumptions toward recognition of the increasingly important role played by international companies under new criteria; and reorientation of the elements of the Department dealing with international business. The argument of this chapter leads to the conclusion that all three steps are needed within a relatively short period, though one would have to expect a bureaucratic miracle to be optimistic about the time that will be required. Even if not all can be accomplished soon they should be taken in order, for those discussed last cannot be successful without the preceding changes.

Improvement in Communication and Cooperation

Those officials with whom we discussed these problems around the world—company, host government, and U.S. embassies—repeatedly emphasized that the first priority in improving government-business relations was a significant change in attitudes on the part of all parties concerned. With a change in these attitudes would come a change in the relationships of business to governments, which would itself reinforce the change of attitudes. As a result of these changes new mechanisms of cooperation and communication would likely be developed out of initiatives on the parts of business, the U.S. government, and host governments.

Attitudes

Many of those we interviewed showed a genuine willingness to change past attitudes and a wide recognition that it is time to do so. Frequently, younger officials made stronger arguments along this line than older ones. Historically most companies have not wanted anything to do with the embassy abroad (save social contacts); others have sought its assistance only in extreme cases; and a few have known how to use it effectively, without harming company or U.S. government activities or image. These attitudes often reflect parent company instructions (or lack thereof); few managers abroad are instructed to work closely *either* with the embassy or the host government, though many general managers soon recognize a need to do so. The lack of instructions reflects the absence of policies of headquarters. And, of course, many ambassadors would prefer not to have to see U.S. businessmen, save in a social relationship.

The needed changes will come sooner and be more effective if they occur also at the top in both business and government. This will require a removal of past biases and a willingness to look at evidence from new viewpoints. None of the players have a monopoly on open and forthcoming attitudes at present; all face the need to change in order to achieve the objectives that are being enunciated. Even host governments will have to adopt new attitudes, but it can be argued that these would be facilitated if the initiatives discussed below were taken on the part of U.S. business and government officials. LDC governments, at least, are not likely to move in this direction for some time without a strong lead from the U.S. government.

While it is not possible to say that there is a single attitude that pervades all of the U.S. government, a strong bias has existed among State Department officials that political issues are more important than economic or commercial.[1] And business is seen as narrowly motivated and incapable of contributing to or assessing wider policy objectives or assuming wider responsibilities for achieving national interests. And, of course, many business speeches and publications continue to argue as though the *only* objective of business is profits. Despite the fact that this is *not* the single objective of companies, and many other objectives are traded off against it, so long as company officials continue to assert that this is the *only* criterion by which they should be judged, and the only objective which they pursue, they will continue to reinforce antipathetical views of government officials.

But business is being induced (forced) to accept wider responsibilities related to political, economic, security, social, cultural, and scientific issues and objectives. As it does so, attitudes of governmental officials may change. However, the change in government attitudes could be accelerated by an earlier recognition by governmental officials that companies are, in fact, not so singularly motivated, or at least reserving judgment on *each* company until the evidence is in as to its motives.

If business can be seen as able to pursue wider objectives than mere profit (that is, to pursue profit with adequate recognition of the cultural, political, ecological, ethical, and social constraints in a country), a much more cooperative attitude is likely to be found on the part of U.S. officials. Some experiments in closer government-business dialogue—such as occurred in the early days of the Council of the Americas (then known as the Business Group for Latin America) between company officials and desk officers—have demonstrated to State Department officials that "businessmen are not so bad; they also have human motivations and social orientations."

Though it is not possible to change attitudes by fiat, efforts should certainly be made to bring about a wider and more intensive dialogue between business and government officials at *all* levels, so that each could understand the motivation and orientations of the other. The not infrequent meetings between government officials and top corporate officials or executives of business associations (NAM, U.S. Chamber, U.S. Council of the I.C.C., Council of the Americas, etc.) have their place, but the dialogue needs to be carried on at much lower (operational) levels by business and government. Personnel exchanges are a means of broadening familiarity and understanding, but they affect relatively few people. What is needed is a closer personal relationship between officials from each side working on similar problems.[a] It is highly unlikely that after such a process (extending over a considerable period), the existing orientations would remain; they would certainly be much more selectively applied than at present. And, hopefully, a gradual recognition will arise that business and government are overlapping more in their goals and responsibilities, rather than being antagonistic.

A similar bias has existed historically in the State Department toward the responsibilities and orientations of relevant segments of the Commerce Department.[2] The Commerce Department has been seen as the mouthpiece for selected business interests and not as taking into account the total national interest. When Commerce has, in fact, had a different orientation, it has been difficult for officials in the State Department, conditioned by past experience, to recognize and reinforce that change. In fact, Commerce has never been a strong spokesman for the business sector, simply because business itself cannot respect a patsy, and quickly recognizes that the Department does not have power or prestige within the councils of the government. For Commerce to become a strong advocate of business interests, it must demonstrate that it is able to fit those interests into the total objectives of the U.S. government. Once having done so, it will achieve greater status not only in the government but with the business community itself. Like the ambassador abroad, the Commerce Department must be an intermediary between the government and U.S. business, explaining each to the other and developing an accommodation that is in accord with the national interest.

These changes in attitude in State, in Commerce, and between them are prerequisites for a further change in State Department attitudes toward coopera-

---

[a] This proposal argues in favor of the OMB suggestion to restructure responsibilities on the basis of industry sectors (as do the French in the ministry of industry) rather than on "macro" and "micro" bases, which reflect academic training biases.

tive methods of policy formation. Many attempts have been made by the State Department to develop mechanisms with other Departments for cooperative policy formation. But interdepartmental jealousies have aborted each of these efforts. In the Kennedy administration an undersecretaries group was formed to coordinate foreign policies affecting departmental interests, but it was never made responsible for policies. Under President Johnson, a senior review group (again of undersecretaries, chaired also by State) attempted to coordinate, but State seemed unable to form policy cooperatively. Consequently, the responsibility shifted to the Council for International Economic Policy (CIEP) in the White House. The responsibility *should* be within State, but only if it can learn how to fulfill it. There is more than enough to be done, and it is necessary to utilize all of the manpower resources available. It is also desirable to obtain all the various inputs from the departments having an interest or responsibility vis-à-vis international business and the conduct of U.S. foreign economic policy. If State cannot change its viewpoints, its responsibilities will be slowly decimated so as to achieve the necessary multiple and cooperative inputs.

These changes must be carried into the field by both business and government, and they will have to be reinforced by attitudes at the top. This means that business speeches should include the necessity to make these changes, starting with company presidents; and governmental speeches, from the president down, should show a similar recognition and will to act. A genuine change of attitudes would produce a new set of relationships which would, in turn, reinforce more favorable attitudes.

New Relationships

Extensive examinations of "modern capitalism" and the new "social contract" between societies and business indicate that a set of new relationships is emerging and should be reinforced. These include an acceptance of the need to pursue mutual objectives on the part of government and business, of social welfare and the efficient use of resources, and of social responsibility *within* the operations of business as well as *to* the community.

Within the mores of American business is the concept that the government's role is to serve the objectives of business. Or, as J. Paul Getty has reportedly asserted, "If America doesn't have business, what has it got?" inferring that the only business of America is business. Though a few such ringing statements can still be heard today, there is increasing recognition that business is not the essence of U.S. society. Rather, business will achieve its goals *only* if it demonstrates to the society that it is a mechanism by which primary social and economic objectives can be achieved. This is not an easy shift for business to make, as evidenced by the fact that in a recent briefing of U.S. businessmen going on a mission to Latin America to discuss problems of investment with government officials, they were instructed by group leaders on how to argue *against* regulations promulgated by the host governments. (A similar approach has characterized representations of U.S. companies to the U.S. Embassy against the alien decrees in developing countries.) Only after it was pointed out to them by an observer that a more fruitful approach would be to discuss with the host government officials how business could *help* achieve governmental objectives of social transformation and economic development did the group see that there was an alternative approach. Though some saw this as a desirable alternative, not all did. (A similar problem of identification is evident in the attitudes of Peruvian business to the revolutionary regime in that country.) If the governmental objectives are seen as representative or valid (even if *not* deemed sound or desirable by foreign companies) business should adopt those same objectives— not seeking ways to avoid doing so in the pursuit of profit. Preferably, business (as one of the social actors) should play a role in helping shape the social (and governmental) goals. Where it does not do so, it is often seen as incapable. Acquisition of this capability and demonstration of a willingness to be constructive in seeking social solutions would alter radically the role of business. (It is not suggested that the moves would be the same in all countries; on the contrary, "constructive" solutions will likely vary considerably from country to country.) Such a shift in roles will undoubtedly reinforce the positive attitudes called for.

As business has successfully assisted countries in achieving a level of abundance and the removal of abject poverty, national goals (and recently international goals) have turned more toward social welfare (public goods) and the effective use of resources. Pursuit of these goals will require changes in company policies and activities and frequently the elimination of a whole product line. For example, the decline of the large, high-powered automobile in the U.S. will bring a potential reallocation of resources away from those with high incomes toward greater variety of goods for those with lower incomes, requiring a shift in business operations and objectives.

A final necessary change in orientation is that of acceptance by business of a social responsibility in the process of pursuing its goals, among which is the maintenance of "satisfactory" profits. Society will no longer accept the argument that socially responsible actions on the part of business can occur *only after* profits have been made. If profits cannot be made in socially responsible activities and operations, then they should not be made. Other companies, doing other things with the same resources, can make profits while at the same time undertaking socially acceptable modes of operation. Acceptance of social responsibilities will not necessarily lower profits; it may merely elicit a more effective set of management decisions, and is likely also to increase the productivity of the workers involved who see themselves as being better treated and receiving greater respect, from which will come a greater contribution to their own or the world community.

These changes need to be made not just from the top but all the way through company activities. Once accomplished, or even begun, the decisions and attitudes mentioned above will be accelerated. And governments will feel reinforced in the view that business can adopt an orientation toward pursuit of mutual objectives.

Mechanisms and Procedures

The changes in attitudes and relationships recommended above are likely to produce some changes in the mechanisms for communication between government and business in the U.S.

The first is that the quality of the dialogue within industry associations and business groups would be improved and turned toward a pursuit of mutual objectives with governments. This is already occurring, as evidenced by the efforts on the part of the international committee of the U.S. Chamber of Commerce, by the reorientation of recommendations coming out of the National Foreign Trade Council, by the reports coming out of the U.S. Council of the International Chamber of Commerce, and the dialogues occurring under the sponsorship of the Council of the Americas. A recognition that government officials would be interested in the results of such communications would elicit a desire on the part of the companies to make inputs on policies prior to the government's conclusion of departmental deliberations. Acceptance of the necessity to pursue mutual objectives would remove the concept that business objectives ought to be determined apart from considerations of government interests and then presented to government in an adversary proceeding.

A second change that should be considered by international companies is that of upgrading the role of the Washington representative. In only a few companies is this official brought into the policy-making council at headquarters.[b] A few are involved in this way and have a high rank within the company; their inputs in terms of governmental interests at home and those of the State Department are given serious consideration in policy formulation by the company. The fact that this individual is fitted into the top council makes his representation more effective in Washington with government officials. He should become an effective officer on the home scene, and should also have the opportunity for frequent trips to regional "management centers" abroad in order to understand better what the emerging problems are there that concern the U.S. government as well as the company.

[b]The representative is *not* in policy groups largely because most companies do not see "Washington relations" as a significant policy issue at present. As they begin to alter this perception the role of the "Washington rep." will change. But, a good and perceptive "Washington rep." would hasten the shift in company policy by showing the relationship between company and government actions and goals.

At present, most Washington representatives have little contact with State Department officials—seeking them out only for information or special problems. There is little felt need on the part of either companies or State for closer contact. But this fact reflects precisely the stand-off attitude that will have to be changed if the problems of business are brought more into the forefront of State's interests and companies are to cooperate more closely in the formation of policies.

To make the dialogue more effective would require a periodic input on the part of companies to the information of country desk officers in State, as well as to economic officers dealing with specific industrial sectors or problem areas. A useful exercise would be the coupling of business advisers to State's country-desk officers; these advisers would not be attached to the Department, but remain in their positions. The objective would not be for the outside advisers to second-guess the decision of the desk officers; it would be to make such advisers available for telephonic or personal communication on actions that the desk officer felt seriously involved business interests abroad. The adviser would, of course, not necessarily be the officer consulted on a problem affecting his own company. Such one-on-one relationships produce a mutual understanding that cannot be gained by large group dialogue, nor do personnel interchanges spread the dialogue widely enough. The same business adviser would take back into the company a much closer appreciation of the problems facing government and better advice to the company as to how to adapt its activities so as to reduce the pressure on governments.

In addition, desk officers (or economic officers) should be invited, as they are now on many occasions, to meetings of the international committees of trade associations, such as the American Motor Association, the Pharmaceutical Manufacturers Association, Machinery and Allied Products Institute, etc. In this way they establish an acquaintance with individual businessmen and have a chance to discuss problems of international business in their sector of responsibility. The objective is to expand contacts and understanding—not to grease a channel for influence. One of the results of the above recommendations would be an improved flow of information from business to the government. Presently, information is obtained from U.S. companies for aggregate statistical purposes or to respond to particular legislative or regulatory problems. Even more desirable would be a continuous flow of information, on an industrial sector or country basis, relative to significant problems created by the activities of international companies both at home and abroad. The determination of what information should be made available, in how much depth, how frequently, and how publicized (if at all) would be easily made if a closer communication existed, as suggested in the prior paragraphs. The absence of such flows has fed the desire of business to protect itself against what were considered unwarranted pressures at home and abroad—such as in the tax legislation of 1962; lack of response to expropriation, resulting in congressional passage of the Hickenlooper amendment; and the more recent Burke-Hartke bill.

Finally, with closer communication, it is conceivable that we would eventually get a resolution of one of the more difficult problems facing U.S. government-business relations abroad—that of the selection of particular companies to support or promote in a foreign country. Historically, the U.S. government has shied away from supporting any one company, on the grounds that there were usually several U.S. companies interested in a particular project or investment situation. Other countries have found it possible to select a given company (usually in rotation under cohesive procedures adopted by the companies themselves—as in Germany, France, The Netherlands, and Japan). As a consequence, the full support of the U.S. government has not been behind U.S. business. At times, U.S. companies have lost out on this ground. Support of particular projects has been at such a high level that the Dutch have used Prince Bernhardt, and former President Pompidou was cited in business journals as pushing hard for the adoption of French color television abroad.

Instructions to U.S. embassies were drafted in 1973 to give them discretionary power to support a single U.S. company *if* it was clear that it had a greater chance of success than others; but the instructions were withheld at the request of the legal counsel in State. Though Commerce has stated it would make such a selection within its programs, not all businessmen feel that this action is equitable in a competitive society. The criteria for making this determination are not clear, and any one company could complain that the criteria were inappropriate or misapplied, and that it was damaged. A closer coordination of the sort suggested here would ease disputes by resolving them within the U.S. before they show up abroad. If this problem of company selection can be solved, the U.S. embassies would put more effort behind particular U.S. business proposals—since there would be no others in the running. At present, they are permitted to stand aside, doing little or nothing except to show an interest in a specific company initiative; worse, the initiative of a company may be given strong support by the embassy, only to see that support weakened when another U.S. company enters the competition for a particular project. (It is likely that this problem cannot be resolved by a general guideline. At times, embassies do give informal preference to one company over another. Wider acceptance of this approach will come only with broad rapport between business and government under more cooperative relations.)

It must be admitted that there are times and conditions in which close cooperation would not be advantageous for one or the other party. A company will not want to appear close to the U.S. government when the latter is in conflict with the host government; the embassy will not want to get close to a company that has been demonstrably acting in bad faith with the host government or influential people in the country. But these are specific cases, and do not violate the rule of desirable closer cooperation. They do emphasize that cooperation must be built on open and honest dealings, which in turn can be demonstrated only through the passage of all relevant and timely information between the parts and to the host government.

No claim is made for the above recommendations that they will bring a new era in business-government relationships. But they would constitute a significant start, toward changing basic attitudes. Without them, it is probably useless to proceed to consideration of the next steps or alternatives available. But with them, the next moves gain considerable force and justification.

Shift in International
Economic Priorities

Recognition of the importance of the activities of international companies for U.S. international economic policy will require a shift in the ranking of priorities. Both State and the embassies will need to recognize the increased significance (absolute and relative) of economic and commercial relations compared to political-military relations, as the threat of armed conflict recedes in the face of greater economic interdependence and the commercial ties stemming from investment and trade. And within economic policies a further shift is occurring from trade to investment.[3] Postwar economic policies of the U.S. were dedicated to a removal of barriers to trade, stability in foreign-exchange rates, and the provision of long-term finance for the reconstruction and development of countries. The initiatives of international companies have relegated these policies to a lower priority. The U.S. government urged licensing of technology and an expansion of investments abroad in the 1950s. The stabilization of exchange rates and the reduction of trade barriers accelerated the integration of operations of international companies at least among the developed countries on the new bases established by licensing and investment.

The result is the development of an international economy better described as "international production" than as "international trade." This phenomenon is causing reorientation of policies and priorities. It leads towards a concern for the allocation and distribution of business activities (extractive, industrial, and service) around the world.

The first shift, therefore, is to consider trade more subservient to investment activities than has historically been the case. The second is to recognize the decline in usefulness of concepts of competition compared to those of cooperation. And the third is to consider policies toward business in an integrated (or sectoral) fashion rather than by separate functional operations, calculating the trade-offs between particular policies directed at specific international companies or industrial sectors rather than simply looking at each policy separately.[4]

Production vs. Trade

There is enough statistical evidence now to indicate that international production is more important quantitatively than the flow of international trade. This is not only true for the world as a whole, but is even more the case for U.S. economic activities abroad. International production amounted to well over $400 billion in 1973, of which half belonged to U.S. international companies, while world exports in 1973 amounted to $350 billion, of which one-fifth was U.S., and 65 percent of U.S. (nonagricultural) exports were at the hands of U.S. companies also investing abroad.

The integration of the world economy is occurring not only through trade, but more important, through the allocation of industrial and service activities by international companies, especially in developed countries. This allocation of activity, under company criteria of efficiency and benefit, is quite different from what would occur if barriers to investment remained and trade were free. The principles guiding such decisions are different from those which guided the formation of the postwar international economy, and U.S. policies must respond to these shifts. The responses will have to take place in the underlying principles and theory of international economic integration as well as in the procedures of policy formation and its implementation.

The first shift that will have to take place is a recognition that the process of integrating the world economy is no longer proceeding as much on the basis of comparative advantage theory as on location theory. This will be a difficult shift to make, if for no other reason than that international economists have been trained much more in trade theory, based on the concept of comparative advantage, than they have on location theory related to business decisions on where to place a given operation. They have only recently concluded that trade is not a complete substitute for factor movements. Once it is recognized that factors of production will move internationally even if there are no barriers to trade, greater attention will have to be paid to the location of industrial and service activities than previously.

Tariff protection has existed around the world as a means of redistributing the benefits of economic growth. The removal of all tariffs will not remove this concern for the distribution of benefits, which will be sought by other interferences such as nontariff barriers (NTBs). And efforts to remove NTBs without addressing the problem of benefit-sharing are doomed to frustration if not failure. Each nation will seek to make certain that industries are located in such a way as to benefit itself. Increasingly, concern for industrial policies guiding the location and development of specific sectors will take precedence over trade policies. Trade patterns and trade policies will themselves largely be determined by the industrial policies.

Trade is already largely a consequence of investment activities around the world. Data from the U.S. Department of Commerce and the U.K. Board of Trade indicate that a substantial portion of U.S. and British exports and imports are at the hands of international companies and are in fact intracompany trade. Industrial trade patterns, therefore, and much of the income arising from international services, are a result of the investment decisions to locate activities in various countries of the world. Reduction of trade barriers, or even an increase, will not necessarily affect the patterns of intracompany trade significantly. As a result of substantial cooperative arrangements within Europe and between Europe and Third World countries on research and development, production, marketing, and technology transfers, more and more trade will be determined by investment activities and interaffiliate relations.

In addition, the expansion of service activities, which lend themselves not to trade but rather to investment abroad, will increase the emphasis on the problems of location of services rather than the trade of goods. Finally, the pattern of resource trade and development will be determined largely by the location of industrial activity, which in turn is influenced by the investment decisions of international companies.

A primary policy shift is likely away from trade toward consideration of the desirability and impact of factor movements. The State Department still has a number of individuals and groups working on trade problems, but an insignificant priority is given to the problems of the different types of capital flow and the resulting complex activities and impacts of international business. For example, the discussions of exchange rate stability and the new international monetary system have taken place with considerable disregard for the impact on company decisions as to investment and the location of industrial activities—decisions that will undoubtedly affect the structure of the U.S. balance of payments and therefore the strength of the dollar.

This myopia on the problems of international business results from two major factors; professional training of economists and organizational structure of the U.S. government. Officials dealing with the problems of business are not predominantly economists, nor predominantly trained in business administration; they come from varied backgrounds through the Foreign Service. But economists are more numerous than business majors in State's offices responsible for foreign economic policy. Academic training of international economists is almost wholly related to problems of finance and trade; only recently has direct investment been included in the texts, and little Ph.D. research has been directed toward policy problems raised by direct investment. The subject has not yet been taken into the body of international economics as a significant element; therefore, those concerned with policy still see as the major issues those of trade and payments. (Each of these subjects is supported by a body of theory that tells them "how" these "should" be carried out: trade under a system of nondiscriminatory market decisions, and payments under a system of "undistorted equilibrium." But both criteria are largely irrelevant to the operational decisions of international companies.) It is understandable that international economists will take as policy issues those that they can fit into their training.

Professionals trained in schools of business administration would not be much better prepared, for few schools require acquaintance with international business and only a few provide specialization in the subject. Both tend to keep their tools, concepts, and problems compartmentalized not only from each other but also apart from political, psychological, or sociological aspects. Holistic approaches are avoided, despite the fact that problems of business are holistic.[5] The Department should encourage generalists with both economic and business administration training to apply, and it should seek to remedy their educational deficiencies, as the OMB report recommends.

The second source of myopia is organizational, resulting from the fact that no single administrative unit has adequate responsibility for the varied problems raised by international business. The Overseas Private Investment Corporation (OPIC) has been trying to promote investment; Commerce's Office of International Investment is promoting two-way direct investment; State's regional bureaus may be required to handle particular problems, such as expropriation; State's Economics-Business (EB) bureau has some responsibility for policy on investment and trade. The White House's CIEP has the entire range of foreign economic policies, but it was (in mid-1974) under a chairman both untrained and inexperienced in problems of international business or economics, with a staff composed largely of lawyers.

Ten years ago, a census of governmental units concerned with business abroad totaled forty-four; a count one year ago showed over eighty having some responsibility or interest. This situation is a prescription for "no policy," which is exactly what exists, for each department or agency jealously guards its prerogatives and position. Since each insists on handling its *former* problems, new ones do not get picked up readily, especially ones that require cross-departmental coordination.

An example of the need for such coordination is seen in the role of labor. The movement of labor or the prevention of its movement among countries is a critical factor in the location of industrial and service activity. This problem has largely been left to the Department of Labor both in terms of its impact on the U.S. and representation on the issues in the International Labor Organization, as well as within the embassies. But, as both the French and Germans have recently argued, it is probably better to take industry to the foreign workers than to bring the workers to France and Germany. Somewhat the same argument was involved in the permission to use border industries in Mexico as plants for the production of products to be used in the U.S. But the result is an increase of investment and a potential shift of jobs from the U.S. to Mexico, affecting not only labor but the volume of trade, pressure on the exchange rates, and the political relations between the U.S. and Mexico. This issue appears to be handled as much as anywhere by the Customs Bureau of the U.S. Treasury Department— as though it were a tariff matter!

We have found that we can move everything around the world except land—and the resources under the land (soil, sand, humus) can be moved, and qualities (fertility) of the land itself can be altered by international movement of chemicals. This mobility of factors reduces *comparative* advantages in trade and has a strong impact on the location of industrial activity over the world and the form of international business arrangements—as witness the contracts made between Japanese business and Australian and Arabian resource suppliers. To the extent that concern for location of industry is included in policy formation at all, it is handled separately by the Department of Commerce or Interior, and there is a special group in State concerned with oil problems, which are presumed to be distinct from other sectoral problems.

Finally, the transfer of technology is itself a factor movement—not generally included within the neoclassical concepts of trade. It is a strong factor in determining not only the structure of trade but also the pattern of investment. This problem has not yet been given a high enough priority within the government, and is dispersed among different groups within it, most of which are more concerned with the methods of developing science and technology than with international transfers.

Related to the possibilities of factor movements is the facilitation of transportation. The continued reduction of transportation costs for all sorts of commodities and factors (including knowledge and personnel) is altering the structure of production around the world and the patterns of trade. Although there is a unit within the State Department concerned with transportation issues, its concern is not integrated into a full-fledged policy concerning the development of international business.

As recognized above, one of the major obstacles to reordering of these priorities is the fact that the officials who have been in charge of State Department policies have often been trained in other matters, and have experience in trade policy rather than in business policy. Considerable effort will be needed to force the required reorientation of personnel—as discussed on pages 165-183. But the task will have to be done if State is to orient its policies toward what is happening on the international economic scene.

Cooperation vs. Competition

The increasing concern among countries over the distribution of the benefits of economic growth—internally as well as among countries—will reorder the priority between the desires for competition as compared to cooperation. This means that the Justice Department (Antitrust Division) will have to be brought into line under a total policy of the U.S. government towards international business. The Justice Department cannot be permitted to pursue the creation of a structure of international market activity dictated by past concepts of what is good within the domestic "competitive" system, when the concept is so out of phase with the structure and operation of international companies. For example, the Andean countries are trying to rationalize their industry on a new integrated pattern, but to do so is likely to require combinations of foreign-owned companies negotiated by the companies themselves. It is not clear how far the Justice Department will permit U.S. companies to participate.

Nor can competition be an effective guiding principle when the market is no longer accepted as the allocation mechanism because of "absolute" scarcities, as occurs for food and other goods in catastrophes or other tight situations. A major economic objective in this case becomes that of allocation of scarce goods and benefits to produce an equitable distribution of the resources.

Even when there is an abundance and no pressure on scarce resources, a substantial inequality in the distribution of the benefits of growth around the world will induce governments to force a redistribution through cooperative arrangements or bilateral monopoly. Criteria for the allocation of goods or resources and the distribution of final products will have to be developed by other than market criteria.

Melding of Policies

The two shifts noted above mean that there will have to be substantial coordination among the different elements of the government responsible for international economic activities. And the historical guiding principle of "multilateral, nondiscriminatory trade and payments" can no longer be employed as the sole policy rule. The problem is to permit the market to determine the patterns of investment and trade in those areas where it is still an acceptable guide, and to employ other means in areas where it is no longer acceptable. An illustrative case is the U.S.-Canadian auto agreement; the efficiency criterion of free trade was supplemented by equity concepts of acceptable location of production (more investment in Canada) and acceptable payments effects (balance in trade in autos and parts). When the balance in auto trade in U.S. accounts with Canada turned into a deficit, the State Department sought a renegotiation of the arrangement. More recently the U.S. government has objected to "unfair" prices in oil, which reflect the scarcity created by a high "reservation price" by producing countries—a "free market" tactic of any supplier. The nonmarket criteria of acceptability will rest on other than (static or solely market) efficiency—including not only equity, but participation in the processes of production and decision making, and a sufficient interdependence to remove the fear of dependence among countries.

At the same time that coordination of policies is achieved, activities of international companies must be disaggregated so as to separate policies directed toward particular industries, services, hotels, banks, and extractive industries, for their impacts are quite different on host countries, and U.S. government goals.[6] How to make the trade-offs involved is a question of policy and will depend on the orientations adopted to reflect the increasing significance of the international companies around the world economic scene. But whether these shifts occur is a question of structural reorientation, for without that no policy change is likely to be implemented.

Structural Reorientation

As suggested by the requirement to meld separate policies directed presently by different departments of the government, a reorientation of various agencies in the Executive Branch will be needed to create a better government-business communication on international issues. Although, historically, it may have been true that international trade was carried out predominantly by one group, while another group conducted international short-term capital movements, another international long-term portfolio movements, and still others some direct investment abroad, this separation no longer reflects business operations abroad. Rather, the same international companies tend to be involved in all these, plus the transfer of technology and management skills, and even the inducement for labor to move. From our discussions with business and government officials, it is clear that the responsibility for a reorientation of governmental structure rests with the State Department, since it has repeatedly been assigned the final responsibility for foreign policy.

Several officials in business and the Department of Commerce argued that the reorientation needed was so drastic that it simply could not be undertaken by State alone, and would not be undertaken if left to State to initiate and implement. Hence, they supported initiatives to take economic policy out of State or at least to place the Commercial Service in Commerce. Both of these alternatives have been examined by the Office of Management and Budget in its study of the economic/commercial responsibilities of the Foreign Service; its assessment of the undesirability of doing so is cogent and persuasive.[7] The overriding reason for retention of the responsibility by State is that foreign policy is increasingly an integrated whole and business activities affect many facets of foreign policy—cultural affairs and public relations, military, science and technology, agriculture, aid, labor, commercial, financial, and political.

A separate service abroad exists for Agriculture, and Treasury has its own attachés at important posts. But Commerce needs a representative at *all* posts, and its activities impinge on all others, while those of the other two departments can be separated fairly distinctly. In addition, the separation of commercial from economic activities is a wholly spurious one, supported only by the unwillingness of State to integrate them properly and by the specious separation that exists within academic disciplines. The separation has adverse implications for international business, because some problems simply fall between the stools. If economic officers (and many ambassadors) are uneager to handle business problems, company officials quickly get the message and do not bring issues to their attention. Commercial officers may be sympathetic but too far from the ambassador to influence him. Where the ambassador has taken an interest or the economic and commercial officers have worked in tandem—as we witnessed in a few posts—some significant issues were being handled (for example, the plight of the pharmaceutical companies in Spain).

If State proves once again that it is unwilling to take appropriate measures—especially after the extensive and detailed recommendations of the OMB report—it will have no argument against those who assert that commercial work and the problems of international business will simply not be met appropriately under State's tender care. The loss of the role of coordinator to a special Assistant in the White House was a direct result of the failure of two efforts at the undersecretary level in State, reflecting a lack of understanding of how to bring other departments into the decision-making process *or* a lack of will to do more than go through the formal motions. Ideally, the White House would not be in the picture as the coordinator; rather, the special assistant to the president would be free to focus on special problems, leaving coordination to State.

A reorientation will require some organizational shifts, but no reorganization on any major scale. But these shifts will have to reflect, and be supported by, strong leadership from the top—the president on down—and woven into the fabric of operations, organization, promotion, assignment, reporting, and assistance to business by State, Commerce, and embassy personnel.

State's Responsibilities

For State to exercise full responsibility in the areas affected by international business, three jurisdictional conflicts require resolution: that between Commerce and EB in State, that between EB and the regional bureaus in State, and that between the commercial attachés and economic officers in the embassies. Only if attention is paid to fairly mundane problems of rank, reporting, promotion, etc. can a new policy orientation be implemented successfully. It will take strong leadership at all levels in State to make the needed changes, but attitudes may simply be too ingrained to permit such changes in the lifetime of any top official.[c]

The unwillingness of State to take a strong initiative in the direction of solving the problems discussed here is illustrated by the fact that it failed on two

---

[c]Deputy Secretary of State Irwin promulgated a twelve-point program for immediate action in August 1972 to strengthen business services and trade promotion, but no great turnaround was evident eighteen-months later. For example, the redesignation of positions as "economic/commercial" rather than "economic" and "commercial" was left to the posts, and few did so.

Apochryphal or not, a story is told that Averell Harriman resigned as Secretary of Commerce to become European Director for ECA partly because he considered that it would take fifteen years to turn Commerce around effectively; a period five times the expected career life of a Secretary.

occasions to implement agreements worked out after painstaking negotiations with Commerce (in 1961 and 1966) on the handling of its responsibilities abroad by the Commercial Service.[d] The 1961 agreement between State and Commerce provided for a separate Commercial Service within the Foreign Service, offering FSOs the opportunity to opt into a separate career ladder, the top of which would be commercial counselor or possibly minister is a few posts (ranks were determined in agreement with Commerce, though agreement was difficult to achieve, post by post). Additional officers were to be placed in the Service to increase the numbers committed to commercial work. Given the long-standing bias in the Foreign Service against commercial work, not enough officers opted into the commercial career, and Congress permitted little expansion of the numbers assigned abroad.

Since the Senate Commerce Committee had failed to pass a bill to create a completely separate Commercial Service (similar to that for Agriculture), and since the separate career ladder within the Foreign Service failed, an agreement was worked out in 1966 recombining the assignments into an integrated economic-commercial career cone, with potential promotion to ministerial ranks.

The 1966 arrangement provided for integration of the economic-commercial tasks and services in the following fashion:

1. Establishment of a separate economic/commercial career ladder within the Foreign Service, with lateral movement between this ladder and others, especially with the political career ladder;

2. Uniform designation of "economic-commercial" for all officers; including minister-counselor, officers, and attachés, rather than "economic," "commercial," or "trade promotion" officers;

3. Making E/C competence and program management capability a required qualification for officer assignments to senior positions abroad that involve these functions and responsibilities to an important degree;

4. Utilizing the position activity profiles of officers in the assignment and promotion process to assure that E/C officers meet the requirements for the position and are rewarded.

The arrangement also provided for cooperative review of the program at the embassies between State and Commerce. It concluded that "If these recommendations are accepted, the negotiation of a State-Commerce agreement to replace that of November 15, 1961, or to formalize the integration of E/C activities and personnel within the Foreign Service, *is not recommended*" (italics in original). This faith in a mere understanding (though written out in detail) which was not codified or made into a formal agreement (treaty?) was, as it

---

[d]Not all the responsibility for failure rested with the State Department in the early case, for Congress and Commerce also failed in some respects, but the final responsibility was still with State. State's failure in the second case was admitted by Deputy Secretary Irwin (Memo of August 1972).

turned out, a mistake. Apparently, State would fulfill only formal agreements, or (like any sovereign) only those seen in its interest. And it has not been seen in the interest of those in authority to alter the low priority of economic/commercial activities or departmental support for them.

The evidence obtained in our interviews was that the projected integration was quite spotty abroad, and within State itself there were many top officials who did not know of the 1966 agreement or its provisions.[e] The OMB concluded in its report of January 1973 that State had failed to implement the agreement, and proposed that it be done forthwith—seven years later! For example, in November 1972 it was considered necessary in a cable outlining a new program related to export opportunities in major foreign projects to stress the desirability of establishing a "country team" subcommittee, composed of economic officers, AID officers, the consular section, Treasury, military, and Agricultural attachés, and other officers having access to information on emerging major projects so as to obtain early evidence of opportunities. Such a combined effort was not considered "standard operating procedure" for business opportunities.

The OMB report made forty recommendations concerning programs in the economic-commercial area and forty-seven recommendations concerning administration, recruitment, promotion, assignment, training, etc. A quick search of the files in the Office of Commercial and Business Affairs in State's EB area showed only one cable to the posts concerning OMB's recommendations—it urged establishment of better communications with American businessmen abroad. In addition, Commerce and State's regional bureaus have been working out new "country commercial programs" for transmission to the posts. A cable sent in December 1973 queried posts as to their procedures and urged consideration of a technique used in Tokyo of holding seminars on particular issues, rather than the long-standing "ambassador's group" in which briefing of businessmen and their debriefing for the ambassador occurred on a monthly basis. (Of course, the commissioning of the present study is itself a strong evidence of concern on the part of some in State for the future of the economic/commercial function.)

Pressure from the Senate Committee on Commerce, reflected in a bill proposed in 1971 and again in 1972 to create a separate International Commerce Service, had been the cause of the OMB study. State testified, again, that it agreed with the need to give strong support for business objectives and problems overseas, but that a separate Commercial Service was not desirable. In testimony before the Senate Committee in June 1973, Deputy Secretary of State Rush

---

[e]To the outside observer this may seem quite curious, but the ways of Washington are such as to produce forgetfulness in many instances. Given the fact of rapid rotation of officers from post to post, abroad and in Washington, institutional memory tends to be rather short. In the case of the State-Commerce Agreement, implementation occurred at only a few embassies, so few officers returning to Washington could bring back experiences of how the agreement worked, or even that it was in existence. In addition, new entrants into the Foreign Service or into the economic-commercial career cone would not necessarily know.

agreed with the recommendations of the OMB report, calling it a "thorough, deliberate, and impartial" study, and affirmed the president's decision to keep the Commercial Service integrated within the Foreign Service.

He noted further that State had upgraded the highest-ranking economic office in the Department from deputy undersecretary to undersecretary, to be filled by William Casey (formerly of the SEC).[8] And the position of assistant secretary for economic and business affairs was filled in February 1972 by Willis Armstrong, with strong business connections. (However, both individuals left their posts in early 1974, providing a continuity of less than a year in one case and just over two years in the other.) Rush also stressed the economic/commercial experience of the director general of the Foreign Service and two deputy directors of personnel in State, without indicating whether they had served in commercial or economic positions under the "coordinated, but not integrated" structure of the past.

On the OMB recommendations he reported that "Secretary Rogers has *urged each mission* to study carefully the possibility of reorganizing its economic and commercial work into a more fully integrated function" (emphasis added). This is, of course, a far cry from laying out the new structure and commanding adherence, but secretaries Kissinger and Rush have since visited many posts emphasizing the need for integration. (One State official pointed to the integrative moves recently in Tokyo, Manila, and the Hague.) Rush further reported that "Commercial Coordinators have been designated in the five regional bureaus in the Department . . . responsible for commercial programs and policies in their bureaus." This is undoubtedly a step in the right direction, but implementation will require considerable diplomacy within the Department and *strong* support from the top in reordering priorities in each bureau. The Deputy Assistant Secretary for Commercial and Business Activities was designated as the coordinator of all commercial programs among the bureaus and with the Department of Commerce.

As to promotion of economic/commercial officers, Deputy Secretary Rush reported that one-fourth of the Deputy Chief of Mission positions would be filled by such officers, and that since this determination five of twenty-seven such assignments had come from this career ladder; nine more officers came from another ladder but had economic/commercial experience.[f] Assignments to executive and program direction positions in the bureaus in State, he stated, were also to be opened up to economic/commercial officers, since they had been formerly almost exclusively reserved for political officers. In addition, overseas positions had been reprogrammed from other areas into commercial activities. Senior officers posted to economic/commercial minister posts in London, Paris, Bonn, Rome, Saigon, and Tokyo were now eligible for rank of career minister by virtue of these assignments. Within "the promotion rating of all Foreign Service

[f]*The Inspection Report* (op. cit., pp. 51-2) had stressed the unequal opportunity of economic/commercial officers to rise to high positions because of a lack of past assignments to the regional bureaus in State which controlled such positions.

Officers" in the future would be a "demonstrated concern for American business interests," with the intent of linking "their performance in assisting U.S. business" to their career path. Finally, in their post inspections, "Foreign Service inspectors have been instructed to pay particular attention to the commercial performance of overseas missions."

The fact that this testimony was deemed necessary and that so much of it hinged on the word "now" demonstrates the gap between the agreement in 1966 and State's performance. In 1966, a deputy assistant secretary of commerce had been brought into the Foreign Service in State and put in a new post of deputy assistant secretary for commercial and business affairs for the express purpose of looking at specific business problems and coordinating the commercial activities between State and Commerce. He found the work exceedingly difficult, given the absence of lines into the regional bureaus. This gap has been filled only recently. And the instruction to the Foreign Service inspectors to examine commercial efforts of the entire embassy repeats one given them in 1961, followed by extensive briefings by the Assistant Secretary of Commerce. This continued delay shows that constant vigilance is required to make progress in this field. State apparently responds only to pressure. But the present official in charge feels that there is a considerably greater favorable response of late both by embassies and inspection teams, but inspections are only once every three years—longer than the career life of most secretarial officers.

As to training of economic/commercial officers, Deputy Secretary Rush testified that, besides the regular twenty-six-week course offered by the Foreign Service Institute twice a year, a new series of one-week seminars had been instituted;[g] increased time to economic and energy matters was being programmed into the Institute and the National War College courses, a new six-week workshop on international business was being developed for commercial officers, economic/commercial conferences were to be planned jointly by Commerce and State (whereas previously they were held separately abroad), ten officers were being sent to universities to study economic and business subjects at the graduate level (continuing past programs), and increasing emphasis would be placed on officer exchanges between State and Commerce.

Further cooperative efforts between State and Commerce have been developed on a variety of commercial programs, including personnel assignments. However, conversations with top economic officers in State brought agreement that present economic officers are not adequately trained to carry out expanded tasks related to overall international business problems, that a bias among them against commercial work remains, and that the lack of effort to carry out the 1966 arrangement was largely a matter of poor institutional memory. But, like the OMB report, they argued that separation of commercial and economic work

[g]Better recruitment and training were also urged in the *Inspection Report* (pp. 17 & 53-4), which found that, despite past efforts, and good accomplishments, economic officers were not prepared adequately to deal with emerging problems in international business.

would simply not be effective, even if commercial activities were defined quite narrowly. This leaves the proposition that integration is necessary to achieve effective and efficient programs, but that it cannot be accomplished without the full and active support of the State Department at *all* levels.

No formal initiatives will be worth much if they are unaccompanied by a change in attitudes—more forthcoming, more eager, more perceptive of the changes needed, and more willing to alter the past separation of assignments at the posts. The key change must occur in the selection boards which reward particular types of activities and orientations. If these are not composed of officers who sense the new directions, no change will occur. (The State official directly in charge of the commercial programs has no representation on these boards.) The reward system must reflect the actions and priorities desired.

To make integration work will require a restructuring of the relations between Commerce and State, between EB and the regional bureaus in State, and within the economic-commercial section of embassies. This restructuring should reflect reassignments of responsibilities and a new pattern of cooperation, which the present institutional attitudes, orientation, and organization makes virtually impossible. They can be changed only with considerable pressure from within State or from higher levels. Some officials argue that the intensified economic and commercial pressures are causing a radical shift in focus, and that the secretarial officers from Kissinger on down are urging more rapid reorientation of work priorities. If so, our visits to the embassies were a few months too early to see evidence of strong shifts.

EB relations with Regional Bureaus. The primary reorientation that is required is that of giving a higher priority within the regional bureaus to economic-commercial problems.[h] The "primary business" of State tends to be centered in these bureaus, and this business has been seen as political-military—that is, the keeping of the peace. But peace-keeping is different from constructing economic or commercial ties (despite the historical belief, oft repeated, that commerce creates peace). Evidence of the low priority given to economic-commercial work is the fact that EB is not invited to numerous top-staff meetings concerning foreign problems, because its interests are not considered integral or it is seen as unable to make a significant input.

The regional bureaus and the particular country desks are the channel through which all important (and many quite unimportant) communications

[h]The *Inspection Report* places primary emphasis on the responsibility of the EB area, and asserts, "If State can adequately perform its role in integrating economic and other aspects of policy, it should not be necessary to concentrate control of international economic policy and operations in a central coordinating body [outside of State]" (pp. 4-5). But it has been just this inability that caused the shift to the special trade representative (STR) and the CIEP. And one reason for the inability was a lack of internal coordination in State and a sufficiently high priority within the regional bureaus for economic/commercial activities. EB cannot coordinate when little is going on in the regional bureaus to coordinate.

have to pass and be approved. Any request of the embassy staff made by EB must be vetted through the relevant country desk, and if the policy affects several countries and has legal, UN, cultural-affairs, aid, and commercial implications, the approval of relevant officials in several subunits or other agencies will be required. (Cables with as many as forty "approving signatures" have been noted, though the usual clearances number *only* ten to fifteen!)

At present, a small percentage of officers tending to regional affairs and country desks have an economic background or economic-commercial assignment. There are a few staff positions in the bureaus calling for economic experience. But the major work of the bureaus does not encompass economic-commercial affairs. Without a higher priority for such work, career officers will not see it to their advantage to pay attention to these activities—neither while in the bureaus nor on foreign assignment. Therefore, this reorientation will have to be dictated from the top and infused throughout the regional bureaus by the process of policy emphasis, secretarial concern, promotion procedures, and post assignments. Presently, the OMB study concludes, State's procedures for promotion and assignment leave much to be desired in bringing about an appropriate reordering of priorities or the implementations of the agreement on economic-commercial integration.

EB Relations with Commerce. Over the past fifteen years Commerce and the economic area of State have had a running disagreement on who should have responsibility for different aspects of foreign economic policy.[i] Commerce had its own Commercial Service attached to the embassies prior to World War II, but it was melded into the Foreign Service in 1945, at a time when U.S. exports were in high demand by all countries and the problem was to get imports into the U.S. to cut the need for economic assistance. The shift to a balance-of-payments deficit in the late 1950s and the continuing drain of dollars brought a reorientation in Commerce's programs and a concern among businessmen over the allegedly unmatched reduction of U.S. tariffs in GATT negotiations.

At the end of the Eisenhower administration a drive was begun to expand

---

[i]The OMB report records the following perceptions of each agency of the other:

One of the most persistent criticisms made by State and Commerce of each other has been that the other agency fails to value the right things. In the view of Commerce and many businessmen, State is overly concerned with preserving good diplomatic relations at the expense of vigorous and direct pursuit of particular interests; with giving undue weight to political and military concerns; with according highest economic/commercial priority to negotiation of treaties, conventions, and other agreements among governments, which comprise the stuff of diplomatic accomplishments; and with remaining rigidly impartial and evenhanded in dealings with particular firms and business interests. Many State officials in turn see Commerce as unquestioningly reflecting the views of the business community; unwilling to recognize the limitations that a basically private enterprise economy places on any government effort to promote exports; and too ready to disrupt diplomatic relations and other foreign policy objectives by pressing hard on particular commercial issues, failing to recognize that other interests must be pursued and that a balance is necessary. [p. 130].

U.S. exports, coordinated under a National Export Expansion Council of businessmen advisers. A Trade Policy Committee (TPC) at the secretarial level was established to coordinate tariff negotiations, and placed under the Secretary of Commerce, shifting that responsibility from State; State, however, kept the Trade Agreements Committee, which did the staff work for the TPC. The Kennedy administration sought to place overall responsibility for foreign economic policy in State, with Commerce responsible for trade promotion. But the disagreement over policy responsibility extended into debates on the Trade Expansion Act of 1962. Commerce argued for the continuation of the Trade Policy Committee; State urged consolidation of all responsibility in it; and the White House, under congressional prodding, finally agreed to a compromise proposal for a special trade representative (STR) reporting to the president, and the TPC was eliminated.[j]

Commerce itself has a split personality in terms of its primary role in foreign economic affairs. It has not wholly resolved its duties of protecting domestic industry and promoting international business, nor the apparent dilemma of promoting exports but also investment (which has been seen as reducing exports), nor that of promoting international business while taking into account contrary economic or political interests. Although Commerce's prime role internationally had for many decades been that of promoting trade (mainly exports), its major role in the 1940s and 1950s had become import promotion, and in the early 1960s the total budget for the Bureau of Foreign Commerce was only $3 million. It was expanded by a factor of three in a period of four years, and the industry desks of the domestic bureau were dedicated to export promotion also when the two bureaus were combined under a single assistant secretary.

At the same time, the policy role of Commerce was expanded with the addition of staff personnel to handle issues of trade, tariffs, investments, licensing and antitrust, balance of payments, etc. State responded by creating an International Business Committee to handle business disputes abroad and by agreeing to a new arrangement in 1961 (mentioned above) on the commercial service. The undersecretaries' meetings were also a response to Commerce initiatives and similar pressure from Agriculture, in an effort to let others participate but still retain State's dominant role.

Under successive secretaries, the Commerce Department has not achieved a

---

[j]Commerce had a last-minute opportunity to retain control through legislative action in the Conference committee reconciling the Senate and House bills. In reference to the provision for responsibility for policy guidance, Congressman Mills turned to Secretary Hodges and asked: "Do you want this in Commerce or the White House?" Hodges turned to an aide and asked the same question. They quickly agreed to let it shift to the White House on the ground that, given the apparent inability of either State or Commerce to act objectively, there should be an intermediary at the White House to reconcile differences of view within the administration. (Agriculture was particularly eager to have the STR in the White House, because it felt that neither State nor Commerce weighed its interests adequately.)

significant role in policy determination in foreign economic policy, save in the area of East-West trade. Successive reorganizations of the Department have emphasized even more its role in trade promotion, and have not equally strengthened its ability to make an imprint on policy positions in foreign economic affairs. (The OMB report points out that the most recent reorganization diffuses the interests of the Department among so many bureaus that coordination by the assistant secretary will be virtually impossible. Consequently, Commerce's voice will depend more on personalities than on institutional strength.)

If Commerce sees its role predominantly in the area of trade promotion, its support for the varied activities of international business will be downgraded. And it does not seem to be organized in such a way as to raise or handle problems arising from international business activities other than trade disputes of a minor sort. Conversely, the Economic Affairs area of State was retitled Economic Business (EB) by Deputy Secretary Irwin in August 1972, showing greater concern for business operations, but not making them primary. (A suggestion that it be titled Business-Economics, showing the primacy of business problems over economic, met with resounding opposition when voiced in one of the meetings of the advisory groups to this research project.) And it has instituted a coordinating committee on emerging business problems likely to lead to expropriation, giving it a chance to influence company behavior or governmental reactions abroad.

The problem of expropriation involves interests that cut across not only State-Commerce but also EB and the regional bureaus within State. It affects AID through the Hickenlooper amendment, and Treasury through the Gonzalez amendment;[k] it raises political issues for the White House; it involves USIA; it affects OPIC; and it alters the general climate for international business and therefore government relations with parent companies in the U.S. It is a clear example of the reason integration of economic and commercial services is the appropriate way to move, rather than separation, *unless* some quite distinct activities can be carved out.

Separation appears to be an objective of at least the Bureau of International Commerce, but Commerce also faces schizophrenia if it tries to make trade promotion (or international marketing) paramount, for it is responsible for trade policy, international finance, and foreign investment as well. It also, therefore, has not yet recognized in its institutional structure the significance of shifts in business operations abroad from trade to international production and from mere investment to the location of business activity around the world. If these movements were recognized, the issues would not be posed so distinctly and

---

[k]The Hickenlooper amendment to the AID legislation requires the termination of assistance to any country that expropriates U.S.-owned property without adequate, prompt, and effective compensation; the Gonzalez amendment requires the U.S. government to oppose loans to any such country by international organizations.

separately. Export promotion is also a question of how to get investment abroad, and what investment, and where. Production abroad is also a question of competitiveness at home and reduction of injury to local interests. Shifts in industry location are also a question of trade policy, facilitating the desired movement of goods and components, and of aid and development policies. And resource development is also a question of East-West trade and coproduction arrangements.

Coordination among these problems appears presently in Commerce to be possible only at the level of the assistant secretary. The questions Commerce's Domestic and International Business Administration appears to seek to answer are the following: how to raise the U.S. share of exports around the world, how to fit the special case of East-West trade into export promotion (without losing key technologies), how to make U.S. industry more competitive in exports, how to offset the impacts of import competition, and how to obtain the needed resources for domestic growth and exports. Minor questions appear to be those related to trade policy, direct investment, and international finance. Commerce appears to be eschewing a role in the needed policy turnaround and to be narrowing the scope of its interests to commercial affairs. It will have to rely even more on the EB area of State, despite the fact that EB is itself not strong enough to press business interests within State.

In order to strengthen the role of EB in commercial affairs, the *Inspection Report* of the Foreign Service recommended that this area pay more attention to management of the Commercial Service than it has in the past, recognizing that the direct responsibilities lie within Commerce and the regional bureaus of State:

EB has no direct responsibility for the performance of commercial services, but it should:

—contribute, on behalf of State, to planning and programming commercial services—not only abroad but also their domestic aspects;

—integrate commercial services with commercial policy—particularly since it is commercial and monetary policy initiatives which shape the environment that determines the effectiveness of commercial services;

—support personnel performing commercial services, e.g., by monitoring their recommendations and initiatives to ensure that they receive full consideration and by acting as their main channel of communication and contact on substantive matters.[9]

The report asserts that the EB area has left these management functions primarily to the regional bureaus and Commerce and has concentrated instead on:

—coordinating economic/commercial reporting requirements and monitoring compliance;

—being the point of contact for the Department with American business;

—following-up *ad hoc* business complaints about foreign commercial services and acting as a liaison with business when other channels of communication fail with posts abroad or with Commerce.[10]

The report does not suggest that these activities be stopped. Rather, it proposes assumption of the managerial tasks alongside of these.[11]

Management of the commercial services, tied as they are to the country programs under the responsibility of the regional bureaus, cannot be a primary responsibility of EB; it can have only a coordinating or integrative role. It is, therefore, all the more necessary that the regional bureaus place a high priority on this work, in cooperation with Commerce, giving EB something to coordinate. The present "country commercial programs" do reflect a more cooperative stance on the part of State, but Commerce has no inputs into the economic programs of State or to the selection of "economic" officers, despite the supposed integration.

Economic-Commercial Section in Embassies. The embassy structure and responsibilities has reflected the hierarchy of relations outlined above. Political officers are the closest to the ambassador and DCM, who likely have come up through the political career cone; few of ministerial rank have come up through economic-commercial assignments. Within the economic and commercial sections, assignments in the larger embassies tend to be clearly distinguished between economic and commercial activities, with the latter further down on the rung of prestige and perquisites. One commercial officer stated that his representation allowance was meager in comparison to others, but was sometimes supplemented by cooperation with CIA officers. (CIA's potential use of a Commercial position as a "cover" has been given as a reason by some businessmen for not using the embassy.)

The commercial work is seen as clerical, mundane, and unexciting, with criteria of performance being numerical—how many reports and contacts made in a given period. Economic assignments have involved policy issues, discussions with governmental officials, and resolution of conflicts between the U.S. and other governments or business and the host government besides normal reporting activities. It is the exceptional post in which commercial officers are permitted to get involved in what are designated as economic assignments—however, if the post is small and work is heavy, the assignments tend to get merged. The OMB report shows a continuing strong perception on the part of both economic and commercial officers that the former have the best assignments and positions and the latter inferior ones. In one post, though the commercial officer outranked the economic officer, he reported through the latter and was evaluated by him for promotion. During discussions of the advisory group for this research, it was asserted that no "self-respecting" economic officer would take a commercial assignment.

The problem of the relative positions in economic and commercial assignments is the result of a vicious circle or a self-fulfilling prophecy: the assignment is seen as mundane and unexciting; therefore, officers less likely to be promoted to ministerial rank are assigned; their qualifications are such as not to expand the scope of the work beyond a narrow definition; performance and interest are seen as low level, perpetuating the assignment of less promotable officers.

This cycle raises problems for both State and Commerce. Both are trying to obtain more relevant, cost-effective, and imaginative commercial programs; to do so they have invited each post to submit projected tasks and assignments. These are reviewed by EB, the country desks, and Commerce. The American Republics Area (ARA) in State has a standing "action team" of the desk officer, an EB officer, and a Commerce official for each country to assess and agree on the Country Commercial Program (CCP) and to evaluate performance.

All recognize that the final key, however, is demonstration that performance on commercial/economic affairs will be a factor in the rating of *all* officers— from the ambassador on down—at each post. How this should be done remains in disagreement. Commerce has insisted on veto of officers going into commercial work so as to upgrade their qualifications and assign better ones to the most important posts; State has agreed only to Commerce having the ability to hold up an assignment pending further discussion—but not a veto. On its part, State sees Commerce as insisting on keeping a good commercial officer in that work (despite the desirability of shifting him to economic or political work to broaden his experience) and as trying to obstruct assignment of an economic or political officer into commercial work to gain experience. Commerce is likely to see such a shift as an attempt to get rid of a problem officer, even if State is in fact trying to assign higher quality personnel into the section. The past experiences are too strong to permit open-handed dealing without strong leadership from the top of each department.

If this leadership is to be exercised, it must run the full range of economic-commercial relations, not only integrating them but also tying them to political responsibilities both within State and the embassy, for the problems of international business will not yield to economic or commercial analysis or techniques alone.

Reconciliation Through Integration. As recognized in the OMB report, the resolution of the difficulties in meeting the problems of international business involving the U.S. government are conceptual and attitudinal—not organizational, in the sense that a complete reorganization of the government is required. The various proposals for reorganization stem from frustration at trying to change orientations within the existing structures. As the OMB also noted, if these changes are demonstrably impossible because of the ossification of viewpoints and attitudes, then reorganization, placing some responsibilities in completely new agencies, will be desirable and necessary. It will be desirable simply because the waste of resources in State and embassies trying to fulfill old assignments will become too burdensome and costly. It will be necessary because the problems raised by international business will have to be met in some different way, for they will not disappear simply because the government is not tooled up to handle them adequately.

The services usually rendered by the U.S. government to U.S. businesses abroad include at least the following three: promotion, assistance, and protection. In addition, the government sets the rules of the game, either unilaterally or in concert with other governments. Although these functions have not changed in seventy years or more, their content and complexity has altered significantly, and they are much more closely tied together in the same company activities within and across national boundaries.

It is conceivable to separate completely the task of promotion of exports, licensing, or investment abroad simply by defining the limits of promotional activity so as to preclude any but those necessary to put U.S. business in contact with foreigners or other U.S. businessmen and the AmCham; "get them through the door," so to speak. This activity would encompass virtually all of what is now being developed under the Country Commercial Program, but promotional activities would cease when interested parties were "introduced," leaving further processing or problem-solving to other embassy staff.

But to carry out these promotional functions it would be highly desirable to involve others than commercial officers. Many opportunities come up through military contacts. Economic and AID officials see opportunities emerging through development plans; science attachés will run upon opportunities in their field; and the ambassador himself discovers some on occasion. Basketball's "full court press" would be a much better strategy in discovering opportunities and promoting them than to leave the function to a single officer or small staff.

It is not possible to conceptualize distinctions among the remaining responsibilities of assistance, protection, and policy (rule-setting) that would permit a separation of responsibilities. The separation of "political" from "economic" work has meant an artificial demarcation of views and activities that will be an obstacle to the solution of emerging problems in international business. These problems cannot be dissociated from the earlier concepts of "political economy," which encompassed not only narrow economics but also social policy, welfare, and commercial and developmental policies. The academic separation of disciplines has too long been copied in the governmental structure, despite the fact that business problems are not labeled as to what elements are included and whether they will yield to one set of techniques or another. Increasingly they yield only to multiple techniques and approaches, involving a number of talents and viewpoints. The ambassador, having responsibility for all facets, should be familiar with and experienced in several aspects of embassy work so as to be able to draw expertly on the knowledge and competence of each of his specialists.

On the road up the promotion ladder, FSOs should be given experience in political, commercial, economic, and probably cultural affairs, as was agreed within the economic-commercial arrangement between State and Commerce in 1966. This is the responsibility of the selection boards, which in turn reflect the predominant interest in promotion and assignment of the regional bureaus. These must work more closely with EB and Commerce, which have places on the boards, in selecting experienced and promotable officers.

The central key to the restructuring of orientations, therefore, lies in the regional bureaus. They must become responsible for the entire country program, including political, economic, and commercial activities, in the sense of negotiating the terms of reference for officials overseas and of becoming committed to the fulfillment of the program agreed upon. They must become interested in the assignment of personnel into economic-commercial work, exchanging personnel in and out of the political and economic-commercial cones. If this is not done, the stigma on economic work will continue in comparison to political, and on commercial as compared to them both.

To accomplish this reorientation will require a reallocation of program time within the regional bureaus away from politico-military matters in favor of economic-commercial. Whether or not peace is built upon closer economic-commercial relationships, international business is tying economies, industries, resources, and service sectors closer together across national boundaries, with serious cultural and political consequences. Therefore, more personnel should be shifted into economic-commercial and out of political tasks.[1]

To force appreciation of these changes, all FSOs should be required to digest and implement the OMB report on economic-commercial assignments. With the assumption of this responsibility, EB could become effectively a staff function to the regional bureaus, but reporting to the undersecretary for economic affairs. It would continue its liaison with Commerce and among the regional bureaus to form a single international economic policy as appropriate. But policies toward different regions are likely to differ significantly, and the need to have expert economic analysis within each bureau will increase. Similarly, problems of different sectors (banking, extraction, services, and industries) will differ among themselves and within regions; hence, sectoral expertise will also be needed. To keep economic and commerical matters substantively out of the responsibility of the regional bureaus is to downgrade their importance in embassy programs, in promotion, in assignments, and therefore in policies. EB (and embassies) will need specialized capabilities on important sectors to support the country programs.

But to pass this responsibility to the regional bureaus without adequate preparation and training will itself produce a debacle. (More needs to be done in mid-career training of FSOs for economic-commercial work, as recommended in the OMB report.) This is the reason why so much emphasis has been given to having ambassadors with wide experience, and why disregard for this advice has

---

[1]This does not mean the kind of action that has already been taken to expand the number of economic-commercial slots simply by retitling a job as "economic-commercial" and proceeding with the same tasks as before—this was done to frustrate the intent of the 1966 agreement to some extent, and was repeated even after Deputy Secretary Irwin's orders in 1972. If a reduction of staff concerned with political-military matters results, this would fit with the recommendations of John F. Campbell in *The Fudge Factory* (N.Y.: Basic Books, Inc., 1971), where he argues that State is too big to function effectively, and that economic affairs should be reduced considerably and made a staff function to the regional bureaus, which should themselves be reduced greatly in size, along with embassy staffs.

produced a feeling of frustration and *déjà vu* with all recommendations to require a larger proportion of ambassadors to have economic-commercial experience.

At the same time that the regional programs are restructured, the terms of reference for the selection boards must be reoriented. Not only must the cone for economic-commercial tasks be one through which more FSOs are passed, but those with predominant experience in that cone must be increasingly tapped for ministerial posts.[m] This will *not* be done without the cooperation of the regional bureaus and the insistence of top-level officers, probably from the president down.

During 1974, the State Department did begin a "big push" to reverse the hierarchy of the past and put the economic/commercial assignments on top of the political/military. The Inspection Service was told to examine all posts with a view to the involvement of all officers in economic/commercial tasks, including the ambassador. And Review Boards for promotion and assignment were told to count more heavily any experience in economic/commercial positions. These are certainly steps in the right direction, but the task is far from completed with these shifts; more will have to be done to eradicate the "buddy system" of promotion and assignments under which senior officers look after each other and special friends in the younger ranks. More structured career planning for younger officers will be necessary, to make certain that they are passed through the appropriate positions. Both the "buddy system" and career advice have previously centered in the regional bureaus. It is there that the critical changes have to be made, shifting economic/commercial responsibilities to the desk officers and matching rewards to performance both in State and at the embassies.

If this move were undertaken, EB could become a specialized staff area, with thirty to forty professionals in longer-term assignments. This would provide a strong institutional memory, which is often lacking at State, and a level of expertise that is lost through frequent rotation. This staff could serve both the assistant secretary and undersecretary for economic affairs, and be liaison for the regional bureaus' economic officers with other departments of the government involved in economic policies or problems.

If these changes were made, the EB area could spend more time in coordination with other departments. The undersecretary for economic affairs should bring policy *coordination* back from the White House, and form an interagency group that functions as a unit to recommend policies to those that have to carry them out—the secretary of state, and through him to the president. The members of the undersecretary's group would be the assistant secretaries for international affairs in the various departments. To support this coordination the

---

[m]A recent decision required that 20 percent of the DCMs come from the economic-commercial cone. This is a step in the right direction, but must be supported by putting men of DCM quality into the cone.

EB assistant secretary should work in concert with assistant secretaries for the regional bureaus and representatives of other departments.

Procedures for effecting this cooperation exist. They have simply not been adopted by State in the past, causing coordination efforts to fail and be moved out of the Department to the White House. The basic procedure is to require inputs from all relevant departments concerning each issue, and to discuss the issue until a policy recommendation is forthcoming by the undersecretary at the meeting.

Once this recommendation is voiced, all participants would have a given period of time (seven to ten days) to object and force the matter to a secretarial meeting or the Cabinet. If no recommendation was forthcoming from any meeting, the agenda would either be held over for further discussion or particular matters dropped as a consequence of "recommendation for no further action," and no action would be taken by State in the absence of further consultation. Without objection, the recommendation would be transmitted to the secretary or president for final approval. Under this arrangement, the presidential assistant on international economic policy would be free to focus on particularly difficult policies, and would not need a duplicate staff. This procedure would keep State as the key agency in foreign economic policy but involve all others in policy formation, as is appropriate.[n]

A subcommittee, such as that chaired by the assistant secretary for EB on potential expropriation cases, could function as a preparatory group to help sharpen the issues and form the agenda of the undersecretary's group. The members of the group chaired by the assistant secretary would be the deputy assistant secretaries in the departments concerned with the particular problems at issue. In this way, the State official would be clearly in charge of raising issues and seeing to the preparation of the positions to be considered.

These sessions should be the means of obtaining administration-wide positions on the problems discussed, including programs that are considered the responsibility of any one department—e.g., resources, labor, export control, balance of payments, aid, financing, transportation, barter programs, antitrust enforcement overseas, commodity agreements, quotas, controls over multinational enterprises, taxation, etc. The same group could constitute a review board for claims by international companies for protection abroad or for appeals for support on major problems, such as resource supply.

Decisions taken under such a procedure would provide guidance to departments facing similar questions or attempting to implement their own programs, achieving a greater degree of coordination than now exists. Meetings of the staffs

[n]At the time of writing (April 1974), the special assistant to the President in charge of CIEP has resigned and a new Secretary of Treasury has been appointed, without the powers of an Economic czar (such as held by Secretary Shultz); some international economic policies will apparently pass to the STR, but what is not clear. The lines of authority are even *less* clear than before.

or officers reporting to assistant secretaries would, of course, be necessary to iron out differences of information or technical matters. Any assistant secretary could ask for an item to be placed on the agenda of the committee.

The success of such an arrangement would depend, of course, on the personalities involved and the allegiances they build up among the officers of the other departments. It would also depend on the backing the undersecretary obtained from the secretary of state and the White House for the recommendations he made after the deliberations of the coordinating committee. Such backing would be provided if the recommendation of the *Inspection Report* is accepted of making the undersecretary for economic affairs the third-ranking State Department official and the highest-ranking economic officer dealing with international affairs. This action should be complemented by the demise of the CIEP, however; or the undersecretary (as well as the secretary) will constantly be overshadowed.

Unless some such coordination is developed, the operating departments across government will assume more responsibility for policy formulation and implementation, leading to contradictory positions toward the same country from different agencies and causing some confusion not only in policies but in operations of embassy personnel in that country. With it, closer coordination would exist within the Executive Branch, with greater willingness to consider the legitimate views of each Department.[o] In addition, it would provide a clearing house for the differing views of those interested groups in the economy that will have made their positions known to the different agencies involved. It would strengthen and steady the voice of the assistant secretaries in presenting the governmental specific position to the specific vested interests in the economy. And finally, it would release the White House economic adviser from having to develop positions, and permit concentration on overall coordination, domestic and international.

Implementation of these changes would reinstitute in State the primary role in foreign economic policy, concentrate effort on economic-commercial matters, and provide for appropriate participation of others. Such a structure would provide the business community with a better understanding of how to communicate with State and the other departments, since the flow of information and responsibilities would be clearer. It would make for more effective communication for groups such as the Council of the Americas to be closely tied to the American Republics Area in State, for the Asian Society to be tied to that region, and for the Business and Industry Advisory Council (BIAC) with reference to OECD Countries. The International committees of the NAM, Chamber, U.S. Council of the ICC, etc. would have their ties with State,

---

[o]Recollections of officials are that a similar procedure worked well under Undersecretary Dillon in the late 1950s, though the situation was less complex and the bureaucracy smaller. This may argue for at least making the staffs smaller and more careful choice of program objectives and reporting requirements—as suggested by all those recently examining the economic/commercial service.

Treasury, and Commerce, as appropriate to their major responsibilities, recognizing that conflicts and major policy issues are to be resolved through the State structure. At the same time, the major responsibilities of Commerce, Agriculture, Treasury, Labor, etc. would not be diluted. Commerce, however, would have a closer tie to State through the regional bureaus than would the other agencies.

If State is unwilling to adapt its structure, orientation, assignments, and promotion to these ends, however, the pressure to pull commercial and eventually economic tasks out of the Department will increase, to the detriment of both economic and political problem-solving. The task calls for leadership that may not exist, or that may exist but be unable or unwilling to see the shift in priorities in the international scene and therefore unwilling to lead in this direction. If so, others will fill the vacuum, from within other departments or the White House.

Policy Implications of Closer
Business-Government Relations

The specific policies that are likely to be adopted as a result of closer government-business relations cannot be predicted, though one can state with assurance that one keystone of U.S. policy will have to be removed and replaced. There is already evidence that the principle of nondiscrimination will be broken so repeatedly that its removal as a basic precept of international economic relations will be evident in practice if not in policy.P Not only has the question of favorable treatment of one company compared to others bidding on a project or licensing or joint-venture arrangement been raised, but also Deputy Secretary Irwin requested examination of the means to provide strong support for the "front runner" among American applicants. The Department has not yet resolved this issue, but it will undoubtedly lead to discrimination among U.S. applicants when any selection among companies is made for support.

The same issue of discriminatory treatment arises in cases of expropriation. The principles of international law which the State Department calls upon include that "nationalization or expropriation (or other substantially equivalent

PThe principle of nondiscrimination means mainly equal treatment of all other nations; but as applied in investment policies, it has included "national treatment"—that is, nondiscrimination between domestic and foreign firms. And, in discussions in the OECD, State officials have argued further for "neutrality" of policies toward investment, which means the adoption of policies that do not "distort" the actions of companies operating in free markets. The concept is, therefore, not singular, and is used in opposition to a wide range of governmental interferences.

The central role played by this concept is recognized in the OMB Report (p. 70): "While business and government perceptions about the proper Government role may have generated misunderstandings, the Government position, although not clearly formulated, is essentially to assure nondiscriminatory treatment for American investors."

governmental interference with private property rights) must be for a public purpose, and not arbitrary or discriminatory. Moreover, prompt, adequate and effective compensation must be paid for the value of the rights so affected." In further definition, "discriminatory" means action that discriminates against the United States or its nationals.

But these principles were not upheld in the cases of expropriation that have been faced, nor can they likely be upheld in the future. It is evident in the IPC case in Peru and certainly in Cuba that United States interests were discriminated against in comparison to the treatment of other nationals. In addition, what is "prompt, adequate and effective compensation" cannot be put on any scale for determination whether U.S. companies were treated differentially poorly. And many of the settlements "accepted" by the U.S. Embassy or other officials were not seen by the U.S. companies involved as offering "prompt, adequate, and effective compensation." These criteria are meaningless, in fact.[q] The principle of nondiscrimination has already been voided in the diverse settlements of many cases. But the Department is reluctant to jettison it—probably largely because it does not want to endanger its retention in other areas.

But it is in equal danger in any decision as to how or how far to protect the interests of a U.S. company abroad. There are no "clearly enunciated principles" as to when or how to protect a company's interests nor what costs to impose on the company. Each time a company obtains protection or representation of its interests, it gains some discriminatory treatment. Discrimination is the essence of such protective acts—not only among companies but among countries. And the criteria that guide the decision to protect or not are also discriminatory—that is, any schedule of acts that "entitle" a company to so-and-so-much protection from the U.S. government would be discriminatory. Discrimination has in fact been codified among different industrial sectors, extraction, and service activities. Given the high U.S. interest in a few sectors, policies affecting them are likely to be discriminatory among countries.[12] Apart from the regulations as written, their implementation is often discriminatory among capital-exporting countries. The procedures for approval are such as to make proof difficult; formal complaints are, therefore, not easily initiated or successful. However, it is

---

[q]The threat of the imposition of these criteria is seen by developing countries as equivalent to "an atomic bomb" in business relations, despite the fact that in only a few cases has the U.S. employed them even equivalent to a piece of field artillery, and in most cases they have equaled only a slingshot.

The inability of the U.S. government to bring its policies into accord with its practices leaves host governments unsure as to the reaction, and therefore eager to set rules (such as those under the Calvo doctrine) designed to separate U.S. business from the protection of the U.S. government. In turn, this attitude of host governments makes U.S. business more wary of what they might do in extreme situations; and guarantees of national treatment are seen as unsatisfactory.

An accommodation of policies with practice is but one of the adjustments that the U.S. government will have to make to the new situation which confronts it because of changing power relations and the spread of international business.

clear from specific cases that host governments have made arrangements with companies of other countries, rather than with U.S. companies, merely because of the country of origin of the U.S. companies. (And it is not necessarily bad for U.S. interests that this is done, for too great an exposure of one country's companies in a given host country will cause undesirable tensions.)

Discrimination is, therefore, increasingly applied and accepted by U.S. officials, both abroad and at home, in dealing with international business. For example, the former capital export controls discriminated among capital-receiving nations, and several foreign governments complained, to little avail. To take up the many specific problems of international companies and to enhance business-government communication will cause distinctions to be made among specific cases. This will increase the chances of discrimination—among industries, among companies, and among countries. Though the U.S. government will probably drag its feet in dropping the principle—and there are reasons for its continued support in a number of situations—it seems clear that, in much practice and policy implementation, the principle is already passé.

This fact makes it all the more necessary for the government to seek to formulate the structure of a new international economic order—a task that it seems to be avoiding like the plague, seeking rather to hark back to principles of Bretton Woods (when convenient to do so) and the proposals of the Williams Commission,[13] which were largely outdated before they were committed to print.[14]

To restructure the world order will, as is recognized by State officials, require a continuing dialogue among governments, business, and labor. The views of the advanced countries are not similar to those of the LDCs, which in April 1974 put before the United Nations their own views of the reorientation needed. The process of including business and labor groups will be easier if done at the international level and will be seen as less threatening to host countries; but it is likely also to be less effective than if the dialogue is conducted at the national level within each country. Yet a close partnership between governments of capital-exporting countries and the international companies will be seen by developing countries as evidence of the imperialistic nature of the advanced economies.

Since many developing country governments are already convinced that the U.S. government and U.S. international companies collaborate closely at all levels and throughout all policies and activities, acceptance of the recommendations of this chapter would reinforce that perception. To demonstrate the reality of the nature and extent of cooperation and its usefulness to the host countries, some concurrent program should be instituted to explain fully the motives and actions of international companies and the role played by the U.S. government. A more forthcoming stance with both business and other governments is required—one that gives a high priority to the interests of the host countries.

The alternative to this approach is for the U.S. government to stand aside on the issues raised by the spread of the international companies. Two scenarios can be described under this alternative: other governments do not stand aside; or they do not interfere in actions of international companies. In the former, the companies would be pulled toward the interests of the more powerful and influential nations. They would be placed under regulations of regional commissions. Both sets of constraints are likely not to utilize the special advantages and capabilities of the international companies (especially the ME form); the present moves toward industrial integration through the international companies would likely be truncated, if not stopped altogether. Finally, the U.S. government is no more likely to stand aside from the issues raised by *inward* foreign investment than are the other host governments; when such investment becomes substantial or appears to be taking over key sectors, its policies will also become interventionist. Other international companies will then be subjected to U.S. policies within the domestic economy directed at constraining them.

The second scenario of all governments refraining from intervention is highly unlikely, simply because it would permit the international companies to determine the extent and form of industrial integration over the world. The level, nature, and sectors of international production would be determined by the decisions of "foreign enterprises," as would the structure and pattern of world trade. These decisions would be made under criteria of company advantage, rather than comparative advantage, or national advantage—with a resulting distribution of benefits that would not be acceptable to governments.

Therefore, guidance and control of the international companies is the only remaining alternative, with governments seeking a dialogue with both companies and labor to determine the most acceptable methods and objectives for these guidelines. The U.S. government alone cannot pursue this cooperative approach with companies, for the U.S. companies would be seen as interlopers abroad, and discrimination against them would result. The U.S. itself will inject discriminatory policies against foreign investors coming into the U.S. when the inward volume becomes critical; it will then seek a means of codifying these "exceptions." The next step would be the formation of new "rules" for the international economic order, within which controls over company behavior would fit.

Notes

Notes

Chapter 2
The International Government-Relations
Function

1. A number of the concepts and facts presented in this chapter are borrowed, with permission of the publisher, from Ashok Kapoor and J.J. Boddewyn, *International Business-Government Relations: U.S. Corporate Experience in Asia and Western Europe* (New York: American Management Association, 1973).

2. This classification borrows from J.N. Behrman, *Decision Criteria for Foreign Direct Investment in Latin America* (New York: Council of the Americas, 1974), 2-9.

3. For more details about Western Europe and a further elaboration of these concepts, see J.J. Boddewyn, "Western European Policies Toward U.S. Investors," *The Bulletin*, 93-95 (New York University, Graduate School of Business Administration, Institute of Finance, March 1974).

Chapter 3
Intelligence Networks: The Collection,
Evaluation, and Dissemination of
Information

1. F.J. Aguilar, *Scanning the Business Environment* (Boston, Mass., Division of Research, Harvard Business School, 1967), 9 and *passim*. Aguilar (p. 69) found that personal sources predominated in 71 percent of the cases, versus 29 percent for impersonal ones. The most useful work in this subject is H.L. Wilensky, *Organizational Intelligence* (New York: Basic Books, 1967), 42ff; but see also John Thackray, "Corporate Planning: Onto the New Drawing Board," *Corporate Financing* (May-June 1973), 27-32; W.W. Cain, "International Planning: Mission Impossible," *Columbia Journal of World Business* (July-August 1970), 53-60; and W.J. Keegan, "Multinational Scanning: A Study of the Information Sources Utilized by Headquarters Executives in Multinational Companies," *Administrative Science Quarterly* (September 1974), 411-22.

2. J.S. Schwendiman, *Strategic and Long-Range Planning for the Multinational Corporation* (New York: Praeger, 1973), 121-23.

3. See, for example, R.B. Stobaugh, Jr., "How to Analyze Foreign Investment Climates," *Harvard Business Review* (September-October 1969), 100-108; S.H. Robock, "Political Risk: Identification and Assessment," *Columbia Journal of World Business* (July-August 1971), 6-20; F.R. Root, "Analyzing Political

Risks in International Business," in Ashok Kapoor and Ph.D. Grub (eds.), *The Multinational Enterprise in Transition* (Princeton: N.J.: Darwin Press, 1972), 354-65; Ashok Kapoor, *Foreign Investments in Asia: Survey of Problems and Prospects in the 1970's* (Princeton, N.J.: The Darwin Press, 1972); L.C. Nehrt, *The Political Climate for Private Foreign Investment* (New York: Praeger, 1970); R.D. Robinson, *International Business Policy* (New York: Holt, Rinehart & Winston, 1964); F.R. Root, "U.S. Business Abroad and the Political Risks," *MSU Business Topics* (Winter 1968), 73-80; F.R. Root, "Attitudes of American Executives Toward Foreign Governments and Investment Opportunities," *Economic and Business Bulletin* (Temple University), XX, 2 (January 1968), 14-23; and Herbert Cahn, "The Political Exposure Problem," *Worldwide P & I Planning* (May-June 1972), 16-22.

4. Pertinent comments about such problems can be found in John Fayerweather, *International Business Management: A Conceptual Framework* (New York: McGraw-Hill, 1969); and Yair Aharoni, *The Foreign Investment Decision Process* (Boston, Mass.: Division of Research, Harvard Business School, 1966).

5. See P.W. Cherrington and R.L. Gillen, *The Business Representative in Washington* (Washington, D.C.: The Brookings Institution, 1962); and J.D. Johnson, "The Washington Representative," *Michigan Business Review* (May 1971), 6ff. For a more light-hearted touch, see the communications from the "Washington Rep" in *Worldwide Projects and Installations Planning.*

6. The new NAM president's "most recent work in organizing and financing worldwide projects is in line with NAM's interest in multinational business operations." *Business Week* (9 December 1972), 35.

7. The former BAC was attached to the U.S. Department of Commerce in 1960, and it had offices in its building, being thereby directly able to influence departmental policies. Secretary of Commerce Hodges removed this presence, and forced the BAC-government meetings to be opened to the press. The group then shifted location, changed its name to Business Council, and redirected its contacts to the White House and to all departments equally. See also: Edward Cohan, "Secrecy in High Places," *New York Times* (29 October 1972).

8. Business was not particularly well represented at the 1972 United Nations Conference on the Human Environment in Stockholm, although the ICC held a conference just before it. Galdwin Hill, "The Pollution Lobby: Influence Peddlers Sell Little at Meetings," *New York Times* (18 June 1972), F5.

9. U.S. Senate, The International Telephone and Telegraph Company and Chile, 1970-71; Report of the Committee on Foreign Relations by the Sub-Committee on Multinational Corporations, 93d Cong., 1st Sess, 21 June 1973. Also M.C. Jensen, "Corporate Infighting Noted," *New York Times,* June 22, 1973, 1ff.

Chapter 4
Issues and Areas in the Influence Process

1. For additional comments on the importance of perceptions and other selected characteristics of the influence process, see Ashok Kapoor, *Planning for*

International Business Negotiations (Cambridge, Mass.: Ballinger, 1975), especially chapter 6; Thomas C. Schelling, *The Strategy of Conflict* (New York: Oxford University Press, 1960), p. 15; Charles T. Goodsell, *American Corporations and Peruvian Politics* (Cambridge, Mass.: Harvard University Press, 1974), especially parts 1 and 4.

2. In seeking information on an issue, the IC does not rely on a single source but uses several sources; for additional comments see Yair Aharoni, *The Foreign Investment Decision Process* (Cambridge, Mass.: Division of Research, Graduate School of Business Administration, Harvard Business School, 1966) and J. Alex Murray, "Intelligence Systems of the MNCs," *Columbia Journal of World Business*, September-October 1972.

3. For a detailed study of the Bechtel proposal to the Indian government, see Ashok Kapoor, *International Business Negotiations: A Study in India* (New York: New York University Press, 1970, and Princeton, N.J.: The Darwin Press, 1973).

4. Efforts to influence must be seen within the broader framework of measures for effective business-government relations; for additional comments see Ashok Kapoor and J.J. Boddewyn, *International Business-Government Relations: US Corporate Experience in Asia and Western Europe* (New York: American Management Association, 1973), especially the concluding chapter; Goodsell, *American Corporations and Peruvian Politics*, op. cit., especially chapter 3.

5. Alternative sources of investments are becoming available to developing countries; for additional comments on the Pacific Basin in relation to U.S. and Japanese competition see Ashok Kapoor, *Asian Business and Environment in Transition* (Princeton, N.J.: The Darwin Press, 1975).

6. For additional comments, see Frank H. Golay (ed.), *Underdevelopment and Economic Nationalism in Southeast Asia* (Ithaca, N.Y.: Cornell University Press, 1969).

7. For various references dealing directly and indirectly with this subject, see Conference Board (NICB) *Cumulative Index*, and David Burtis et al. (eds.) *Multinational Corporation-Nation State Interaction; An Annotated Bibliography* (Philadelphia: Foreign Policy Research Institute, 1971).

8. References to different situations are provided in J.N. Behrman, *U.S. International Business and Governments* (New York: McGraw-Hill Book Company, 1971); Chitoshi Yanaga, *Big Business in Japanese Politics* (New Haven, Conn.: Yale University Press, 1968); and Kapoor, *Planning for International Business Negotiations*, op. cit. offers several detailed studies and analyses.

Chapter 5
Actors in the Influence Process

1. For detailed case studies and analysis reflecting many characteristics of the influence process, see A. Kapoor, *Planning for International Business Negotiations* (Cambridge, Mass.: Ballinger, 1975).

2. The international company uses several different groups to influence the host government; for additional comments on Southeast Asia see I-Tjhih, "Business-Government Relations in Southeast Asia: A Study of Singapore and Malaysia" (unpublished Ph.D. dissertation, Graduate School of Business Administration, New York University, 1972).

3. See C. Fred Bergsten, "Coming Investment Wars," *Foreign Affairs*, October 1974, and Zuhayer Mikdashi, "Collusion Could Work," *Foreign Policy*, Spring 1974.

4. For a Canadian example, see John Fayerweather, *The Mercantile Bank Affair* (New York: New York University Press, 1974).

5. For an excellent discussion of the role of interest groups in decision making of the Japanese government, see Chitoshi Yanaga, *Big Business in Japanese Politics* (New Haven, Conn.: Yale University Press, 1968).

6. For examples of varying degrees of involvement of the U.S. government, see A. Kapoor, *Planning for International Business Negotiations*, op. cit.

Chapter 6
Criteria of Sucess of Government-Business
Relations

1. Theodore Moran, "Transnational Strategies of Protection and Defense by Multinational Corporations," *International Organization*, Spring 1973, 273-87.

2. See John Fayerweather, "The Mercantile Bank Affair," *Columbia Journal of World Business*, 1971, 41-51.

Chapter 7
U.S. Government Alternatives

1. For corroboration of this point, see the *Inspection Report, Economic Functions*, Office of Inspector General, Foreign Service, January 1973, 18-29, 48.

2. For corroboration of this point, see Staff Report, *Commercial and Economic Representation Abroad*, Office of Management and Budget; Executive Office of the President, January 1973, pp. 130-39.

Commerce has biases also in that it is organized so that different units pursue different objectives overseas; the views of different commerce officials concerning the "cooperation" received from State varies considerably. And State's view of the support it gets from Commerce differs from perceptions of various Commerce officials.

This report by the OMB was read after our own interviews; its analysis and conclusions were corroborated by our own results. It is an excellent study, commended to all interested parties.

3. The significance of these shifts is discussed at length in a monograph by J.N. Behrman, "Toward a New International Economic Order," Paris: The Atlantic Institute, 1974.

4. These shifts are supported also by the analysis of the OMB, chapter 2.

5. A strong argument for a changed orientation is made by Carl Madden (economist for the U.S. Chamber of Commerce) in *Clash of Cultures: Management in a Changing Society* (Washington, D.C.: National Planning Association, 1973).

6. For suggestions as to appropriate criteria for disaggregation, see the monograph by J.N. Behrman on "Decision-Criteria for Direct Investment in Latin America," New York: Council of the Americas, 1974, chapter 1.

7. OMB, chapter 6.

8. This was in line with the recommendation of the *Inspection Report on Economic Functions* (op. cit.). The earlier removal of this post and later replacement at the deputy undersecretary level had clearly signaled a reduction in importance within the Department.

9. Ibid., p. 36.

10. Ibid., p. 37.

11. A much longer *Inspection Report, Commercial Services* was made by the Office of the Inspector General, Foreign Service, July 1972, recommending changes in the commercial programs and their management by State.

12. Just as taxes on large autos in Japan and Europe discriminated against U.S. auto exports. Discrimination is likely also in attempting to reconcile different sets of restrictions; see J.N. Behrman, *Conflicting Constraints on International Business* (N.Y.: Fund for Multinational Management Education, 1974), see also his paper prepared for the Asia Society's SEADAG conference in California (December 1973) entitled "Actors and Factors in Decisions on Foreign Direct Investment," and published in *World Development*, August 1974, 1-14.

13. Report to the President, *United States International Economic Policy in an Interdependent World* (Washington, D.C., July 1971).

14. One study of the problems facing the formation of a new international economic order has been made by C. Fred Bergsten, *The Future of the International Economic Order* (Lexington, Mass.: Lexington Books, D.C. Heath, 1973); another by J.N. Behrman, "Toward a New International Economic Order," Paris: Atlantic Institute, 1974; Richard N. Cooper's contribution (*A Re-ordered World* (N.Y.: Basic Books, 1973) is a collection of articles which do not compose an holistic approach to reordering the world economy, many of which are rooted in outmoded principles.

Index

195

About the Authors

Jack N. Behrman was Assistant Secretary of Commerce for Domestic and International Business under the Kennedy and Johnson Administrations. He had previously published path-breaking studies on foreign licensing and direct foreign investment and has since continued to write on problems of foreign investment and the multinational enterprise. His most recent works include *National Interests and the Multinational Enterprise, U.S. International Business and Governments*, and *The Role of International Companies in Latin American Integration*. He also made a study for the State Department on "Multinational Co-Production Consortia: Lessons of the NATO Experience."

J.J. Boddewyn is Professor of International Business at Baruch College (City University of New York). His teaching and research have centered on international comparative management and marketing as well as on environmental and managerial topics, with emphasis on international business-government relations and external affairs about which he advises multinational companies and governments. He is the author of *Comparative Management and Marketing, Organizing for External Affairs in Europe*, and *Western European Policies Toward U.S. Investors*; a coauthor of *World Business Systems and Environments*, and *International Business-Government Relations: A Study of U.S. Corporate Experience*; and coeditor of and contributor to *Public Policy Toward Retailing: An International Symposium*.

Ashok Kapoor is professor of marketing and international business at the Graduate School of Business Administration of New York University, and also serves as an adviser to governments and international companies. He is an innovator in developing international business negotiation simulations as teaching, research, and training tools. Dr. Kapoor is the author of numerous articles and of *International Business Negotiations: A Study in India; Change and Uncertainty in Asia: Implications for the International Company*. In addition, he is a coauthor of *Managing International Markets, International Business-Government Relations: A Study of U.S. Corporate Experience, Foreign Investments in Asia, World Business Systems and Environment*, and *Planning for International Business Negotiation*; coeditor of *The Multinational Enterprise in Transition*; and editor of and contributor to *Asian Business and Environment in Transition*.

DATE DUE